Multilevel Security for Relational Databases

Multilevel Security for Relational Databases

Osama S. Faragallah

El-Sayed M. El-Rabaie • Fathi E. Abd El-Samie

Ahmed I. Sallam • Hala S. El-Sayed

CRC Press
Taylor & Francis Group
Boca Raton London New York

CRC Press is an imprint of the
Taylor & Francis Group, an **informa** business

AN AUERBACH BOOK

CRC Press
Taylor & Francis Group
6000 Broken Sound Parkway NW, Suite 300
Boca Raton, FL 33487-2742

First issued in paperback 2019

© 2015 by Taylor & Francis Group, LLC
CRC Press is an imprint of Taylor & Francis Group, an Informa business

No claim to original U.S. Government works

ISBN-13: 978-1-4822-0539-8 (hbk)
ISBN-13: 978-1-138-37490-4 (pbk)

Library of Congress Cataloging-in-Publication Data

Faragallah, Osama S.
    Multilevel security for relational databases / Osama S. Faragallah, El-Sayed M. El-Rabaie, Fathi E. Abd El-Samie, Ahmed I. Sallam, and Hala S. El-Sayed.
        pages cm
    Summary: "Most database security models focus on protecting against external unauthorized users. Because multilevel secure databases provide internal security according to user access type, they are a viable option for the security needs of modern database systems. Covering key concepts in database security, this book illustrates the implementation of multilevel security for relational database models. It considers concurrency control in multilevel database security and presents encryption algorithms. It also includes simulation programs and Visual studio and Microsoft SQL Server code for the simulations covered in the text"-- Provided by publisher.
    Includes bibliographical references and index.
    ISBN 978-1-4822-0539-8 (hardback)
    1. Database security. I. Title.

QA76.9.D314F37 2014
005.8--dc23   2014020608

Visit the Taylor & Francis Web site at
http://www.taylorandfrancis.com

and the CRC Press Web site at
http://www.crcpress.com

Contents

Preface

In this book we try to look at encryption-based multilevel database security through the eyes of database security researchers. Multilevel security for relational databases is an interesting information security topic. Most of the security models available for databases today protect them from outside, unauthorized users. A multilevel secure database provides internal security in relationship with the user's type of access to the database. A multilevel secure database system has been proposed to address the increased security needs of database systems. Researchers are in need of new algorithms in this area with their software implementation.

We summarize the main contributions of this book as follows:

1. This book is devoted to the issue of multilevel security in the relational database.
2. Multilevel security for relational database models is considered in this book, with a comparison between them using different evaluation metrics.
3. Modifications are presented to an existing multilevel security model in the relational database either to speed or to enhance performance.

4. Formal analysis for data manipulation operations in multilevel security database models and mathematical proofs of soundness, completeness, and security are studied.
5. Simulation experiments are presented for validation of the discussed algorithms and modifications and also for investigating the performance of multilevel database models.
6. The C# and Microsoft SQL server source codes for most of the simulation experiments in this book are included at the end of the book.

Finally, we hope that this book will be helpful for database and information security.

About the Authors

Osama S. Faragallah received B.Sc. (Hons.), M.Sc., and Ph.D. degrees in computer science and engineering from Menoufia University, Menouf, Egypt, in 1997, 2002, and 2007, respectively. He is currently associate professor in the Department of Computer Science and Engineering, Faculty of Electronic Engineering, Menoufia University. He was a demonstrator from 1997 to 2002 and has been assistant lecturer from 2002 to 2007. Since 2007, he has been a member of the teaching staff of the Department of Computer Science and Engineering at Menoufia University. He is the co-author of about 100 papers in international journals, conference proceedings, and two textbooks. His current research interests include network security, cryptography, internet security, multimedia security, image encryption, watermarking, steganography, data hiding, medical image processing, and chaos theory.

El-Sayed M. El-Rabaie was born in Sires Elian, Egypt in 1953. He received a B.Sc. degree (Hons.) in radio communications from Tanta University, Tanta, Egypt in 1976, an M.Sc. degree in communication systems from Menoufia University, Menouf, Egypt in 1981, and a Ph.D. degree in microwave device engineering from Queen's University of Belfast, Belfast, U.K. in 1986. Until 1989, Dr. El-Rabaie was a postdoctoral fellow in the Department of Electronic Engineering, Queen's University of Belfast. He was invited to become a research fellow in the College of Engineering and Technology, Northern Arizona University, Flagstaff in 1992, and a visiting professor at the Ecole Polytechnique de Montreal, Montreal, QC, Canada in 1994. He has authored and co-authored more than 180 papers and 18 textbooks. He has been awarded the Salah Amer Award of Electronics in 1993 and the Best (CAD) Researcher from Menoufia University in 1995. He acts as a reviewer and member of the editorial board for several scientific journals. Professor El-Rabaie was the head of the Electronic and Communication Engineering Department at Menoufia University, and later, the Vice dean of Postgraduate Studies and Research. Dr. El-Rabaie's research interests include CAD of nonlinear microwave circuits, nanotechnology, digital communication systems, and digital image processing. He is a member of the National Electronic and Communication Engineering Promotion Committee and a reviewer of quality assurance and accreditation of Egyptian higher education.

Fathi E. Abd El-Samie received his B.Sc. (Hons.), M.Sc., and Ph.D. degrees from Menoufia University, Menouf, Egypt in 1998, 2001, and 2005, respectively. Since 2005, he has been a member of the teaching staff in the Department of Electronics and Electrical Communications, Faculty of Electronic Engineering, Menoufia University. He is currently a researcher at KACST-TIC in radio frequency and photonics for the e-Society (RFTONICs). He is a co-author of about 200 papers in international conference proceedings and journals and 4 textbooks. His current research interests include image enhancement, image restoration, image interpolation, super-resolution reconstruction of images, data hiding, multimedia communications, medical image processing, optical signal processing, and digital communications. In 2008, Dr. Abd El-Samie was the recipient of the Most Cited Paper Award from the journal *Digital Signal Processing*.

Ahmed I. Sallam was born in Tanta, Al Gharbia, Egypt in 1982. He received a B.Sc. degree (Hons.) in computer science and engineering from Al Azhar University, Faculty of Engineering in 2005 and an M.Sc. degree in computer science and engineering from Menoufia University, Faculty of Electronic Engineering, Egypt in 2012. He is a senior software engineer at Qarun Petroleum Company. His research interests include database, database security, cryptography, multimedia security, and image encryption.

Hala S. El-Sayed received her B.Sc.(Hons.), M.Sc., and Ph.D. degrees in electrical engineering from Menoufia University, Shebin El-kom, Egypt in 2000, 2004, and 2010, respectively. She is currently assistant professor in the Department of Electrical Engineering, Faculty of Engineering, Menoufia University. She was a demonstrator from 2002 to 2004 and an assistant lecturer from 2004 to 2010. Since 2010, she has been a member of the teaching staff in the Department of Electrical Engineering, Faculty of Engineering, Menoufia University. Her research interests are database security, network security, data hiding, image encryption, signal processing, wireless sensor network, robotics, secure building automation systems, and biometrics.

1

CONCEPTS OF DATABASE SECURITY

1.1 Database Concepts

A database system is a computerized system whose overall purpose is to store and organize the data in a way that can be accessed, managed, and modified on demand. A database system becomes an important part of information management systems that enhances the ability of organizations to manage their important data in an easy way. A database system has many benefits that are described as follows:

- Reducing the amount of data redundancy by ensuring that the data are stored in one location and can be accessible to all authorized users
- Improving data access to users through use of host and query languages
- Enhancing data security
- Decreasing data entry, storage, and retrieval costs
- Allowing more flexibility for manipulating data
- Presenting greater data integrity and independence from applications programs

The interaction between the user, other applications, and the database itself can be performed through a software system called a database management system (DBMS) [1], which is specially designed to help the user to capture and analyze the stored data. The general purpose of the relational database management system is to be used as a tool to define, create, and manage the relational database.

Databases are classified according to their organizational approach. The most common approach is the relational database [2]. In relational databases, all data are stored in a collection of relations.

A relation contains a group of rows that have the same attributes. A row represents an object and information about that object. A relation is defined as a table, which is organized into rows (tuples) and columns (attributes). All the data in the same attribute have the same domain and stratify the same constraints. A domain presents the possible values for an attribute in the relation and the constraints make some restrictions on the domain of an attribute.

In the relational database, a relation cannot contain duplicate tuples because that would create ambiguities in retrieval.

In the relational database, to ensure uniqueness, each relation should have an attribute (or a set of attributes), called the primary key, that uniquely identifies every tuple of the relation [3]. A primary key is called a simple key if it is a single attribute and it is called a composite key if it is made up of several attributes.

In the relational database, a foreign key is an attribute (or collection of attributes) in one relation that uniquely identifies a tuple of another relation. In other words, a foreign key is an attribute or a group of attributes used to establish and enforce a link between the data in two relations.

A relational database consisting of independent and unrelated relations serves little purpose. The power of a relational database lies in the relationship that can be defined between relations. The most crucial aspect in designing a relational database is to identify the relationships among relations [4]. The types of relationship include:

- One to many: The primary key relation contains only one tuple that relates to no, one, or many tuples in the related relation.
- Many to many: Each tuple in both relations can relate to any number of tuples (or no tuples) in the other relation. Many-to-many relationships require a third relation, known as an associate or linking relation, because relational systems cannot directly accommodate the relationship.
- One to one: Both relations can have only one tuple on either side of the relationship. Each primary key value relates to only one (or no) tuple in the related relation.

In the relational database, a stored procedure is an executable code that is stored in the relational database. Stored procedures group common operations, like inserting a tuple into a relation or encapsulating complex business logic and calculations. Stored procedures are more performance than writing application code, for the following reasons:

- There is no communication between the relational database and other external applications.
- There is no need to compile and execute the stored procedure for each instance, as the stored procedure is compiled once.

In the relational database, structured query language (SQL) is the standard computer language for managing data in the relational database [5]. All relational database management systems, like Oracle, Informix, and SQL Server, use SQL as a basic database language. The SQL operation for manipulating the relation is described as follows:

- Select operation: This operation is used to get groups of tuples from the relation database. The SQL command for the select operation is described as follows:

```
SELECT [A₁,A₂, ...,Aₙ]
FROM R
WHERE P
```

where R is a relation, $A_1, A_2, \ldots, A_n$ are the attributes from relation R, and P is the condition of the select statement that defines the tuples to be retrieved.
- Insert operation: This operation is used to insert tuples in the relation. The SQL command for the insert operation is described as follows:

```
INSERT
INTO R [A₁,A₂, ...,Aₙ]
VALUES [a₁,a₂, ...,aₙ]
```

where R is a relation, $A_1, A_2, \ldots, A_n$ are the attributes from relation R, and $a_1, a_2, \ldots, a_n$ are values from domains of $A_1, A_2, \ldots, A_n$ that will be inserted.

- Update operation: This operation is used to modify tuples in the relation. The SQL command for the update operation is described as follows:

```
UPDATE R
SET [A₁=a₁,A₂=a₂, ...,Aₙ=aₙ]
WHERE P
```

where R is a relation, $A_1, A_2, \ldots, A_n$ are attributes from relation R, $a_1, a_2, \ldots, a_n$ are values from domains of $A_1, A_2, \ldots, A_n$ that will be updated, and P is the condition of the update statement that defines tuples that are to be updated.

- Delete operation: This operation is used to delete tuples from the relation. The SQL command for the delete operation is described as follows:

```
DELETE
FROM R
WHERE P
```

where R is a relation and P is the condition of the delete statement that defines tuples that are to be deleted.

The internal mechanisms of SQL statement processing in the relational database management system (RDBMS) are presented in the following five steps:

- The RDBMS parses the SQL statement by dividing it into individual words and validating the statement syntax.
- The statement is then checked by the RDBMS against the information schema. In addition, it ensures the user privileges to execute the statement.
- The next step is the optimization of the SQL statement. The query optimization process is defined as finding the efficient way to execute the SQL statement.
- The next step is the generation of the execution plan for the SQL statement based on the optimization process performed during the previous step.
- The set of binary instructions created in the previous step is executed by the RDBMS.

1.2 Relational Database Security Concepts

In recent years, the need for securing relational databases has been increased because of increased database attacks. Most companies and organizations store their sensitive data in their own relational databases. In recent years, attackers have been able to target large relational databases that belong to large companies or large banks. In the past, relational database attacks were common, but were fewer than attacks on networks. Now, due to the increasing access of relational databases by many people, the chances of relational database attacks have increased. The reason for these attacks is to obtain money by getting sensitive information like credit card numbers or Social Security numbers. Thus, it is important to protect relational databases against these risks, and this is where database security comes into place.

Relational database security can be defined as a system that protects the confidentiality, integrity, and availability of the database [6]. Unauthorized access to a relational database indicates a loss of confidentiality, unauthorized modification to the available data indicates a loss of integrity, and lack of access to relational database services indicates a loss of availability. Loss of one or more of these basic facets will have a bad impact on the security of the relational database.

The protection of the confidentiality, integrity, and availability of the relational database will be illustrated in more detail as follows:

- *Confidentiality* can be defined as a process for preventing unauthorized access to the sensitive data that is stored in the relational database. It can be ensured by applying encryption to the data stored in the relational database. Encryption is a process in which the information is encrypted in a way that only authorized users can manage. The different levels for encryption are described as follows:
  - Data in transit means that an attacker can get access to the sensitive information by observing the network between the sender and the receiver.
  - Data at rest means that an attacker can attack the information stored in the relational database.

There are many algorithms for encryption, such as data encryption standards (DES), triple DES, and advanced encryption standards (AES).

- *Integrity* can be defined as a process for preventing unauthorized alteration to the sensitive data stored in the relational database. The integrity of data is not only whether the data is correct, but also whether it can be trusted and relied upon. Database integrity ensures the accuracy and the consistency of the data entered into the relational database.
- *Availability* can be defined as a process for preventing loss of access to relational database services. Databases must have no unplanned downtime.

In relational databases, many layers of security can be used to ensure database security [7]. The security layers can be classified into the following:

- *Authentication* can be defined as the concept of verifying the identity of a user that needs to access the relational database. Each user should identify himself before having access to data stored in the relational database system. Authentication may happen at different levels; for example, authentication can be performed by the relational database itself or allow other external methods to authenticate users.
- *Access controls (authorization)* can be defined as setting rules that define whether the user has access to the data in the relational database. Authorization rules manage the modification of data in the relational database. Access controls are procedures that are defined to manage authorizations of the data in the relational database.
- *Integrity* can be defined as a group of rules that present the correct state of the relational database during the database modification.
- *Auditing* can be defined as keeping track of all security relevant actions issued by a user.

In this book, the main focus is directed toward aspects related to access controls. An access control mechanism ensures data confidentiality. Whenever a subject tries to access a data object, the access control mechanism checks the rights of the user against a set of authorizations, usually stated by some security administrator. Access control ensures that all direct accesses to database objects occur only according to the rules governed by protection policies. There are two different ways to enforce access control: discretionary access control and mandatory access control.

1.3 Access Control in Relational Databases

Preventing unauthorized access to the relational database is the main goal in implementing a secure database management system. Most of the database users need only a specific permission on some parts in the relational database to perform their jobs. Allowing them access to the whole database is undesirable. So, a security policy should be developed effectively to enable a group of users to access only required parts of the database. Once the security policy is developed, it should be enforced to achieve the level of security required. Three main approaches in DBMS for access control are discretionary access control, mandatory access control, and role-based access control.

1.3.1 Discretionary Access Control

Discretionary access control (DAC) is based on granting and revoking privileges for the usage of system objects (elations, views, columns, etc.) [8]. The privileges are granted to (or revoked from) every subject (user, account, program) separately. Discretionary access control policies allow access rights to be propagated from one subject to another. This is called discretionary in the sense that the owner of data has complete discretion regarding granting/revoking access privileges to his data.

In the DAC, granting/revoking privileges can be performed by the database administrator (DBA) [9]. The DBA has the following responsibilities:

- Creating accounts for users that want to log on to the relational database system
- Granting/revoking privileges for users that want to access the relational database system

- Monitoring the relational database performance
- Managing the backup and recovery procedures of the relational database

The types of DAC privileges are described as follows:

- The account privilege: Each user holds privileges that are independent of the relations in the database. For example, the DBA grants/revokes privileges to a user to CREATE TABLE, CREATE VIEW, DROP, and ALTER.
- The relation privilege: The DBA can specify the privilege to modify each individual relation in the relational database. For example, the DBA grants/revokes privileges to a user to SELECT/MODIFY/REFERENCE privilege on specific relation R. Discretionary access controls can be granted to many objects in the relational database system, such as the database, group of relations, one relation, set of the attributes of one relation, and group of tuples of one relation.

Making a discretionary access controls decision based on the content of data is called data dependent access control [10,11]. For example, some users cannot see salaries that are over than $100,000. The two approaches for implementing access controls in the relational databases are described as follows:

- View-based access control: A relation is the physical location in the relational database that stores the data in the relational database. A view is the logical set of the stored query on the data. Unlike the physical table in the relational database, a view is a logical table computed from data in the relational database dynamically when access to that view is requested.
- Query modification: A query that is written by a user is altered to include the limitation determined by the user's privileges. For example, the DBA grants user A to select only the employees that are in the material department from the relation of employees by the following grant statement:

```
GRANT SELECT ON Employees TO A
WHERE Department = 'material'
```

When user A needs to select all records from the employee's relation, his query will be changed and his privileges will be added as follows:

```
SELECT * FROM Employees; Will be changed to:
SELECT * FROM Employees
WHERE Department = 'material';
```

In SQL, granting is performed by means of the GRANT statement, which has the following general format:

```
GRANT privileges
[ON relation]
TO users
[WITH GRANT OPTION]
```

For example:

```
GRANT SELECT
ON Employees
TO A
```

In SQL, revoking is performed by means of the REVOKE statement, which has the following general format:

```
REVOKE privileges
[ON relation]
FROM users
```

For example:

```
REVOKE SELECT
ON Employees
FROM A
```

DAC suffers from some drawbacks when applied to the relational database:

- Enforcement of the security policy: DAC depends on the concept of ownership of the data. In DAC, the user who creates the object in the relational database is the owner of this object and can grant access to other users on this object. This has the disadvantage that the enterprise cannot manage and enforce its security requirements without including all the users that create all the objects in the relational database.

- Cascading authorization: For example, consider three users: U_1, U_2, and U_3. User U_2 has the privilege on object O from U_1 and grants this privilege to U_3. Later, U_1 grants privilege to U_3 on the same object O, but U_2 revokes privilege from privilege U_3 for some reason. The effect of these operations is that U_3 still has the access privilege (from U_1) to access object O although U_2 revoked privilege.
- Trojan horse attacks: A Trojan horse can be used to grant a certain privilege of a user on an object to another user without knowing any information about the user.
- Update problems: In DAC, view-based protection is a logical query that has no physical data in the relational database. The disadvantage of view-based protection is that not all data can be updated through certain views.

1.3.2 Mandatory Access Control

While DAC is concerned with ensuring the privilege to access data in the relational database, mandatory access control (MAC) is in addition ensuring the flow of data in the relational database system. MAC depends on the security level associated with each object in the relational database and each user. A security level on an object is defined as a security classification, while the security level on a user is defined as a security clearance. MAC is defined as multilevel security (MLS); because of each user and each object, one of the multiple security levels can be assigned.

A complete understanding of MLS will not happen without understanding its origins [12]. The U.S. military has a historical isolated database that contains its sensitive information. The sensitive data are classified into different security levels and must be processed on dedicated systems that do not provide access to users outside the intended security level. The main limitations can be described as follows:

- Redundant databases: To store data in the relational database into different security levels, a different database should be created for each security level.
- Redundant workstations: There is a need to have different workstations to get each type of datum.
- High cost of IT infrastructure: There is a risk in sharing the network resources.
- Inefficiency: Users need to get privileges on several relational database systems to perform their duties.

Multilevel security was the solution. MLS allows the data in different security classification levels to be accessed by users that have different security clearance levels.

The Bell and LaPadula model was the basic model that introduced the concept of MLS [13]. This model depends on definitions of objects and subjects. An object like relation, a tuple, or an attribute is a passive entity. A subject like user or program is an active process that needs to have a privilege on objects. Every object is assigned to a security level (classification), and every subject is assigned to a security level (clearance). Security levels are defined as labels. A label contains two components: a hierarchical component and a group of unordered categories. The hierarchical component presents the security levels of the data. For example, a company might define the security levels of its sensitive data as top secret, secret, confidential, or unclassified. The unordered categories are used to define the sensitivity of the leveled data.

Multilevel security is based on the Bell and LaPadula model and formalized by two rules. LaPadula rules are described as follows [14]:

- The simple property (no read up): A subject is allowed to read an object if the subject's security clearance level is greater than or equal to the object's security classification level.
- The star property (no write down): A subject is allowed to write to an object if the object's security classification level is greater than or equal to the subject's security clearance level.

The star property allows a lower security level subject to write data to a higher security level object. This can result in overwriting and therefore modifying of higher security level objects by lower security level subjects. Thus, MLS enforces a stronger star property to restrict each subject to write at his own security level:

- Strong star property: A subject is allowed to write to an object if the subject's security clearance level is equal to the object's security classification level.

1.3.3 Role-Based Access Control

The main motivation behind role-based access control (RBAC) is the necessity to simulate the structure of the natural security policies of the organization. RBAC is based on the roles that users have. Roles are similar to those of the user groups in access controls.

In RBAC, a role is defined as a group of actions and duties belonging to a specific activity [15]. The role may present a user's job (e.g., buyer), or it may define an action that the user should do (e.g., order material). Instead of defining all the permissions to each one of the users that performs the same task, permissions on objects can be defined for roles. The user that is assigned to a role can perform all actions that the role is authorized to do. The components of RBAC can be described as follows:

- Role–permission relationships: This component manages granting/revoking permission to a specific role.
- User–role relationships: This component defines how to assign users to a specific role.
- Role–role relationships: This component defines how to make a role a member of another role.

RBAC has three security principles:

- Least privilege: RBAC allows a user to access objects with the least privilege required for the specific task that is needed to be performed. This minimizes the Trojan horses attack.
- Separation of duties: RBAC ensures that no user has enough privileges to misuse the system on his own.
- Data abstraction: This is supported by means of abstract privileges such as credit and debit for an account.

In RBAC, database administrators can manage access at a level of abstraction that is identical to the way that organizations perform their business. This is achieved by organizing users' tasks through the implementation of roles, role hierarchies, relationships, and constraints.

In role-based access control, roles can have overlapping duties and privileges, so users assigned many roles may need to do common tasks. Some general tasks may be done by all users. In this situation, there is no need to repeat these common tasks for each role created. Role hierarchies can be performed to present the real structure of an enterprise.

RBAC has two types of role hierarchies:

- General hierarchical RBAC is based on the concept of multiple inheritances that present the ability to obtain permission inheritance from more than one role and to inherit user membership from more than one role.
- Limited hierarchical RBAC is limited to a single descendant. Limited role hierarchies do not support multiple inheritances.

1.4 Work Objectives

In the digital world nowadays, database security has become increasingly important since the database is the primary repository of information for organizations and governments. More and more research has been developed in database security to protect the data from possible unauthorized instructions. Most of the security models available for databases today protect them from outside and unauthorized users.

Multilevel security for relational databases provides internal security in relationship with the user's access to the relational database. Relational database multilevel security systems have been proposed to address the increased security needs of relational database systems. Although multilevel concepts were originally developed to support confidentiality in military systems, there are now many commercial systems that use multilevel security policies.

Although many models have been developed to support multilevel security in the relational database, there are many problems in implementing multilevel security policies. These problems included complexity in designing multilevel security for the relational database and increasing the database size according to the classification level columns added to the original database to support multilevel security in the database.

This book will introduce the concept of multilevel security in the relational database, will present a comparative study for previous models that support multilevel security policies in the relational database, and will show the weakness and the strength of each model.

Also, in this book a prototype will be implemented to be used as a research tool for a performance evaluation of multilevel security for relational database (MLS/DBMS) models.

This book will give a complete view of an encryption-based multilevel security database model, which is a combination of multilevel security for the relational database and encryption system by encrypting each record with an encryption key according to its security class level. This model is characterized by three achievements:

- Utilizing an encryption system as a second security layer over the multilevel security layer for the database
- Reducing the multilevel database size
- Improving the response time of data retrieval from the multilevel database

The goal of these three achievements is to increase robustness against database attacks and enhance the performance of data manipulating operations such as select, insert, update, and delete in the multilevel database. The effectiveness of an encryption-based multilevel security database model is verified through the mathematical proof of the soundness of, completeness of, and security for multilevel security for relational database system.

The encryption-based multilevel security database model achieves good quality because it satisfies integrity properties such as entity integrity, polyinstantiation integrity, data borrowing integrity, foreign key integrity, and referential integrity of the multilevel database. Also, this book will illustrate the C# and Microsoft SQL server source codes for the implementation of the encryption-based multilevel security database model.

Concurrency control is used in relational databases to manage the concurrent execution of operations by different subjects on the same data object. This book will explain the concept of concurrency control and will define its impacts on multilevel security for relational databases. It will create a survey for studying the secure concurrency control protocols that are proposed in multilevel security for relational databases and will implement a prototype to be used to perform a series of experiments to measure the performance cost for applying the concurrency control in multilevel relational databases.

This book will also define the implementation of the data manipulation operations for the instance-based multilevel security model (IBMSM) since the IBMSM proposes two layers: the instance layer and the class layer.

1.5 Book Organization

- In Chapter 2, the basic concept of multilevel relational database security will be discussed. This chapter will explain the models that support multilevel database security and will introduce a comparative study between the multilevel database security models.
- In Chapter 3, the implementation of multilevel relational database security models will be illustrated and the performance study will be instrumented to compare the multilevel secure database (MLS/DBMS) models.
- In Chapter 4, an overview of the encryption algorithms that are applied will be presented.
- In Chapter 5, the encryption-based multilevel security database model will be described and the implementation of a working prototype to be used as a research tool for studying principles and mechanisms of the model will be explored.
- In Chapter 6, the formal model for the data manipulation operations in the encryption-based multilevel security database model will be presented and the mathematical proofs of soundness, completeness, and security will be proved.
- In Chapter 7, the concept of concurrency control in multilevel security for relational databases will be introduced.
- In Chapter 8, the implementation of the data manipulation operations for the instance-based multilevel security model (IBMSM) will be defined.
- In Chapter 9, the C# and Microsoft SQL server source codes for the implementation of multilevel relational database security models will be presented.

2

BASIC CONCEPT OF MULTILEVEL DATABASE SECURITY

2.1 Introduction

Mandatory access control (MAC) is a method of restricting unauthorized users from accessing objects that contain some sensitive information. An implementation of MAC is multilevel security (MLS), which has been developed mainly for computer and database systems at highly sensitive government organizations such as the intelligence community or the U.S. Department of Defense.

In multilevel security, each datum is defined as an object and has a security class level (classification), and each user is defined as a subject and has a security class level (clearance). The class level of an object or a subject A is called a label and is denoted as L (A). The access control in multilevel security is based on the Bell–LaPadula model [16], which has the following properties:

- The simple security property: A user, s, is allowed a read access to an object, o, only if L (s) is higher than or identical to L (o).
- The *-property: A user, s, is allowed a write access to an object, o, only if L (s) is identical to or lower than L (o).
- The strong * property: A user, s, is allowed a write access to an object, o, only if L (s) is identical to L (o).

The goal of the simple security property is to prevent a subject with low clearance from accessing a higher object (that is, no read-up), while the goal of the *-property, as shown in Figure 2.1, is to prevent a subject with a high clearance from writing data to a subject that is cleared at a lower level (that is, no write-down).

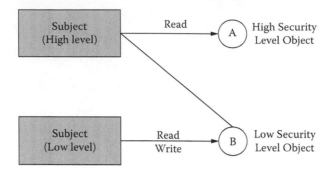

Figure 2.1   Illegal information flow in multilevel secure data model.

2.2 Multilevel Database Relations

A relational database consists of a relation schema and a relation instance. The relation schema can be defined as the structure of the relational database that consists of the relation's name, the name of each attribute (or column), and the domain of each attribute. A relation schema is denoted as $R(A_1; \ldots; A_n)$, where each A_i is an attribute in the relational schema. An instance of a relation can be defined as a set of tuples (rows) in which each tuple has the same number of attributes as the relation schema. A relation instance is denoted as $r(a_1; \ldots; a_n)$.

In the multilevel relational database, each data attribute in the schema is associated with a security classification attribute called the classification attribute [17]. Also, the multilevel relational database schema contains an additional attribute, called tuple classification, that identifies the security classification of each tuple. The multilevel relation database schema can be denoted as $R(A_1; C_1; \ldots; A_n; C_n; TC)$, where each A_i is a data attribute, each C_i is a classification attribute for A_i, and TC is the tuple-class attribute. The primary data attribute is denoted as PK and its corresponding classification attribute can be denoted as C_{PK}.

For simplicity, the multilevel security hierarchy has four levels of increasing sensitivity. These levels, from lowest to highest, are unclassified (U), confidential (C), secret (S), and top secret (TS). Data in relational multilevel database security are labeled with their own security classification. Users who need to access data should have the appropriate security classification level.

Table 2.1   Employee Relation in Multilevel Form

EMPLOYEE	DEPARTMENT	SALARY	TC
Ahmed U	Accounting U	7,000 U	U
Ahmed U	Sales S	7,000 U	S
Ahmed C	IT C	10,000 C	C
Mohamed TS	Telecom TS	5,000 TS	TS

Table 2.2   Employee Relation Instance for a C User

EMPLOYEE	DEPARTMENT	SALARY	TC
Ahmed U	Accounting U	7,000 U	U
Ahmed C	IT C	10,000 C	C

Table 2.1 shows a multilevel relation employee, which has three data attributes: employee (employee name; the primary key), department (department), and salary (salary). In addition to data attributes, it has the tuple class attribute TC. Instead, the security class of each attribute is shown to the right of its data value. According to the simple security property of the Bell–LaPadula model, a multilevel relation should be differently viewed by different users, depending on their clearances. For instance, a user with L clearance will see the filtered relation instance employee, as shown in Table 2.2, while a TS user will see the entire relation of Table 2.1.

2.3 Polyinstantiation

The covert channel represents the problem of the possibility that a lower level user can predict some unauthorized information from a higher security level [18]. Assume that the database contains an employee named Ahmed (with security level C) and that another user (with security level U) decides to insert a tuple that contains Ahmed as the name of the employee. If that insert is rejected, a U level user can know that there is an employee named Ahmed that exists in the multilevel relational database on some higher security level. A poly-instantiation integrity property can solve the covert channel problem that would be opened "by default" every time the lower level user tries to insert a tuple with the primary key attribute that already exists in the database on some higher security level.

In the multilevel relational database, the relation can be polyin-stantiated when it contains two or more tuples with the same primary key values. Polyinstantiation occurs in the following two situations:

- *Invisible polyinstantiation* can occur when a user with a low security level inserts data in an attribute that already contains data with a higher security level.
- *Visible polyinstantiation* can occur when a user with a high security level inserts data in an attribute that already contains data at a lower security level.

2.3.1 Invisible Polyinstantiation

The invisible polyinstantiation (polylow) can occur when a user at a low level of security needs to insert a new tuple that contains the same primary key as in an existing tuple with a high security level [19]. In the invisible polyinstantiation, the multilevel relational database security has three choices:

- Informing the user that the new tuple exists at a higher security level and therefore the insertion of the new tuple will be rejected: This choice leads to the covert channel problem because the user with a low security level gets unauthorized information at a high level of security.
- Replacing the existing tuple at a high security level with the new tuple being inserted with a low security level: This choice allows the user with a low security level to overwrite data not visible to him and thus break the data integrity.
- Inserting the new tuple with a low security level without modifying the existing tuple at the high security level: This choice leads to the polyinstantiation of the tuple because there are two tuples in the relation with the same primary key but in different security levels.

For example, consider the following scenario:

- A user with an S security level updates the salary to be 10,000 in Table 2.3. U user sees no change in the relation, as shown in Table 2.3, but S user sees the relation after an update, as shown in Table 2.4.

Table 2.3   Employee Relation in MLS Form

EMPLOYEE	DEPARTMENT	SALARY
Ahmed U	Accounting U	Null U

Table 2.4   S User View for Employee Relation after Updating the Salary to 10,000 by S User

EMPLOYEE	DEPARTMENT	SALARY
Ahmed U	Accounting U	10,000 S

Table 2.5   U User View for Employee Relation after Updating the Salary to 7,000 by U User

EMPLOYEE	DEPARTMENT	SALARY
Ahmed U	Accounting U	7,000 U

Table 2.6   S User View for Employee Relation after Updating the Salary to 7,000 by U User

EMPLOYEE	DEPARTMENT	SALARY
Ahmed U	Accounting U	7,000 U
Ahmed U	Accounting U	10,000 S

- Next, a U user updates the salary to be 7,000. The modification cannot be rejected because this leads to the covert channel problem.
- Thus, there are two options left: The first option is that the salary attribute can be overwritten in place at the cost of destroying secret data. This results in breaking the data integrity, as shown in Table 2.5. The second option is the invisible polyinstantiation, which will modify the relation in Table 2.4 to the relations in Table 2.6.

2.3.2 Visible Polyinstantiation

The visible polyinstantiation (polyhigh) can occur when a user at a high level of security needs to insert a new tuple that contains the same primary key as in an existing tuple with a low security level [20].

In visible polyinstantiation, the multilevel relational database security has three choices:

- Notifying the user that the new tuple exists at a lower security level and therefore the insertion of the new tuple will be rejected: This choice leads to the denial of service problem because the new tuple that needs to be inserted by the user with high security is rejected by a user in the low level of security.
- Replacing the existing tuple at a high security level with the new tuple being inserted with a low security level: This choice leads to the covert channel problem because the user with a low security level gets unauthorized information at a high level of security.
- Inserting the new tuple with a low security level without modifying the existing tuple at the high security level: This choice leads to the polyinstantiation of the tuple because there are two tuples in the relation with the same primary key but in different security levels.

2.3.3 Types of Polyinstantiation

There are two different types of polyinstantiation [21]:

- Entity polyinstantiation: In the multilevel relational database, the entity polyinstantiation can occur when a relation contains more than one tuple with the same primary key values, but with different access class values for the primary key. As shown in Table 2.7, there are two tuples with the same primary key (Ahmed) but with two different classes.
- Attribute polyinstantiation: In the multilevel relational database, the attribute polyinstantiation can occur when a relation contains two or more tuples with an identical primary key and its security level values, but with different values for one

Table 2.7   Entity Polyinstantiation

EMPLOYEE	DEPARTMENT	SALARY
Ahmed U	Accounting U	7,000 U
Ahmed S	Sales S	10,000 S

or more remaining attributes. As shown in Table 2.8, there are two tuples with the same primary key (Ahmed) and the same classes (U), but with different classes in the next two attributes (Department, Salary).

2.3.4 Architectural Considerations in Supporting Polyinstantiation

There are two different architectures of polyinstantiation:

- No MAC privileges architecture: As shown in Figure 2.2, the no MAC privileges (NMP) architecture has separated the relational database into smaller relational databases. This separation depends on the security level of each relational database. Also, the relational database management system has divided the process into a smaller process that can access all databases with data at or below its level. This architecture has bad data retrieval performance because a user will get the data from multiple single-level database fragments [22].
- Trusted subject architecture: As shown in Figure 2.3, the trusted subject architecture has a single database to be used in saving data at multiple security levels, and the database management system is trusted to guard against illegal information flows [23].

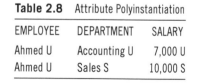

Table 2.8   Attribute Polyinstantiation

EMPLOYEE	DEPARTMENT	SALARY
Ahmed U	Accounting U	7,000 U
Ahmed U	Sales S	10,000 S

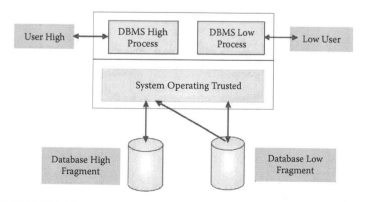

Figure 2.2   No MAC privileges architecture.

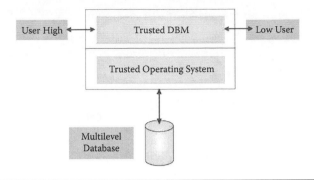

Figure 2.3   Trusted subject architecture.

Table 2.9   Comparison between Polyinstantiation Architectures

CRITERIA MODEL	POLYINSTANTIATION	TRUSTED DBMS	DATABASE FILES	PERFORMANCE
No MAC privileges architecture	Implicitly	Does not demand trust in DBMS	Multiple of single database files	Bad data retrieval performance
Trusted subject architecture	Explicitly	Demands trust in DBMS	Single database is used to save data at multiple security levels	Improved data retrieval performance

Table 2.9 gives a comparison between the previous two approaches to illustrate the advantages and disadvantages of each approach.

2.4 Multilevel Database Security Models

There are many multilevel relational database security models—for example, SeaView and those proposed by Sandhu–Jajodia, Smith–Winslett, etc. This section will present an overview of these models and identify the strengths and the weaknesses of each model.

2.4.1 SeaView Model

In the secure data views (SeaView) model, security levels are assigned to each data element in the attributes of the tuples in the relation, as shown in Table 2.7. In the SeaView model, data are stored in a set of single-level fragments and the multilevel relations are implemented as views over these single-level relations [24].

There are two algorithms that are used in the implementation of the SeaView model:

- The decomposition algorithm divides the multilevel relation into single-level fragments.
- The recovery algorithm reconstructs the original multilevel relation from the fragments.

In the SeaView model, the decomposition of the multilevel relations into single-level ones is performed by applying two different types of fragmentation: horizontal and vertical. Thus, the multilevel relation in Table 2.8 will be stored as five single-level fragments (one primary key group relation and four attribute group relations), as shown in Table 2.10.

The SeaView model has many problems due to the decomposition and recovery algorithms. These problems will be mentioned as follows:

- Repeated joins: Due to the vertical fragmentations that are used in the SeaView model, the query that involves multiple attributes will use a lot of repeated left outer joins between the several single-level relations to get the result.

Table 2.10   SeaView Decomposition of
Table 2.8 into Five Single-Level Base Relations

A

EMPLOYEE	
Ahmed U	

B

EMPLOYEE	*DEPARTMENT*
Ahmed U	Accounting U

C

EMPLOYEE	*SALARY*
Ahmed U	7,000 U

D

EMPLOYEE	*DEPARTMENT*
Ahmed U	Sales S

E

EMPLOYEE	*SALARY*
Ahmed U	10,000 S

- Spurious tuples: When the SeaView recovery algorithm is applied to the single-level relations, additional tuples will be inserted into the original relation. These additional tuples are called spurious tuples and are a result of repeated joins between single-level relations.
- Incompleteness: The SeaView decomposition algorithm puts limitations on the capability of the database. Several relation instances that have realistic and useful interpretations in real life cannot be realized in the SeaView model.
- Left outer joins: The SeaView recovery algorithm is based on the left outer join of relations. It is well known that join is a high-cost operation and should be avoided as much as possible.

2.4.2 Jajodia–Sandhu Model

The Jajodia–Sandhu model is derived from the SeaView model. It modifies the algorithm that decomposes a multilevel relation into single-level fragments and it also modifies the recovery algorithm that reconstructs the original multilevel relation [25].

In the Jajodia–Sandhu model, the decomposition algorithm uses only horizontal fragmentation since no vertical fragmentations are required. This results in improving the recovery algorithm in the Jajodia–Sandhu model over the recovery algorithm in the SeaView model because it is possible to reconstruct the multilevel relation without having to perform join operations; only union operations are required to reconstruct the multilevel relation.

For example, the relation in Table 2.8 will be decomposed into two single-level fragments, as shown in Table 2.11. This provides

Table 2.11 Jajodia and Sandhu Decomposition of Table 2.8 into Two Single-Level Base Relations

A

EMPLOYEE	DEPARTMENT	SALARY	TC
Ahmed U	Accounting U	7,000 U	U

B

EMPLOYEE	DEPARTMENT	SALARY	TC
Ahmed U	Sales S	10,000 S	S

the simplicity of tuple level labeling, combined with the flexibility of element-level labeling.

There are two major problems in the Jajodia–Sandhu model [26]:

- Semantic ambiguity: Suppose that there are two tuples in the relations with security levels U and S and there is no tuple with security level TS. If a user with security level TS needs to get information from the relation, he cannot decide which is the correct information because the values from the U tuple and the S tuple in the relation will be retrieved in the result of the query.

- Operational incompleteness: Suppose that there are two incomparable security levels, M1 and M2, whose least upper bound is the security level S and greatest lower bound is the security level U. There is no way for a user at security level S to insert tuples that contain attributes with security levels at U, M1, and M2.

2.4.3 Smith–Winslett Model

In the Smith–Winslett model, the multilevel relational database is seen as a set of ordinary relational databases where all the databases share the same schema. This model does not support security at the level of each single attribute. The security level can be assigned only to the primary key attributes and the tuples as a whole [27].

The multilevel relational scheme is given as $R(A_{PK}, C_{PK}, A_1 ...,$ $A_n, TC)$, where A_{pk} is denoted as the primary key data attribute, C_{pk} is the primary key classification attribute that contains the security level of the primary key data attribute, $A_1 ... A_n$ is denoted as the data attributes, and TC is denoted as the tuple classification attribute that contains the security level of the tuple.

An example relation is given in Table 2.12, where a user can see the tuples from his own security level and the tuples from all lower security levels. A user accepts the tuples from his own security level only.

Table 2.12   Smith–Winslett Model

EMPLOYEE	DEPARTMENT	SALARY	TC
Ahmed U	Accounting	7,000	U
Ahmed S	Sales	10,000	S

According to these rules, an update and read access are defined. A database modification (insert, delete, and update) from a user can only alter data at the user's security level. A query from a user at security level L can access data from exactly those databases whose level is not higher than the level L.

In this model, a semantics based on the concept of belief has been added. The Smith–Winslett model is also known as the belief-based semantics model and also introduced the concept of a base tuple. The base tuple is the lowest security level of database tuple where the existence of an entity is asserted. As such, the update procedure eliminates the problems present in the Jajodia–Sandhu model, but restricts the scope of an update to a single entity.

2.4.4 MLR Model

The multilevel relation (MLR) model presents the concept of data-borrow integrity, which ensures upward information flow. Modifications to the data at a lower security level can be automatically propagated to higher security levels that need to borrow those data [28].

This model is concerned with eliminating the semantic ambiguity problem in the Jajodia–Sandhu model. A user with a security level can accept data that consist of two parts: data that have the same security level and data that are borrowed from lower security level users. The data a subject can see are those accepted by subjects at the data's level or at levels below that.

The multilevel relational scheme is given as $R(A_{PK}, C_{PK}, A_1, C_1, \ldots, A_n, C_n, TC)$, where A_{pk} is denoted as the primary key data attribute, C_{pk} is the primary key classification attribute that contains the security level of the primary key data attribute, $A_1 \ldots A_n$ is denoted as the data attributes, $C_1 \ldots C_n$ is denoted as the data classification attributes that contain the security level of the primary key data attributes, and TC is denoted as the tuple classification attribute that contains the security level of the tuple.

In Table 2.13 we can see that a user with S security level has used the UPLEVEL command to indicate that he believes the first tuple and insert the second tuple with S security level. However, there is no way for the user with high-level security to define his belief or disbelief in the tuple.

Table 2.13 MLR Model

EMPLOYEE	DEPARTMENT	SALARY	TC
Ahmed U	Accounting U	7,000 U	U
Ahmed U	Accounting U	7,000 U	S
Mohamed U	Sales U	10,000 U	U

2.4.5 Belief-Consistent Multilevel Secure Data Model

In the belief-consistent multilevel secure (BCMLS) data model, each attribute is associated to another security level attribute [29]. The security level attribute is a security label that has one or more letters and each letter defines a security level. Each security level letter in the label should be greater than the security level to its left letter. The first letter defines the security level at which the value of the attribute was entered and is called the primary security level of that attribute. Information that has a security level equal to the primary security level of the label is believed to be true by users. The letters that follow the first letter of the label are called secondary levels and they define the security levels for users that believe the information, and this belief can be either true or false. No symbol (–) before the letters means that there are secondary levels where the information is believed to be true. If there is a symbol (–) before the letters, this means that there are secondary levels where the information is believed to be false. A lower level tuple can be interpreted by a higher level user as true or false. The false tuple can be interpreted as a cover story tuple or mirage tuple.

If a lower level tuple presents the same entity as other higher security level tuples, the lower security level tuple is defined by a higher security level user as a false tuple that defines a cover story tuple.

If a false tuple does not correspond to any real-world entity in the belief of a higher security level user, such a tuple defines a mirage tuple for the higher level user.

Information that is labeled would be defined as true by users with U and C security levels and as false by users on the S security level. The BCMLS model defines the primary security level as the level where the tuple was originally inserted into the database and this tuple is called a base tuple. In Table 2.14, the UC-S label indicates U and C beliefs of true in the information and S belief of false in the same information. The user sees and believes the contents of

Table 2.14   Belief-Consistent Multilevel Secure Relational Data Model

EMPLOYEE	DEPARTMENT	SALARY	TC
Ahmed U	Accounting U	7,000 U	U
Mohamed UC-S	Sales UC-S	10,000 UC-S	UC-S

the database at his own security level and also can access the contents of the database at lower levels. The user also has access to the beliefs of users at lower levels. Users can define their beliefs through the new verify mechanism. The users at each security level can decide what information is accepted. The great advantage of the BCMLS model is the fact that the accepted information does not need to be replicated or borrowed.

2.5 Performance Study

This section describes the performance study of relational multilevel database models—SeaView, Jajodia–Sandhu, Smith–Winslett, MLR, and belief-consistent models—and illustrates the impact of varying the size and structure of the relational multilevel database on the performance of these models.

The machine that is used for the implementation of the performance study consists of CPU speed of 2.2 GHz, physical RAM size of 3 GB, and hard disk size of 320 GB. The software that is used in the implementation is Microsoft SQL server 2008 R2 and the experiments' measurements were captured at the machine using a monitoring tool provided by the Microsoft SQL server. The experiments measure the impact of changing the number of tuples, the number of attributes, and the number of security levels on the performance of the relational multilevel database models. These experiments define the CPU response time (in seconds) as metric. For each query, the monitoring tool observes the time that is taken for the system to give the result of the query.

2.5.1 Experimental Database Structure

An experimental database, the timesheet database, consisting of four relations, was created and populated to facilitate the performance study. The employee relation provides information about employees, the departure relation is used to store the departure notice of each employee when he leaves the site of the work, the timesheet relation is used to store the timesheet of each employee every day, and the annual rights relation is used to store the rights of each employee every year.

2.5.2 Impact of Varying the Number of Tuples

This experiment was designed to determine if the cost of processing varying numbers of tuples has an impact on the performance of the multilevel database models. We chose this experiment because the size of a database is, in part, based on the number of its tuples (records), and the number of tuples processed during each transaction could determine how long it takes to return a response to a user (Figure 2.4).

2.5.3 Impact of Varying the Number of Attributes

This experiment was designed to determine if the cost of processing varying numbers of attributes has an impact on the performance of the multilevel database models (Figure 2.5).

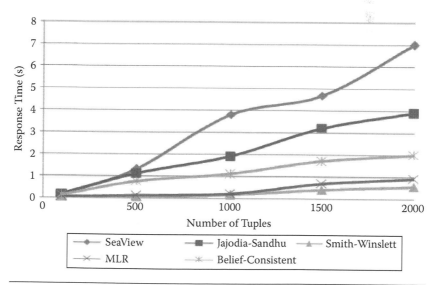

Figure 2.4   The impact of varying the number of tuples on the performance of a multilevel database.

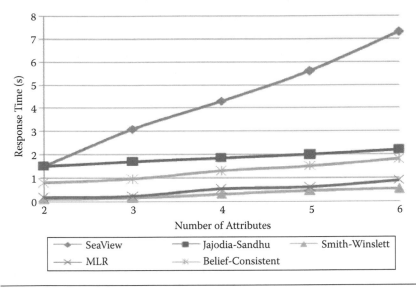

Figure 2.5　The impact of varying the number of attributes on the performance of a multilevel database.

2.5.4 Impact of Varying the Number of Security Levels

This experiment was designed to determine if the cost of processing varying numbers of security levels has an impact on the performance of the multilevel database models (Figure 2.6).

2.5.5 Analysis of Experimental Results

From the previous experimental results, the performance of the Smith–Winslett model is the best because it does not support security classification at the level of each single attribute; the access classes can be assigned only to key attributes and to tuples as a whole. The MLR model offers less performance than the Smith–Winslett model because it supports classification at the level of each single attribute. The belief-consistent model offers less performance than the MLR model because it supports a combination of classification levels for each single attribute to enable the user to assert his beliefs of lower level users' information. The Jajodia–Sandhu model has performed badly because of the impact of union operation between single-level relations in the recovery algorithm. The SeaView model performs very badly because of the impact of join operation between vertical, single-level relations

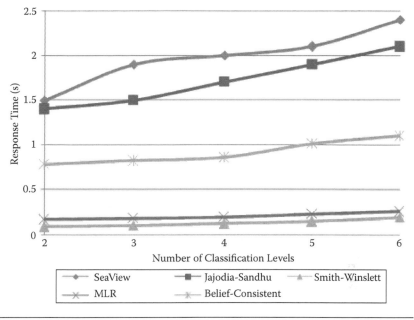

Figure 2.6 The impact of varying the number of classification levels on the performance of a multilevel database.

and union operation between horizontal, single-level relations in the recovery algorithm.

2.6 Summary

This chapter introduced a survey of relational database security and focused on the mandatory access control models. Then this chapter gave a survey about relational multilevel database security management systems, explained the use of polyinstantiation in relational databases with multilevel security, and defined how the polyinstantiation can occur and the types of polyinstantiation. Also, this chapter presented the most common models for multilevel secure RDBMS (relational database management systems) and made a comparative study to explain the strength and weakness of each model. According to this comparative study, the MLR data model is a simple, unambiguous, and powerful model for implementing multilevel secure RDBMS.

3

IMPLEMENTATION OF MLS/ DBMS MODELS

3.1 Introduction

The goal of multilevel security (MLS) for a relational database is to prevent the unauthorized access of the data by preventing any user from accessing any data to which he has no access. A lot of multilevel security database management system (DBMS) models have been proposed to apply the concept of multilevel security for the relational database.

This chapter will illustrate the implementation of the multilevel security database management systems (MLS/DBMS) models. Also, this chapter will provide the flow charts that explain the procedure of implementing data manipulation language (DML) operations such as SELECT, INSERT, UPDATE, and DELETE for each model of the MLS/DBMS models.

3.2 SeaView Model

3.2.1 Selected Operation Procedure

The SQL command for the selected operation is described as follows:

```
SELECT [A₁,A₂,...,Aₙ]
FROM R
WHERE P
```

where R is a multilevel security relation, $[A_1, A_2, \ldots, A_n]$ are the attributes of the relation R, and P is the condition of the select statement that defines the tuples to be retrieved. If a user with a security class level L executes a command to select tuples from an MLS relation R, the selection operation is implemented as follows [30]:

- Step 1: get the security class level of the user that runs the select operation.

- Step 2: make a logical view over the stored single security level relations by performing join between vertical single security class level relations and union between horizontal single-level relations.
- Step 3: get all tuples from the logical view that have security levels below or equal to the security class level of the subject that runs the selection operation.

Figure 3.1 illustrates the flow chart for the selection operation in the SeaView model.

3.2.2 Insert Operation Procedure

The SQL statement for the insert operation is described as follows:

```
INSERT
INTO R  [A₁,A₂, ...,Aₙ]
VALUES  [a₁,a₂, ...,aₙ]
```

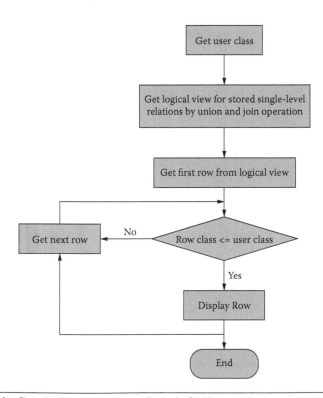

Figure 3.1 Flow chart for selection operation in the SeaView model.

where R is an MLS relation, $A_1, A_2, \ldots, A_n$ are the attributes from R, and $a_1, a_2, \ldots, a_n$ are values from domains of $A_1, A_2, \ldots, A_n$. If a subject with the security class level L runs a command to insert a tuple in an MLS relation R, the insertion operation is implemented as follows [30]:

- Step 1: get the security level of the subject that runs the insert operation.
- Step 2: if the attribute is included in the attributes list in the insert statement, this attribute will be set to its value from the values list in the insert statement.
- Step 3: the security level of all attributes will be equal to the security level of the subject that runs the insert operation.
- Step 4: insert into single-level relations, with the security level equal to the security level of the user, values that are included in the values list of the insert statement and that correspond to the attributes of these single-level relations.

Figure 3.2 illustrates the flow chart for the insert operation in the SeaView model.

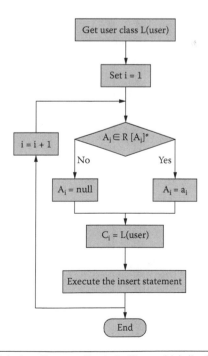

Figure 3.2   Flow chart for insertion operation in SeaView and Jajodia–Sandhu models.

3.2.3 *Update Operation Procedure*

The SQL statement for the update operation is described as follows:

```
UPDATE R
SET [A₁ = a₁, A₂ = a₂, ...,Aₙ = aₙ]
WHERE P
```

where R is an MLS relation, $A_1, A_2, \ldots, A_n$ are attributes from R, $a_1, a_2, \ldots, a_n$ are values from domains of $A_1, A_2, \ldots, A_n$, and P is an update condition that defines the tuples needed to be updated.

If a subject with the security class level L runs a command to update an MLS relation R, for all $t \in R$, if t satisfies P, the update operation is implemented as follows [30]:

- Step 1: get the security level of the subject that runs the update operation.
- Step 2: get all tuples that satisfy update condition P in the update statement and have a security level equal to or below the security level of the user.
- Step 3: for each tuple in the tuples in step 2, if the security level of a primary key is equal to the security level of the user, the tuple in the single-level relation that contains the attributes in the set clause will be updated.
- Step 4: for each tuple in the tuples in step 2, if the security level of a primary key is lower than the security level of the user, the tuple in the single-level relation that contains the attributes in the set clause will be polyinstantiated at the security level of the user.

Figure 3.3 illustrates the flow chart for the update operation in the SeaView model.

3.2.4 *Delete Operation Procedure*

The SQL statement for the delete operation is described as follows:

```
DELETE
FROM R
WHERE P
```

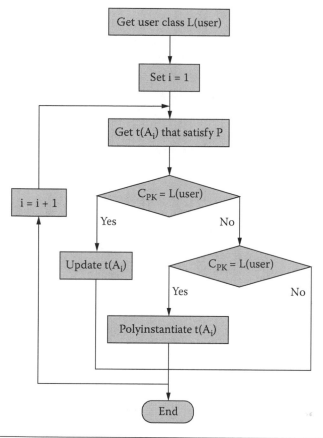

Figure 3.3 Flow chart for update operation in SeaView and Jajodia–Sandhu models.

where R is an MLS relation and P is a delete condition that defines the tuples that are to be deleted. If a subject with the security class level L runs a command to delete tuples from MLS relation R, for all $t \in$ R, if t satisfies P, the delete operation is implemented as follows [30]:

- Step 1: get the security level of the subject that runs the delete operation.
- Step 2: delete all tuples from single-level relations that satisfy delete condition P in the delete statement and have a security level equal to the security level of the user.

Figure 3.4 illustrates the flow chart for the delete operation in the SeaView model.

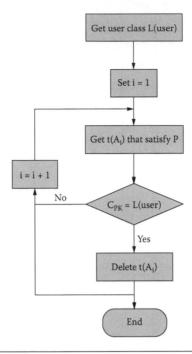

Figure 3.4   Flow chart for delete operation in SeaView and Jajodia–Sandhu models.

3.3 Jajodia–Sandhu Model

3.3.1 Select Operation Procedure

The SQL statement for the select operation is described as follows:

```
SELECT [A₁,A₂,...,Aₙ]
FROM R
WHERE P
```

where R is an MLS relation, $[A_1, A_2, \ldots, A_n]$ are the attributes from R, and P is the select condition that defines tuples to be retrieved.

If a subject with the security class level L runs a command to select tuples from an MLS relation R, the selection operation is implemented as follows [31]:

- Step 1: get the security level of the subject that runs the select operation.
- Step 2: make a logical view over the stored single-level relations that perform the union operation between horizontal single-level relations.

- Step 3: get all tuples, from the logical view, that have a security level below or equal to the security level of the subject that runs the select operation.

Figure 3.5 illustrates the flow chart for a selection operation in the Jajodia–Sandhu model.

3.3.2 Insert Operation Procedure

The SQL statement for the insert operation is described as follows:

```
INSERT
INTO R  [A₁,A₂, ...,Aₙ]
VALUES  [a₁,a₂, ...,aₙ]
```

where R is an MLS relation, $A_1, A_2, \ldots, A_n$ are the attributes from R, and $a_1, a_2, \ldots, a_n$ are values from domains of $A_1, A_2, \ldots, A_n$.

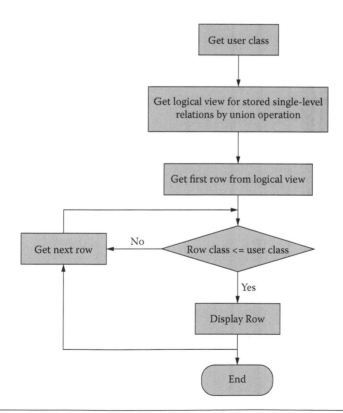

Figure 3.5   Flow chart for selection operation in Jajodia–Sandhu model.

If a subject with the security class level L runs a command to insert a tuple into an MLS relation R, the insertion operation is implemented as follows [31]:

- Step 1: get the security level of the subject that runs the insert operation.
- Step 2: if the attribute is included in the attribute list in the insert statement, this attribute will be set to its value from the values list in the insert statement.
- Step 3: the security level of all attributes will be equal to the security level of the subject that runs the insert operation.
- Step 4: insert into the single-level relation, with the security level equal to the security level of the user, values that are included in the values list of the insert statement and correspond to the attributes of these single-level relations.

Figure 3.2 illustrates the flow chart for the insertion operation in the Jajodia–Sandhu model.

3.3.3 Update Operation Procedure

The SQL statement for the update operation is described as follows:

```
UPDATE R
SET [A₁ = a₁, A₂ = a₂, ..., Aₙ = aₙ]
WHERE P
```

where R is an MLS relation, $A_1, A_2, ..., A_n$ are attributes from R, $a_1, a_2, ..., a_n$ are values from domains of $A_1, A_2, ..., A_n$, and P is an update condition that defines the tuples that are to be updated.

If a subject with the security class level L runs a command to update an MLS relation R, for all $t \in R$, if t satisfies P, the update operation is implemented as follows [31]:

- Step 1: get the security level of the subject that runs the update operation.
- Step 2: get all tuples that satisfy update condition P in the update statement and have security levels equal to or below the security level of the user.

- Step 3: for each tuple in the tuples in step 2, if the security level of the primary key is equal to the security level of the user, the tuple in the single level will be updated.
- Step 4: for each tuple in the tuples in step 2, if the security level of the primary key is lower than the security level of the user, the tuple in the single level will be polyinstantiated at the security level of the user.

Figure 3.3 illustrates the flow chart for the update operation in the Jajodia–Sandhu model.

3.3.4 Delete Operation Procedure

The SQL statement for the delete operation is described as follows:

```
DELETE
FROM R
WHERE P
```

where R is an MLS relation and P is a delete condition that defines the tuples that are to be deleted.

If a subject with the security class level L runs a command to delete tuples from an MLS relation R, for all $t \in R$, if t satisfies P, the delete operation is implemented as follows [31]:

- Step 1: get the security level of the subject that runs the delete operation.
- Step 2: delete all tuples that satisfy delete condition P in the delete statement and have a security level equal to the security level of the user.

Figure 3.4 illustrates the flow chart for the delete operation in the Jajodia–Sandhu model.

3.4 Smith–Winslett Model

3.4.1 Select Operation Procedure

The SQL statement for the selected operation is described as follows:

```
SELECT [A₁,A₂,...,Aₙ]
FROM R
WHERE P
```

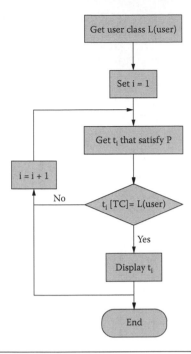

Figure 3.6   Flow chart for select operation in Smith–Winslett and MLR models.

where R is an MLS relation, $[A_1, A_2, \ldots, A_n]$ are the attributes from R, and P is the select condition that defines the tuples to be retrieved.

If a subject with the security class level L runs a command to select tuples from an MLS relation R, the selection operation is implemented as follows [32]:

- Step 1: get the security level of the subject that runs the selected operation.
- Step 2: get all tuples that have a security level below or equal to the security level of the subject that runs the selected operation.

Figure 3.6 illustrates the flow chart for a selection operation in the Smith–Winslett model.

3.4.2 Insert Operation Procedure

The SQL statement for the insert operation is described as follows:

```
INSERT
INTO R  [A₁,A₂, ...,Aₙ]
VALUES  [a₁,a₂, ...,aₙ]
```

where R is an MLS relation, $A_1, A_2, \ldots, A_n$ are the attributes from R, and $a_1, a_2, \ldots, a_n$ are values from domains of $A_1, A_2, \ldots, A_n$. If a subject with the security class level L runs a command to insert a tuple into an MLS relation R, the insertion operation is implemented as follows [32]:

- Step 1: get the security level of the subject that runs the insert operation.
- Step 2: if the attribute is included in the attributes list in the insert statement, this attribute will be set to its value from the values list of the insert statement.
- Step 3: the security level of the primary key will be equal to the security level of the subject that runs the insert operation.
- Step 4: insert the new tuple into the multilevel relation.

Figure 3.7 illustrates the flow chart for the insertion operation in the Smith–Winslett model.

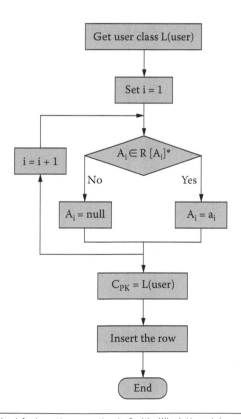

Figure 3.7   Flow chart for insertion operation in Smith–Winslett model.

3.4.3 Update Operation Procedure

The SQL statement for the update operation is described as follows:

```
UPDATE R
SET [A₁ = a₁, A₂ = a₂, ..., Aₙ = aₙ]
WHERE P
```

where R is an MLS relation, $A_1, A_2, \ldots, A_n$ are attributes from R, $a_1, a_2, \ldots, a_n$ are values from domains of $A_1, A_2, \ldots, A_n$, and P is an update condition that defines the tuples that are to be updated.

If a subject with the security class level L runs a command to update an MLS relation R, for all $t \in R$, if t satisfies P, the update operation is implemented as follows [32]:

- Step 1: get the security level of the subject that runs the update operation.
- Step 2: update all tuples that satisfy update condition P in the update statement and have a security level equal to the security level of the user.

Figure 3.8 illustrates the flow chart for the update operation in the Smith–Winslett model.

3.4.4 Delete Operation Procedure

The SQL statement for the delete operation is described as follows:

```
DELETE
FROM R
WHERE P
```

where R is an MLS relation and P is a delete condition that defines the tuples that are to be deleted.

If a subject with the security class level L runs a command to delete tuples from MLS relation R, for all $t \in R$, if t satisfies P, the delete operation is implemented as follows [32]:

- Step 1: get the security level of the subject that runs the delete operation.
- Step 2: delete all tuples that satisfy delete condition P in the delete statement and have a security level equal to the security level of the user.

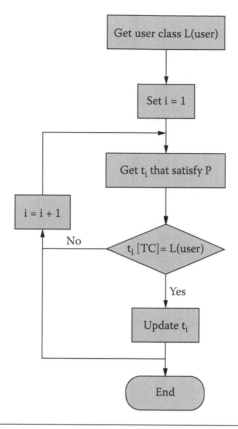

Figure 3.8   Flow chart for update operation in Smith–Winslett model.

Figure 3.9 illustrates the flow chart for the delete operation in the Smith–Winslett model.

3.5 Multilevel Relational (MLR) Model

3.5.1 Select Operation Procedure

The SQL statement for the select operation is described as follows:

```
SELECT [A₁,A₂,...,Aₙ]
FROM R
WHERE P
```

where R is an MLS relation, $[A_1, A_2, \ldots, A_n]$ are the attributes from R, and P is the select condition that defines the tuples to be retrieved. If a subject with the security class level L runs a command to select

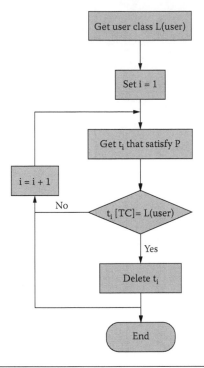

Figure 3.9   Flow chart for delete operation in Smith–Winslett model.

tuples from an MLS relation R, the selection operation is implemented as follows [33]:

- Step 1: get the security level of the subject that runs the select operation.
- Step 2: get all tuples that have a security level below or equal to the security level of the subject that runs the select operation and that satisfy selection condition P.

Figure 3.6 illustrates the flow chart for the selection operation in the MLR model.

3.5.2 Insert Operation Procedure

The SQL statement for the insert operation is described as follows:

```
INSERT
INTO R [A₁,A₂,...,Aₙ]
VALUES [a₁,a₂,...,aₙ]
```

where R is an MLS relation, $A_1, A_2, \ldots, A_n$ are the attributes from R, and $a_1, a_2, \ldots, a_n$ are values from domains of $A_1, A_2, \ldots, A_n$. If a subject with the security class level L runs a command to insert a tuple into an MLS relation R, the insertion operation is implemented as follows [33]:

- Step 1: get the security level of the subject that runs the insert operation.
- Step 2: if the attribute is included in the attributes list in the insert statement, this attribute will be set to its value from the values list in the insert statement; otherwise, the value of this attribute will be null.
- Step 3: the security level of all attributes will be equal to the security level of the subject that runs the insert operation.
- Step 4: insert a new tuple with the attribute's values and its security level into the multilevel relation.

Figure 3.10 illustrates the flow chart for the insertion operation in the MLR model.

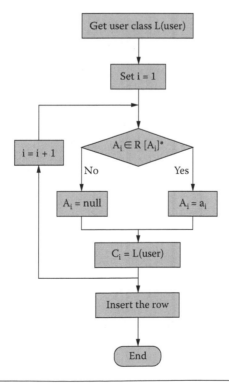

Figure 3.10   Flow chart for insertion operation in MLR and belief-consistent models.

3.5.3 Update Operation Procedure

The SQL statement for the update operation is described as follows:

```
UPDATE R
SET [A₁ = a₁, A₂ = a₂, ..., Aₙ = aₙ]
WHERE P
```

where R is an MLS relation, $A_1, A_2, \ldots, A_n$ are attributes from R, $a_1, a_2, \ldots, a_n$ are values from domains of $A_1, A_2, \ldots, A_n$, and P is an update condition that defines the tuples that are to be updated. If a subject with the security class level L runs a command to update an MLS relation R, for all $t \in R$, if t satisfies P, the update operation is implemented as follows [33]:

- Step 1: get the security level of the subject that runs the update operation.
- Step 2: if no attribute of the primary key is in the SET clause, update all tuples in multilevel relations that satisfy the update condition P in the update statement and have a security level equal to the security level of the user. Also, all borrowed tuples by higher level users that satisfy update condition P in the update statement will be updated.
- Step 3: if some attribute of the primary key is in the SET clause, update all tuples in multilevel relations that satisfy update condition P in the update statement and have a security level equal to the security level of the user. Delete all borrowed tuples by higher level users that satisfy update condition P in the update statement.

Figure 3.11 illustrates the flow chart for the update operation in the MLR model.

3.5.4 Delete Operation Procedure

The SQL statement for the delete operation is described as follows:

```
DELETE
FROM R
WHERE P
```

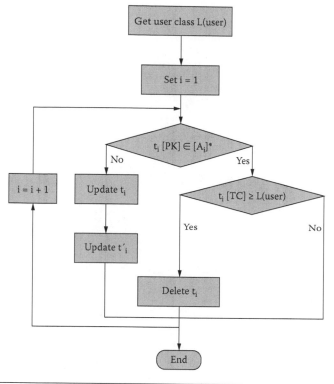

Figure 3.11 Flow chart for update operation in an MLR model.

where R is an MLS relation and P is a delete condition that defines the tuples that are to be deleted. If a subject with the security class level L runs a command to delete tuples from MLS relation R, for all $t \in$ R, if t satisfies P, the delete operation is implemented as follows [33]:

- Step 1: get the security level of the subject that runs the delete operation.
- Step 2: delete all tuples from multilevel relations that satisfy delete condition P in the delete statement and have a security level equal to the security level of the user.
- Step 3: if there is a tuple that satisfies the delete condition P in the delete statement and is borrowed by a high-level user, the high-level user will be notified by exceptions or warnings to delete this borrowed tuple.

Figure 3.12 illustrates the flow chart for the delete operation in the MLR model.

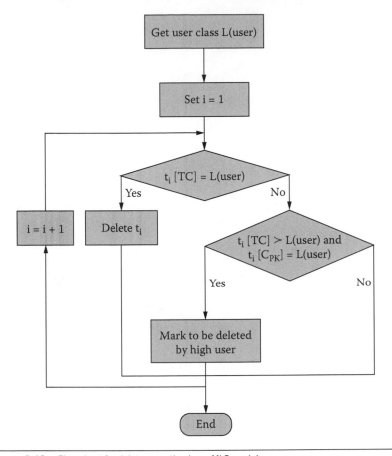

Figure 3.12   Flow chart for delete operation in an MLR model.

3.5.5 Uplevel Operation Procedure

The SQL statement for the uplevel operation is described as follows:

```
UPLEVEL R
GET [A₁,A₂,...,Aₙ] FROM [C₁,C₂,...,Cₙ]
WHERE P
```

where R is an MLS relation, $A_1, A_2, \ldots, A_n$ are the attributes from R, $C_1, C_2, \ldots, C_n$ are the classification level of $A_1, A_2, \ldots, A_n$, and P is an uplevel condition that defines the tuples that are to be upleveled. A user on the security level L issues an UPLEVEL command to indicate that he believes the tuples in the lower level. If a subject with the security class level L runs a command to uplevel tuples from

MLS relation R: for all $t \in$ R, if t satisfies P, the uplevel operation is implemented as follows [33]:

- Step 1: get the security level of the subject that runs the uplevel operation.
- Step 2: get all tuples from the multilevel relation that satisfy uplevel condition P in the uplevel statement and have a tuple security level lower than or equal to the security level of the user.
- Step 3: for each tuple t' in the tuples in step 2, a user tuple t is constructed as follows. The primary key of tuple t and its security level are equal to the primary key of the tuple t' and its class level. For each nonprimary key attribute in the tuple t' attribute, if the attribute is in a GET clause, the attribute of tuple t and its security level will be equal to this attribute of the tuple t' and its class level. If the attribute is not in the GET clause, the attribute of tuple t will be null and its security level will be equal to the security level of the user.
- Step 4: if there is a tuple with a primary key and tuple class equal to the primary key and tuple class of the user tuple t, this tuple will be replaced by the user tuple. If there is no tuple, the user tuple will be inserted into the multilevel relation.

Figure 3.13 illustrates the flow chart for the uplevel operation in the MLR model.

3.6 Belief-Consistent Multilevel Secure Relational Data Model

3.6.1 Basic Procedures for Operations

3.6.1.1 Xview (Label) Procedure This procedure returns the visible part of the security label for the user who executes it [34].

- Step 1: get the label as input parameter for the procedure.
- Step 2: break the label into parts.
- Step 3: get the security level of the subject that runs the procedure.
- Step 4: set the counter equal to 1.
- Step 5: while (counter ≤ user level), pack the new label with parts that the user can see.
- Step 6: increment the counter by 1.
- Step 7: return the new label.

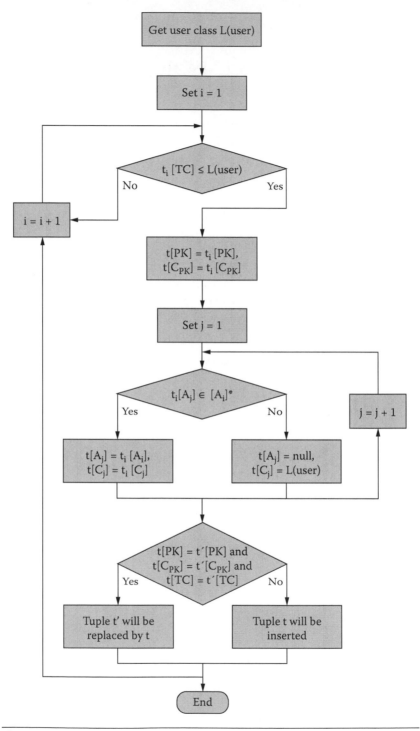

Figure 3.13 Flow chart for uplevel operation in an MLR model.

Figure 3.14 illustrates the flow chart for the Xview (label) procedure in the belief-consistent model.

3.6.1.2 Pl (Label) Procedure   This procedure returns the primary level of the security label [34]—for example, L = ucs, Pl (L) = u.

- Step 1: get the label as input parameter for the procedure.
- Step 2: break the label into parts.
- Step 3: return the first part that has a belief value equal to true.

Figure 3.15 illustrates the flow chart for the Pl (label) procedure in the belief-consistent model.

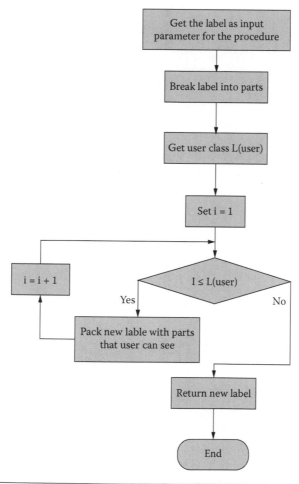

Figure 3.14   Flow chart for Xview (label) procedure in a belief-consistent model.

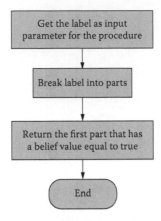

Figure 3.15 Flow chart for Pl (label) procedure in a belief-consistent model.

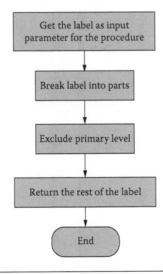

Figure 3.16 Flow chart for Sl (label) procedure in a belief-consistent model.

3.6.1.3 Sl (Label) Procedure This procedure returns the secondary level of the security label [34]—for example, L = ucs, Sl(L) = cs.

- Step 1: get the label as input parameter for the procedure.
- Step 2: break the label into parts.
- Step 3: exclude the primary level.
- Step 4: return the rest.

Figure 3.16 illustrates the flow chart for the Sl (label) procedure in the belief-consistent model.

3.6.1.4 Ib (Label) Procedure This procedure returns the belief of a user from the security level L about information labeled by the label L [34]—for example, L = ucs, Ib (S, L) = s.

- Step 1: divide the security class levels into parts.
- Step 2: get the security level of the subject that runs the procedure.
- Step 3: set the counter equal to 1.
- Step 4: while (counter ≠ user − level), the return value will be equal to mod (L, number of class levels) and L will be equal to L/number of class levels.
- Step 5: increment the counter by 1.
- Step 6: return value.

Figure 3.17 illustrates the flow chart for the Ib (label) procedure in the belief-consistent model.

3.6.2 Select Operation Procedure

The SQL statement for the select operation is described as follows:

```
SELECT [A₁,A₂,...,Aₙ]
FROM R
WHERE P
```

where R is an MLS relation, $[A_1, A_2, \ldots, A_n]$ are the attributes from R, and P is the select condition that defines the tuples to be retrieved. If a subject with the security class level L runs a command to select tuples from an MLS relation R, the selection operation is implemented as follows [35]:

- Step 1: get all tuples that have an Xview (tuple class) not equal to zero and satisfy selection condition P.
- Step 2: for each attribute in the attributes of each tuple in the tuples in step 1, get Xview (attribute class).

Figure 3.18 illustrates the flow chart for the selected operation in the belief-consistent model.

3.6.3 Insert Operation Procedure

The SQL statement for the insert operation is described as follows:

```
INSERT
INTO R [A₁,A₂,...,Aₙ]
VALUES' [a₁,a₂,...,aₙ]
```

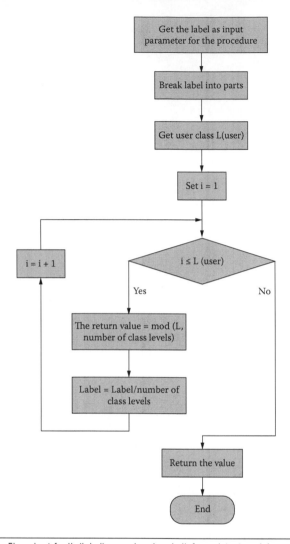

Figure 3.17 Flow chart for lb (label) procedure in a belief-consistent model.

where R is an MLS relation, $A_1, A_2, \ldots, A_n$ are the attributes from R, and $a_1, a_2, \ldots, a_n$ are values from domains of $A_1, A_2, \ldots, A_n$. If a subject with the security class level L runs a command to insert a tuple in an MLS relation R, the insertion operation is implemented as follows [35]:

- Step 1: get the security level of the subject that runs the select operation.
- Step 2: if the attribute is included in the attributes list in the insert statement, this attribute will be set to its value from

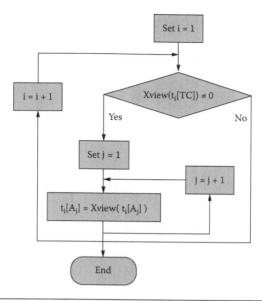

Figure 3.18 Flow chart for select operation in the belief-consistent model.

the values list in the insert statement; else the value of this attribute will be null.

- Step 3: the security level of all attributes will be equal to the security level of the subject that runs the insert operation.
- Step 4: insert a new tuple with attribute values and a security level into the multilevel relation.

Figure 3.10 illustrates the flow chart for insertion operation in the belief-consistent model.

3.6.4 Verify Operation Procedure

The SQL statement for the verify operation is described as follows:

```
VERIFY (TRUE/FALSE) R
WHERE P
```

where R is an MLS relation and P is an update condition that defines the tuples that are to be verified. In the belief-consistent MLS model, users are able to define their beliefs and disbeliefs specifically through the verify operation [35]:

- Step 1: get the security level of the subject that runs the select operation.

- Step 2: for each attribute in the attributes of tuple t, break its security level into parts.
- Step 3: for each security level part in parts in step 2, if this part of the security level is equal to the security level of the user, it will be asserted by user beliefs.
- Step 4: pack the new attribute class level.
- Step 5: return the attribute class level.

Figure 3.19 illustrates the flow chart for the verify operation in the belief-consistent model.

3.6.5 Update Operation Procedure

The SQL statement for the update operation is described as follows:

```
UPDATE R
SET [A₁ = a₁, A₂ = a₂, ..., Aₙ = aₙ]
WHERE P
```

where R is an MLS relation, $A_1, A_2, \ldots, A_n$ are attributes from R, $a_1, a_2, \ldots, a_n$ are values from domains of $A_1, A_2, \ldots, A_n$, and P is an update condition that defines the tuples that are to be updated. If a subject with the security class level L runs a command to update an MLS relation R for all $t \in R$, the update operation is implemented as follows [35]:

- Step 1: get the security class level of the subject that runs the update operation.
- Step 2: if Pl (t [tuple class]) is equal to the security class level of the subject L, tuple t will be updated.
- Step 3: if Pl (t [tuple class]) is lower than the security level of the user, ib(security level of user, t [tuple class]) = security level of the user. A new tuple t′ based on tuple t will be inserted on the level equal to the security level of the user. The attribute values of tuple t will not be changed.
- Step 4: if Pl (t [tuple class]) is lower than the security level of the user, Ib (security level of user, t [tuple class]) = 0. If existing tuples t_i from R have t_i [primary key] = t[primary key] and Pl (t_i [primary key]) = Pl(t[primary key]) and Pl (t_i [tuple class]) < the security level of the user, the user will choose a tuple, t′, and a new tuple, t″, based on t′ will be inserted on the user

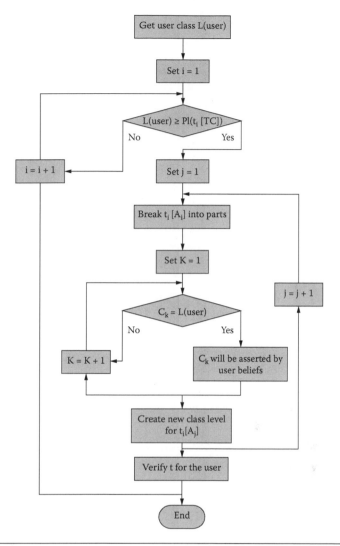

Figure 3.19 Flow chart for verify operation in the belief-consistent model.

level, while the attribute values of t′ itself will not change. If no tuples t_i from R that have t_i [primary key] = t[primary key] and Pl (t_i [primary key]) = Pl(t[primary key]) and Pl (t_i [tuple class]) < the security level of the user exist, a new tuple, t″, based on tuple t will be inserted on a level equal to the security level of the user, while the attribute values of tuple t will not be changed.

Figure 3.20 illustrates the flow chart for the update operation in the belief-consistent model.

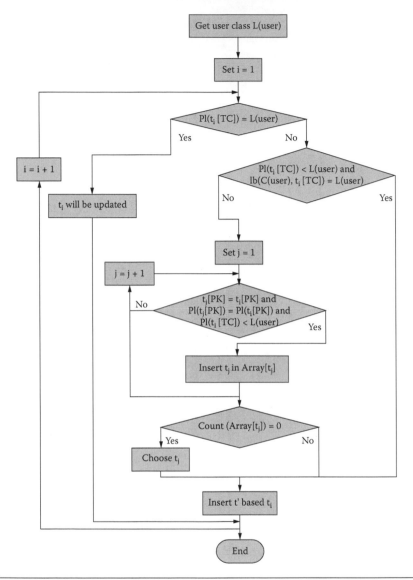

Figure 3.20 Flow chart for update operation in the belief-consistent model.

3.6.6 Delete Operation Procedure

The SQL statement for the delete operation is described as follows:

```
DELETE
FROM R
WHERE P
```

where R is an MLS relation and P is a delete condition that defines the tuples that are to be deleted. If a subject with the security class level L runs a command to delete tuples from MLS relation R: for all $t \in R$, if t satisfies P and Pl is equal to the security class level of the user L, the delete operation is implemented as follows [35]:

- Step 1: get the security level of the subject that runs the delete operation.
- Step 2: if Sl (Xview(Tuple Class)) is NULL, the tuple will be deleted.
- Step 3: if Sl (Xview(Tuple Class)) is not NULL, unverify the tuple for the current user and set the flag for higher level users.
- Step 4: unverify all tuples with the same primary key and its security level as the deleted tuple having Ib(tc) = 1 (belief: false).

Figure 3.21 illustrates the flow chart for the delete operation in the belief-consistent model.

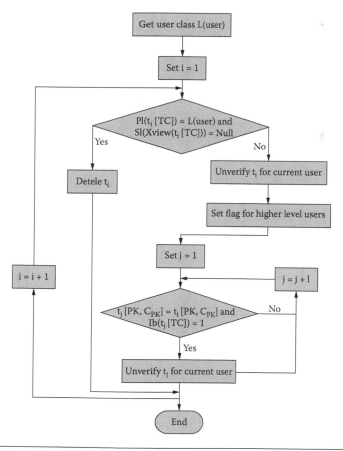

Figure 3.21   Flow chart for delete operation in the belief-consistent model.

Table 3.1   Comparative Study for Multilevel Database Models

PROBLEM MODEL	PROLIFERATION PROBLEM	SEMANTIC AMBIGUITY	RESTRICTION OF THE SCOPE OF AN UPDATE	DISBELIEF IN A TUPLE	SIMPLICITY
SeaView	Not solved	Not solved	Solved	Not solved	Very simple
Jajodia–Sandhu	Solved	Not solved	Solved	Not solved	Simple
Smith–Winslett	Solved	Solved	Not solved	Not solved	Simple
MLR	Solved	Solved	Solved	Not solved	Complex
BCMLS	Solved	Solved	Solved	Solved	Very Complex

3.7 Comparative Study for Multilevel Database Models

Table 3.1 illustrates the strengths and weaknesses of each model of the multilevel security database models.

3.8 Summary

Many multilevel relational models have been proposed; different models offer different advantages. In this chapter, we explained the implementation of DML operations such as SELECT, INSERT, UPDATE, and DELETE for each model of the multilevel secure database models. From the implementation procedures we found that MLR is secure, unambiguous, and powerful because it provides multilevel relations with element-level labeling as a natural extension of the traditional relational data model. MLR introduces several new concepts (notably, data-borrow integrity and the UPLEVEL statement) and significantly redefines existing concepts (polyinstantiation and referential integrity as well as data manipulation operations).

4

FUNDAMENTALS OF INFORMATION ENCRYPTION

4.1 Introduction

Nowadays, information has a good value in our world, so information should be secured. Computer networks made a revolution in information usage possible. An authorized user can exchange the information from a distance using computer networks. To secure the information, we need to be able to hide it from unauthorized access, which is called confidentiality; protect it from unauthorized modification, which is called integrity; and make it available to an authorized entity, which is called availability [36].

This chapter gives the main basics of the design of cryptographic algorithms. A review of the various issues found when selecting, designing, and measuring a cryptographic algorithm is presented. Diffusion-based cipher algorithms, along with their modes of operation, are covered in this chapter. Chaotic encryption with a Baker map is also discussed.

4.2 Basic Concepts of Cryptography

4.2.1 Goals of Cryptography

Cryptography should accomplish the following four goals [37,38]:

- Confidentiality
- Data integrity
- Authentication
- Nonrepudiation

Confidentiality protects the information from unauthorized access. An unauthorized party is called an adversary, which should not have the ability to access the network.

Data integrity ensures that the information has not been modified in an unauthorized way. If the data are modified, all parties through the network can detect this modification.

Authentication methods are classified into two categories: entity authentication and message authentication. Entity authentication is the process that one party uses to ensure the identity of the second party in the communication protocol. Message authentication is the term used with data origin authentication. It provides that the data received is the original message source.

Nonrepudiation means that the receiver can prove that he receives the original information as the sender sends it.

Knowing the techniques that are used to break an existing cryptography is called *cryptanalysis.* Because the cryptography depends on the cryptanalysis, users refer to cryptology as a joint study of cryptography and cryptanalysis.

4.2.2 *Principles of Encryption*

The basic idea of *encryption* is to modify the message in such a way that only a legal recipient can reconstruct its content [37,38]. A discrete-valued cryptosystem can be characterized by:

- A set of possible plaintexts, P
- A set of possible ciphertexts, C
- A set of possible cipher keys, K
- A set of possible encryption and decryption transformations, E and D

An encryption system is also called a *cipher,* or a cryptosystem. The message for encryption is called *plaintext,* and the encrypted message is called *ciphertext.* Denote the plaintext and the ciphertext by P and C, respectively. The encryption procedure of a cipher can be described as

$$C = E_{K_e}(P) \tag{4.1}$$

Figure 4.1   General encryption and decryption of a cipher.

where K_e is the encryption key and E is the encryption function. Similarly, the decryption procedure is defined as

$$P = D_{K_d}(C) \tag{4.2}$$

where K_d is the decryption key and D is the decryption function. The security of a cipher should only rely on the decryption key, K_d, since an adversary can recover the plaintext from the observed ciphertext once he gets K_d. Figure 4.1 shows a block diagram for encryption/decryption of a cipher.

4.3 Classification of Encryption Algorithms

Encryption algorithms are classified in various ways: according to their structures of the algorithms, according to keys, or according to their percentage of encrypted data [39,40].

4.3.1 Classification according to Encryption Structure

Encryption algorithms are classified as block ciphers and stream ciphers.

A **block cipher** is a kind of symmetric-key encryption algorithm that converts a fixed-length block of plaintext data to a block of ciphertext data of the same length. The fixed length is called the block size. For several block ciphers, the block size is 64 or 128 bits. The larger the block size is, the more secure is the cipher, but the more complex are the encryption and decryption algorithms and devices. Modern block ciphers have the following features [41]:

1. Variable key size
2. Mixed arithmetic operations, which can provide nonlinearity
3. Data-dependent rotations and key-dependent rotations

4. Lengthy key schedule algorithm
5. Variable plaintext/ciphertext block sizes and variable numbers of rounds

Block ciphers can be characterized by:

1. Block size: The greater security is, the larger are the block sizes.
2. Key size: Larger key sizes mean greater security.
3. Number of rounds: Multiple rounds increase security.
4. Encryption modes: These define how messages larger than the block size are encrypted.

Unlike block ciphers that operate on large blocks of data, *stream ciphers* typically operate on smaller units of plaintext, usually bits. So, stream ciphers can be designed to be exceptionally fast—much faster than a typical block cipher. Generally, a stream cipher generates a sequence of bits as a key (called key stream) using a pseudo random number generator (PRNG) that expands a short secret key (e.g., 128 bits) into a long string (key stream; e.g., 10^6 bits), and the encryption is accomplished by combining the key stream with the plaintext. Usually, the bitwise XOR operation is chosen to perform ciphering, basically for its simplicity [42,43]. Stream ciphers have the following properties [44]:

1. They do not have perfect security.
2. Security depends on the properties of the PRNG.
3. The PRNG must be unpredictable; given a consecutive sequence of output bits, the next bit must be hard to predict.
4. Typical stream ciphers are very fast.

4.3.2 Classification according to Keys

According to keys, there are two kinds of ciphers following the relationship of K_e and K_d. When $K_e = K_d$, the cipher is called a private-key cipher or a symmetric cipher. For private-key ciphers, the encryption/decryption key must be transmitted from the sender to the receiver via a separate secret channel. When $K_e \neq K_d$, the cipher is called a public-key cipher or an asymmetric cipher. For public-key ciphers, the encryption key, K_e, is published and the decryption key, K_d, is kept private, and no additional secret channel is needed for key transfer. In conventional encryption, as shown in Figure 4.2, the sender encrypts the data (plaintext) using the encryption key and the receiver decrypts the encrypted data (ciphertext) into the original data (plaintext) using the decryption key. In symmetric encryption, encryption and decryption keys are identical. Figure 4.3 shows the public key encryption (asymmetric encryption) in which the encryption and decryption keys are different. Public key cryptography solves the problem of conventional cryptosystems by distributing the key [45,46]. Table 4.1 shows a comparison between symmetric encryption and asymmetric encryption.

There are two types of cryptosystems:

- Symmetric (private) key cryptosystems
- Asymmetric (public) key cryptosystems

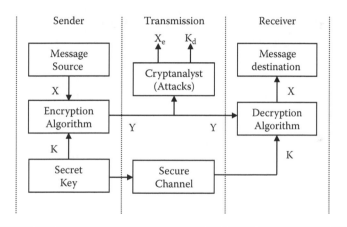

Figure 4.2   Model of symmetric encryption.

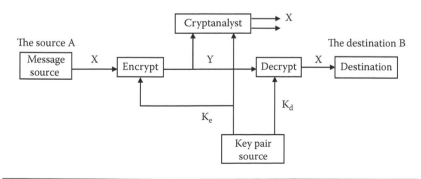

Figure 4.3   Asymmetric-key encryption.

Table 4.1   Comparison between Symmetric Encryption and Asymmetric Encryption

CONVENTIONAL ENCRYPTION (SYMMETRIC ENCRYPTION)	PUBLIC-KEY ENCRYPTION (ASYMMETRIC ENCRYPTION)
Requirements to work: • Use the same algorithm with the same key for the encryption and the decryption process. • The algorithm and the key should be shared by the sender and receiver. Requirements for security: • The key should be secret. • It must be impossible to decrypt the message if no information is available. • Discovering the algorithm and samples of the ciphertext should be insufficient to determine the key.	Requirements to work: • One encryption and decryption algorithm is used for encryption and decryption and two keys, one for encryption and one for decryption. • The sender and receiver should have one of the two keys. Requirements for security: • The key should be secret. • It must be impossible to decrypt the message if no information is available. • Discovering the algorithm and samples of the ciphertext should be insufficient to determine the key.

Most people have chosen to call the first group simply symmetric key cryptosystems, and the popular name for the second group is just public key cryptosystems.

4.3.3 Classification according to Percentage of Encrypted Data

The encryption algorithm can be divided into full encryption and partial encryption according to the percentage of the data encrypted.

4.4 Cryptanalysis

Cryptanalysis is the art of decrypting an encrypted message without knowing the decryption key [47–50]. Some of the most important ones, for a system implementer, are described next, and they are summarized in Table 4.2:

In a *ciphertext-only attack,* the adversary has access only to some encrypted messages.

A *brute-force attack* is a kind of ciphertext-only attack. It is based on a key search and well-designed cryptosystems should be computationally infeasible to attack.

In a *known-plaintext attack,* an adversary has some information about the plaintext and the corresponding given ciphertext. This may be helpful to determine the decryption key.

Table 4.2 Types of Attacks on Encrypted Information

TYPE OF ATTACK	PREREQUISITES FOR THE CRYPTANALYST
Ciphertext only	• The algorithm of encryption • Ciphertext to be decrypted
Known plaintext	• The algorithm of encryption • Ciphertext to be decrypted • Plaintext message and ciphertext generated with the secret key
Chosen ciphertext	• The algorithm of encryption • Ciphertext to be decrypted • Ciphertext chosen by the cryptanalyst with its plaintext generated with the decryption algorithm and the decryption key
Chosen plaintext	• Encryption algorithm • Ciphertext to be decoded • Plaintext chosen by the cryptanalyst with its ciphertext generated with the encryption algorithm and the encryption key

4.5 Conventional Symmetric Block Ciphers

This section gives a brief overview of the construction of some popular conventional encryption algorithms. Each of the following encryption algorithms is a symmetric block cipher algorithm. Symmetric means that the key used for encryption and decryption is the same, while block means that the data (information) to be encrypted is divided into blocks of equal length [51,52].

4.5.1 Data Encryption Standard (DES)

The DES is the most well-known symmetric key block cipher and it has enjoyed widespread use internationally [53].

The DES is a block cipher, which encrypts data in 64-bit blocks. A 64-bit block of the plaintext comes at one end of the algorithm and a 64-bit block of ciphertext goes out at the other end of the algorithm. The same algorithm and the same key with 56 bits are used in the encryption and decryption processes except for minor differences in the key schedule. The key is a 64-bit number. In every 8 bits, 1 bit (the least significant bit) is used for parity checking and can be ignored.

The DES is based on four basic operations: expansion, permutation, XOR, and substitution. The data to be encrypted are first divided into

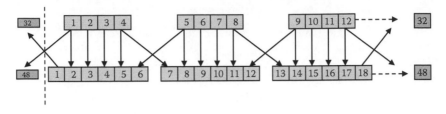

Figure 4.4   Expansion process.

64-bit blocks and fed into an initial permutation (IP) stage, in which each block is divided into two sub-blocks, each with 32-bit length. The right sub-block is fed into a Feistel function (f-function), which is depicted in Figure 4.4. It operates on half a block (32 bits) at a time and contains four stages as shown in Figure 4.5.

1. Expansion. The half-block with 32 bits is expanded to 48 bits, using the permutation of the expansion, defined as E in the diagram, by duplicating half of the bits. The output contains eight 6-bit [8 × 6 = 48 bits] pieces, each consisting of a copy of four corresponding input bits and a copy of the immediately adjacent bit from each of the input pieces to either side.
2. Key mixing. A subkey is combined with the result of the first step using an XOR operation. A key schedule mechanism is used to derive 16 subkeys with 48 bits from the main key.
3. Substitution. First the block is divided into eight 6-bit pieces and, after that, processed by the substitution boxes (S-boxes). The six input bits of each one of the eight S-boxes are replaced with four output bits using a nonlinear transformation, provided in the form of a look-up table. The S-boxes present the basis of the security of the DES. Without them, the cipher would be breakable.
4. Permutation. The 32 S-boxes' outputs will be rearranged using a fixed permutation. The P-box is designed so that, after expansion, each group of S-box output bits is spread across six different S-boxes in the next round.

4.5.2 Double DES

The way to improve security of the block cipher algorithm is to encrypt every block twice using two different keys. The first step is to encrypt

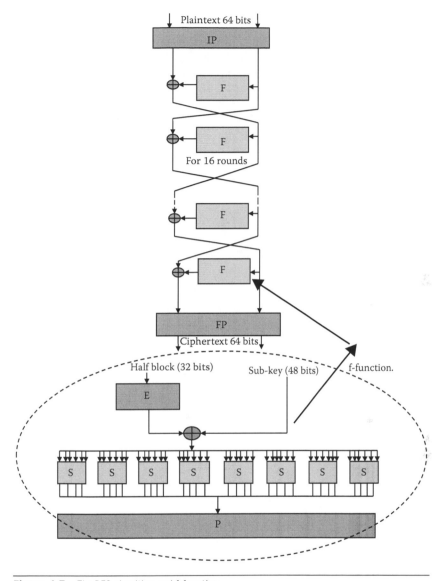

Figure 4.5   The DES algorithm and f-function.

a block using the first encryption key and then encrypt the resulting ciphertext with the second encryption key. The decryption is a process conducted in reverse.

The resulting ciphertext block should be very difficult to be decrypted. Instead of 2^{56} attempts, it requires 2^{128} attempts to find the key and 2^{112} attempts to break the encryption. In 1981, Merkle and Hellman declared the "meet-in-the-middle attack," which proved the weakness of the double DES algorithm [54]. The meet-in-the-middle attack requires that the attacker have both a known piece of plaintext and its corresponding ciphertext. The attack needs to store 2^{56} results when trying to discover a datum that has been encrypted with the double DES. Merkle and Hellman presented a time–memory trade-off, which could break this double-encryption scheme in 2^{56+1} encryptions, rather than 2^{112} encryptions.

4.5.3 Triple DES

The dangers of the Merkle–Hellman attack (meet-in-the-middle attack) can be overcome by conducting three block encryption operations. This method is called triple DES and is performed by executing the DES three times, producing an effective key size of 168 bits. In the triple DES, each 64-bit block of data is encrypted three times with the DES algorithm.

The triple DES is performed as follows:

1. Use key 1 for encryption.
2. Use key 2 for decryption.
3. Use key 3 for encryption.

To decrypt, reverse the steps:

1. Use key 3 for decryption.
2. Use key 2 for encryption.
3. Use key 1 for decryption.

For several applications, both keys 1 and 3 can be the same without creating a significant vulnerability. The choice among single, double, and triple DES is a trade-off between performance and security requirements [55].

4.5.4 International Data Encryption Algorithm (IDEA)

The IDEA cipher was first presented by Lai and Massey in 1990 under the name of proposed encryption standard (PES). After Biham and Shamir presented differential cryptanalysis, the authors named it the improved proposed encryption standard (IPES). The IPES name was changed to international data encryption algorithm (IDEA) in 1992.

The algorithm was intended as a replacement of the DES. IDEA is a block cipher that depends on 64-bit plaintext blocks. The key is 128 bits long. There are eight identical rounds, and the encryption and decryption algorithms are the same. The design behind the algorithm is based on mixing operations from different algebraic groups. Three algebraic groups—XOR, addition modulo, and multiplication modulo—are mixed in this algorithm [56,57]. All of these operations operate on 16-bit sub-blocks.

4.5.5 Blowfish

The blowfish algorithm is a 64-bit block cipher using a variable-length key. It was designed in 1993 by Schaneier [58]. The algorithm contains two parts: key expansion and data encryption. Key expansion divides a key of 448 bits into different subkey arrays of 4168 bytes. Data encryption contains a function iterated for 16 rounds. Each round contains a key-dependent permutation and a key- and data-dependent substitution. All operations are additions and XORs on 32-bit words. The additional operations are four indexed array data lookups per round. The keys should be computed before any data encryption or decryption process.

4.5.6 RC5 Algorithm

The iterated block RC5 was introduced by Rivest, Shamir, and Adleman in 1994 [58]. The main feature of the RC5 is the heavy use of data-dependent rotations. RC5 has a variable word size, w, a variable number of rounds, r, and a variable secret key with b bytes. It is represented as RC5 $w/r/b$. The nominal value of w is 32 bits, and RC5 encrypts blocks of two words. The RC5 is composed of encryption, decryption, and key expansion. The expanded key contains $t = 2 \times (r + 1)$ words. The primitive operations of the RC5 are illustrated in Table 4.3. Generally, RC5 is a fast symmetric block cipher that is suitable for hardware and software implementations with low memory requirements. It provides high security when good parameters are chosen.

4.5.6.1 RC5 Encryption Algorithm   We assume that the input block is given in two w-bit registers, A and B, and we also assume that key

Table 4.3 Primitive Operations of RC5

$a + b$	Integer addition modulo $2w$
$a - b$	Integer subtraction modulo $2w$
$a \oplus b$	Bitwise XOR of w-bit words
$a * b$	Integer multiplication modulo $2w$
$a <<< b$	Rotate the w-bit word a to the left by the amount given by the least significant l_g w bits of b
$a >>> b$	Rotate the w-bit word a to the right by the amount given by the least significant l_g w bits of b

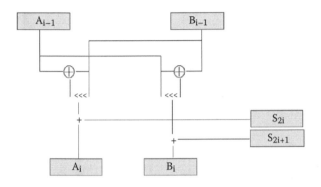

Figure 4.6 RC5$_{w/r/b}$ symmetric block cipher diagram.

expansion has already been performed so that $S[0]$, $S[1]$, ..., $S[t-1]$ have been computed. The steps of the encryption algorithm can be summarized as follows:

```
A = A+S [0];
B = B+S [1];
For i = 1 to r do
A = ((A ⊕ B) <<< B) +S [2i];
B = ((B ⊕ A) <<< A) +S [2i+1];
End
```

In each round of RC5, both registers *A* and *B* are updated as shown in Figure 4.6.

4.5.6.2 RC5 Decryption Algorithm The decryption step can be summarized as follows:

```
For i = r downto 1 do
B = ((B - S [2i+1]) >>> A) ⊕ A;
A = ((A - S [2]) >>> B) ⊕ B;
```

```
End
B = B-S [1];
A = A-S [0];
```

4.5.6.3 RC5 Key Expansion   Key expansion expands the user's secret key, *K*, to fill the expanded key array *S*, which makes *S* similar to an array of $t = 2(r + 1)$ random binary words. Two magic constants, P_w and Q_w, are used in this process. These constants are defined as

$$P_w = Odd\left((e-2)2^w\right) \qquad (4.3)$$

$$Q_w = Odd\left((\phi-1)2^w\right) \qquad (4.4)$$

where
   e = 2.718281828459....(base of natural logarithms)
   ϕ = 1.618033988749....(golden ratio)
   and *Odd(x)* is the odd integer nearest to *x*
   For *w* = 16 and 32, these constants are given in hexadecimals:

$$P_{16} = b7e1;\ Q_{16} = 9e37$$

$$P_{32} = b7e15163;\ Q_{32} = 9e3779b9$$

The expansion begins by copying the secret key $K[0...b-1]$ into an array $L[0...c-1]$ that has c = $\lceil b/u \rceil$ words, where $u = w/8$ is the number of bytes per word. *u* consecutive key bytes of *K* are used to fill up each successive word in *L* in a low-order to high-order byte manner. All unfilled byte positions of *L* are zeroed.

   To initialize the array *S*, we follow these steps:

```
S [0]  = Pw;
For i = 1 to t-1 do
S [i] = S [i-1] + Qw;
End
```

The last step is to mix the user secret key in three passes over the arrays *S* and *L* as follows:

```
i = j = 0;
A = B = 0;
Do 3*max (t, c) times:
```

```
A = S [i] = (S [i] +A+B) <<<3;
B = L[j] = (L[j] + A+ B) <<< (A+B);
i = (i+1) mod (t);
j = (j+1) mod (c);
```

4.5.7 RC6 Algorithm

The RC6 block cipher is a modified version of RC5, which uses four working registers instead of two, as well as integer multiplication as an additional primitive operation. The integer multiplication process greatly enhances the diffusion achieved per round, which leads to greater security, fewer rounds, and increased throughput. The key schedule of RC6-*w/r/b* is similar to the key schedule of RC5-*w/r/b*. The only difference is that for RC6-*w/r/b*, more words are derived from the user-supplied key for use during encryption and decryption. The user supplies a key of *b* bytes, where $0 \leq b \leq 255$. From this key, $2r + 4$ words (w bits each) are derived and stored in the array $S[0, ..., 2r + 3]$. This array is used in both encryption and decryption [59]. Generally, RC6 consists of two Feistel networks whose data are mixed via data-dependent rotations. The operations in a single round of RC6 contain two applications of the squaring function $f(x) = x (2x + 1) \bmod 2^{32}$, two fixed 32-bit rotations, two data-dependent 32-bit rotations, two XORs, and two additions modulo 2^{32}. The steps of RC6 encryption and decryption are summarized next and the block diagrams or RC6 encryption and decryption are shown in Figures 4.7 and 4.8, respectively.

4.5.7.1 RC6 Encryption Algorithm   Input: Four w-bit plaintext values are stored in registers *A, B, C,* and *D*.

Number r of rounds
w-bit round keys $S[0..., 2r + 3]$
Output: Four w-bit ciphertext values are stored in registers *A, B, C,* and *D*.
Procedure:

```
B = B + S [0];
D = D + S [1];
For i = 1 to r do
{t = (B x (2B + 1)) <<< lg w;
u = (D x (2D + 1)) <<< lg w;
```

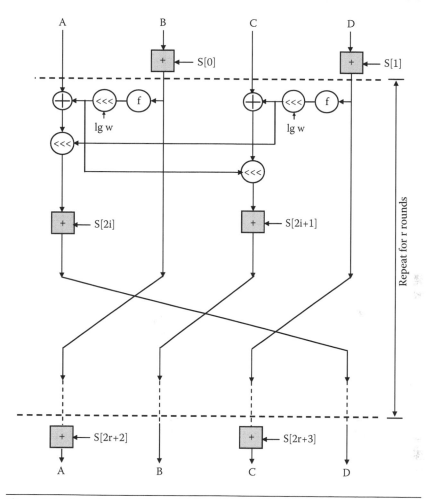

Figure 4.7   Encryption with RC6$_{w/r/b}$ algorithm.

```
A = ((A ⊕ t) <<< u) + S [2i];
C = ((C ⊕ u) <<< t) + S [2i + 1];
(A, B, C, D) = (B, C, D, A);}
End
A = A + S [2r + 2];
C = C + S [2r + 3];
```

4.5.7.2 RC6 Decryption Algorithm   Input: Four *w*-bit ciphertext values are stored in registers *A, B, C,* and *D.*

Number of rounds *r*

w-bit round keys *S*[0, ..., 2*r* + 3]

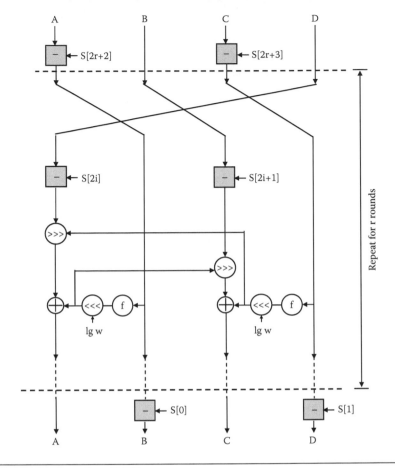

Figure 4.8   Decryption with RC6$_{w/r/b}$.

Output: Four w-bit plaintext values are stored in registers A, B, C, and D.

Procedure:

```
C = C - S [2r + 3];
A = A - S [2r + 2];
for i = r downto 1 do
        {(A, B, C, D) = (D, A, B, C);
            u = (D × (2D + 1)) <<< lg w;
            t = (B × (2B + 1)) <<< lg w;
            C = ((C - S[2i + 1]) >>> t) ⊕ u;
            A = ((A - S[2i]) >>> u) ⊕ t;}
        End
            D = D - S [1];
            B = B - S [0];
```

4.5.8 The Advanced Encryption Standard (AES)

The AES is based on the Rijndael algorithm, which is an iterated block cipher algorithm with a variable block size and a variable key size. The block size and the key size can be independently 128, 192, or 256 bits. The intermediate resulting ciphertext is called a state and it is in the form of a rectangular array of four rows and a number of columns equal to the block size divided by 32. The cipher key is similarly a rectangular array with four rows and a number of columns equal to the key size divided by 32. The number of rounds performed on the intermediate state is related to the key size. For key sizes of 128, 192, and 256 bits, the number of rounds is 10, 12, and 14, respectively. Each round consists of a fixed sequence of transformations, except the first and the last round [36,37].

The AES consists of rounds. Any round, except the final one, consists of subBytes, ShiftRows, MixColumns, and AddRoundKey operations. In the final round, no MixColumns operation is performed. In the subBytes step, a linear substitution for each byte is performed according to Figure 4.9. Each byte in the array is updated using an 8-bit S-box, which provides the nonlinearity in the cipher system.

The S-box is derived from the multiplicative inverse over the finite Galois field GF(28), known to have good nonlinearity properties. To avoid attacks based on simple algebraic properties, the S-box is chosen to avoid any fixed points and also any opposite fixed points [37].

The ShiftRows is based on the rows of the state. It shifts the bytes in each row. For the AES, the first row is left unchanged. Each byte of the second row is shifted a single byte to the left. The third

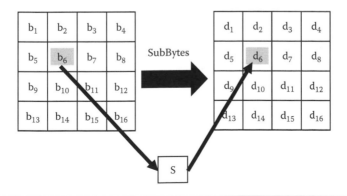

Figure 4.9 SubBytes step.

and the fourth rows are shifted by offsets of two and three bytes, respectively. For the block of size 128 bits and 192 bits, the shifting pattern is the same [40].

In the case of the 256-bit blocks, the first row is unchanged and the shifting for second, third, and fourth rows is 1 byte, 3 bytes, and 4 bytes, respectively, as shown in Figure 4.10.

In the MixColumns step, the four bytes of each column of the state are combined using an invertible linear transformation. The MixColumns function takes four bytes as input and outputs four bytes, where each input byte affects all the four output bytes. With ShiftRows, MixColumns provides diffusion in the cipher system. Each column is treated as a polynomial over $GF(2^8)$ and is then multiplied with a fixed polynomial $c(x) = 3x^3 + x^2 + x + 2$. The MixColumns step can also be viewed as a multiplication by a particular matrix, as shown in Figure 4.11 [36,37].

In the AddRoundKey step, the subkey is combined with the state. For each round, a subkey is derived from the main key using the algorithm key schedule. Each subkey has the same size as the state.

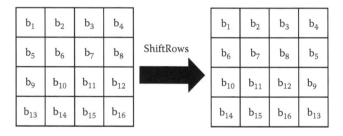

Figure 4.10   ShiftRows step.

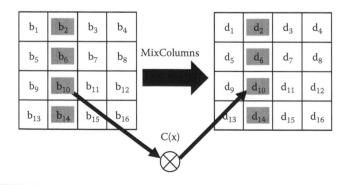

Figure 4.11   MixColumns step.

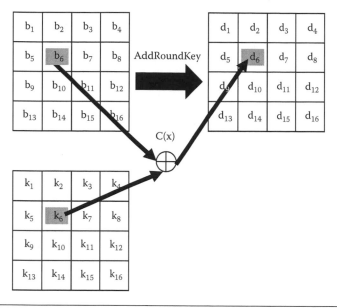

Figure 4.12   AddRoundKey step.

The subkey is added by combining each byte of the state with the corresponding byte of the subkey using a bitwise XOR [36,37]. The AddRoundKey step is shown in Figure 4.12. We will apply the AES with a fixed block size of 128 bits and a key size of 128 bits.

4.6 Modes of Operation

Block ciphers can be run in different modes of operation, allowing users to choose appropriate modes to meet the requirements of their applications. Using a certain mode in the encryption process restricts the decryption process to using the same mode. In this section, we discuss different possible ways in which block codes can be utilized to implement a cryptosystem. The possible block cipher modes of operation that we treat are identified by the acronyms ECB, CBC, CFB, and OFB. In each case, we assume that we have a block cipher of block length n, with enciphering map, E_K, and deciphering map, D_K, for each key K.

4.6.1 The ECB Mode

ECB is the simplest mode of operation for encryption algorithms where the data sequence is divided into blocks of equal sizes and

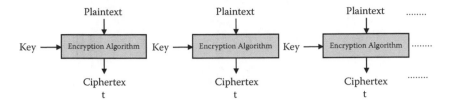

Figure 4.13 Using a block cipher in the ECB mode.

each block is encrypted, separately, with the same encryption key. As illustrated in Figure 4.13, the plaintext is divided into blocks $(P_1, P_2, P_3, \ldots)$ of size n bits, which are encrypted to ciphertext blocks $(C_1, C_2, C_3, \ldots)$. The encryption algorithm is

$$C_j = E_K(P_j) \tag{4.5}$$

and the decryption algorithm is

$$P_j = D_K(C_j) \tag{4.6}$$

where $j = 1, 2, 3, \ldots, E_K$ is the encryption map with the key K, and D_K is the decryption map with the same key K.

The ECB mode has several advantages. There is no need to encrypt a file progressively; the middle blocks can be encrypted first, then the blocks at the end, and finally the blocks at the beginning. This is important for encrypted files that are accessed randomly, like a database. If a database is encrypted in the ECB mode, then any record can be added, deleted, encrypted, or decrypted independently, assuming that a record consists of independent encryption blocks.

The disadvantage of this mode is that identical plaintext blocks are encrypted to identical ciphertext blocks; it does not hide data patterns. The advantage is that error propagation is limited to a single block. The disadvantage of ECB mode appears well in image encryption if we have an image with large areas of the same color or repeated patterns so that there are many blocks of the same plaintext. This may reveal much information about the original image from the encrypted image. This disadvantage is treated in CBC, CFB, and OFB modes. So, all with those kinds of images are better than the ECB mode.

4.6.2 *The CBC Mode*

The CBC mode uses an IV of size equal to the size of each block of pixels. In this mode, each block of plaintext is XORed with the previous ciphertext block before being encrypted. This way, each ciphertext block is dependent on all plaintext blocks up to that point. In decryption, the same XOR operation is repeated so that its effect is cancelled. This mechanism is shown in Figure 4.14.

The main disadvantage of the CBC mode is that an error in (or attack upon) one ciphertext block impacts two plaintext blocks upon decryption. On the other hand, if we have an image that has blocks of the same input data, these blocks are encrypted to totally different ciphertext data. So, the CBC mode is a better approach in encrypting images in the spatial domain, especially when these images contain large areas of the same activity. In the CBC mode, the encryption algorithm is

$$C_j = E_K(C_{j-1} \oplus P_j) \tag{4.7}$$

and the decryption algorithm is

$$P_j = D_K(C_j) \oplus C_{j-1}, j = 1, 2, 3, \ldots \tag{4.8}$$

$$C_0 = IV \tag{4.9}$$

4.6.3 *The CFB Mode*

In contrast to the CBC mode, the CFB mode begins by encrypting the IV, and then an XOR operation is performed between the

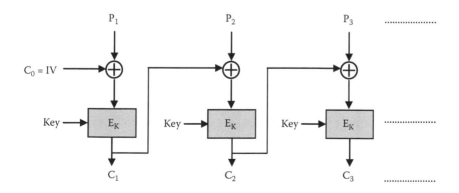

Figure 4.14 Using a block cipher in the CBC mode.

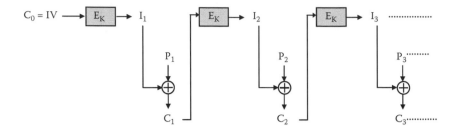

Figure 4.15   Using a block cipher in the CFB mode.

bits of the encrypted IV and the corresponding bits of the first block of the image. The result is the encrypted version of the first block. For the encryption of each of the next plaintext blocks, the previous ciphertext block is encrypted and the output is XORed with the current plaintext block to create the current ciphertext block. The XOR operation conceals plaintext patterns.

Common to the CBC mode, changing the IV to the same plaintext block results in different outputs. Though the IV need not be secret, some applications would see this as desirable [36,37]. Figure 4.15 shows the CFB mode. The encryption algorithm is

$$C_j = P_j \oplus I_j \tag{4.10}$$

and the decryption algorithm is

$$P_j = C_j \oplus I_j \tag{4.11}$$

$$I_j = E_K(C_{j-1}), \; j = 1,2,3, \ldots \tag{4.12}$$

$$C_0 = IV \tag{4.13}$$

4.6.4 The OFB Mode

This mode is similar to the CFB mode. It begins by encrypting the IV. The bits of the encrypted IV are XORed with the corresponding bits of the first plaintext block to get the corresponding ciphertext block. Also, the output of the encryption algorithm is used as an input to the next encryption step instead of the IV. This process continues until the last block. Changing the IV for the same

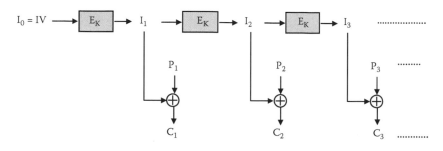

Figure 4.16   Using a block cipher in the OFB mode.

plaintext block results in different ciphertext blocks. Figure 4.16 shows the OFB mode. The encryption algorithm is

$$C_j = P_j \oplus I_j \tag{4.14}$$

and the decryption algorithm is

$$P_j = C_j \oplus I_j \tag{4.15}$$

$$I_j = E_K(I_{j-1}), \ j = 1, 2, 3, \ldots \tag{4.16}$$

$$I_0 = IV \tag{4.17}$$

5

ENCRYPTION-BASED MULTILEVEL MODEL FOR DBMS

5.1 Introduction

This chapter presents the concept of the encryption-based multilevel model for relational database management systems (DBMS). This model is a combination of the multilevel relation model and an encryption system. The encryption system is used to encrypt each tuple (row) in the relation (table) with an encryption key that depends on the security level of the tuple (tuple classification). The encryption-based multilevel security (MLS) model is characterized by three achievements:

1. Utilizing an encryption system as an additional security layer over the multilevel security layer for the relational database
2. Reducing the multilevel database size
3. Improving the response time of data retrieval from the multilevel database

Also, this chapter summarizes the efforts of implementing a working multilevel relational database security prototype. This prototype is used as a research tool for studying principles and mechanisms of the encryption-based multilevel model and other multilevel relational database security models (SeaView, Jajodia–Sandhu, Smith–Winslett, multilevel relational [MLR], and belief-consistent models) [60]. The prototype that is implemented is used to make various experiments to determine the relative performance of the multilevel relational database security models and the performance cost for applying the encryption system in multilevel relational database security.

5.2 The Encryption-Based Multilevel Database Model

In the encryption-based multilevel database model, a symmetric key is created for each unique security level and used to encrypt or decrypt the data in the multilevel relational database. This key is defined automatically by the model during the creation of the security level. The user can use the keys that are defined to the security levels lower than or equal to his security level. A multilevel relation scheme is denoted by $R(E_{C_1}(A_1), E_{C_2}(A_2), \ldots, E_{C_n}(A_n), TC)$, where each A_i is a data attribute over domain D_i, each C_i is a classification attribute for A_i, and $E_{C_i}(A_i)$ is the encryption function for A_i by the key according to the classification security level C_i.

In this model, the classification attributes for the multilevel relational database are removed and each attribute is encrypted by using the encryption key that corresponds to the tuple security classification level (tuple level encryption).

This removing of the classification attributes from the multilevel database results in reducing the multilevel relational database size.

Tables 5.1 and 5.2 illustrate an example showing how the data are stored in the MLR model and in the proposed encryption-based multilevel model. In the proposed model, adding the encryption system to the MLR model led to solving the problems in the MLR model by removing the classification attributes from the multilevel database and then reducing the multilevel database size and making the database administration easier.

The encryption algorithm is supported in several commercial database management systems like DB2 (IBM) and ORACLE. In DB2 (IBM) [61], encryption has been performed by implementing SQL functions and stored procedures that help to encrypt and decrypt the data. The user will supply the encryption key to be used in encrypting the data during the insertion into the relational database. When the data are retrieved, the same password should be supplied to decrypt the data. In ORACLE [62], transparent data encryption helps to encrypt the sensitive data stored in relations in the database. Only the user who has access to the encrypted data can decrypt it.

Table 5.3 shows a comparison between the encryption-based multilevel database model and the commercial database systems like

Table 5.1 Multilevel Relational Database

EMPLOYEE	C-EMPLOYEE	DEPARTMENT	C-DEPARTMENT	SALARY	C-SALARY	TC
Ahmed	U	Accounting	U	7,000	U	U
Ahmed	S	Accounting	S	7,000	S	S
Mohamed	TS	Sales	TS	10,000	TS	TS

Table 5.2 Encryption-Based Multilevel Relational Database

EMPLOYEE	DEPARTMENT	SALARY	TC
타越丽聲攏峒5日	타越丽聲攏峒5日	타越丽聲攏峒5日	U
鑕캭 伍朕鉅 옴	鑕캭 伍朕鉅 옴	鑕캭 伍朕鉅 옴	S
嗅乄嶨葆摧瑳吽쿼	嗅乄嶨葆摧瑳吽쿼	嗅乄嶨葆摧瑳吽쿼	TS

Table 5.3 Comparison between Encryption-Based Multilevel Database Model and Commercial Database Systems such as DB2 (IBM) and ORACLE

MODEL/CRITERIA	ENCRYPTION-BASED MULTILEVEL DATABASE	DB2 ENCRYPTED FIELDS	ORACLE TRANSPARENT DATA ENCRYPTION
Encryption in multilevel security	Supported	Not supported	Not supported
Encryption type	Row-based encryption (one password per row)	Column-based encryption (one password per column)	Column-based encryption (one password per column)
Encryption key	Key is managed by database engine	Key provided by the user at runtime	Key provided by the user at runtime

DB2 (IBM) and ORACLE that support encryption in their database management systems.

The symmetric encryption keys are stored as a hidden property for the security classification levels of the multilevel database security. The database administrator cannot read the encryption keys. He can only read the security classification levels of the multilevel database security.

In the encryption-based multilevel database model, caching has an impact that should be taken into consideration as a plain text. The impact of the caching is due to storing the decrypted data during the transaction execution in the memory, which is a problem.

The encryption-based multilevel database model solves the problem of caching as follows:

- It causes the part of the memory that holds the decrypted data to be blocked so that it can be accessed only from the database engine instance.
- It supports multilevel security to the data so that the user can see only the data in his level and a lower security level. Supporting multilevel security in this model overcomes the problem of caching because it generates a security layer that manages the data access in the memory.

The encryption-based multilevel database model offers several major contributions to the field:

- Adding an encryption system as an additional security layer over the multilevel security layer for the database, which provides a high level of security and robustness against database attacks
- Reducing the multilevel database size by removing the classification attributes and encrypting the tuples by the encryption key according to its security level
- Reducing the complexity of design of the multilevel database security because the database designer does not need to create additional columns for attribute classification.

5.3 Manipulation

The data manipulation statements in the encryption-based multilevel database model are INSERT, DELETE, SELECT, UPDATE, and UPLEVEL [63].

5.3.1 *The INSERT Statement*

The INSERT statement executed by a user with security level L has the following general form:

```
INSERT INTO R [A₁,A₂,...,Aₙ]
VALUES [a₁,a₂,...,aₙ]
```

where R is the relation name and $[A_1, A_2, \ldots, A_n]$ are the attribute names. Each INSERT data manipulation can insert, at most, one tuple into the relation R. The inserted tuple, t, is constructed as follows:

For all attributes in a database relation:

- If there is an attribute A_i in the attribute list of the INTO clause, the data value a_i will be encrypted by an encryption key according to C_i, the security class level of the subject who executes the insert statement.
- If A_i is not in the attribute list of the INTO clause, set the data value to null.
- The tuple class will be set to the class level of the subject who executes the insert statement.

Figure 5.1 illustrates the flow chart for the insertion operation in the encryption-based multilevel database model.

5.3.2 The DELETE Statement

The DELETE statement executed by a user with security class level L has the following general form:

```
DELETE FROM R
WHERE P
```

where R is the relation name, assuming relation R has attributes $[A_1, A_2, \ldots, A_n]$; r is the database relation instance; and P is a predicate expression that may include conditions involving classification attributes.

Only tuples $t \in r$ with $t[TC] = L$ are decrypted by key, according to the security classification level of the user who executes the DELETE statement.

For those tuples $t \in r$ that satisfy the P predicate expression, r is changed as follows:

- Create a temporary tuple for the decrypted data to store the deleted tuple during the execution of the DELETE statement.
- The tuple that satisfies the predicate expression will be deleted.
- If there is a borrowed tuple in the high-security level that has an attribute that depends on the attribute in the deleted tuple, the value of this attribute will be set to null.

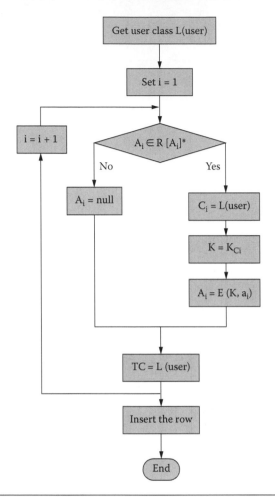

Figure 5.1   Flow chart for insertion operation in the encryption-based multilevel database model. (A. Rask, D. Rubin, and B. Neumann. 2005. Implementing row- and cell-level security in classified databases using SQL server. Available at http://technet.microsoft.com/en-us/library/cc966395. aspx; accessed April 2011.)

Figure 5.2 illustrates the flow chart for the delete operation in the encryption-based multilevel database model.

5.3.3 *The SELECT Statement*

The SELECT statement executed by a user with security class level L has the following general form:

```
SELECT [A₁,A₂,...,Aₙ] FROM R
WHERE P
```

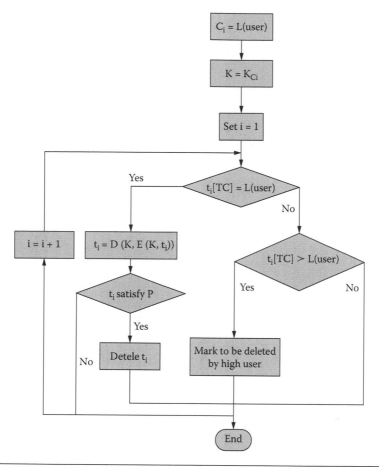

Figure 5.2 Flow chart for the delete operation in the encryption-based multilevel database model. (Y. Elovici et al. 2004. *Proceedings of International Conference SDM*, 28–40.)

where R is the relation name; $[A_1, A_2, \ldots, A_n]$ are the attribute names; and P is a predicate expression that may include conditions involving the security classification attributes. Only those tuples $t \in r$ that have $t[TC] \leq L$ will be decrypted by key according to the classification level of the subject that executes the SELECT statement and will be taken into the calculation of P.

For those tuples $t \in r$ that satisfy the P predicate expression:

- If a decrypted tuple satisfies the predicate expression, this tuple will be included in the result of the SELECT statement.

Figure 5.3 illustrates the flow chart for the select operation in the encryption-based multilevel database model.

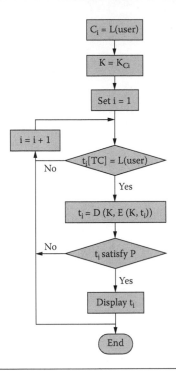

Figure 5.3   Flow chart for the select operation in the encryption-based multilevel database model. (X.-D. Zuo, F.-M. Liu, and C.-B. Ma. 2007. *Proceedings of the Sixth International Conference on Machine Learning and Cybernetics,* Hong Kong, 2158–2163.)

5.3.4 *The UPDATE Statement*

The UPDATE statement executed by a subject with security class level L has the following general form:

```
UPDATE R SET [A₁ = a₁, A₂ = a₂, ..., Aₙ = aₙ]
WHERE P
```

where R is the relation name; $[A_1, A_2, \ldots, A_n]$ are the attribute names; and P is a predicate expression that may include conditions involving classification attributes. Only tuples $t \in r$ with $t[TC] = L$ will be decrypted by key according to the classification level of the subject that executes the select statement and will be taken into the calculation of P.

For decrypted tuples $t \in r$ that satisfies the predicate P, r is updated as follows:

- Create a temporary tuple for decrypted data to store the deleted tuple during the execution of the DELETE statement.

- If there are no attributes of the primary key in the SET clause, for attributes in the SET clause:
  - Encrypt the attribute value and update the tuple.
- If there is a tuple that has an attribute that depends on the attribute in the updated tuple, the value of this attribute will be encrypted and updated.
- If there are attributes of the primary key in the SET clause:
  - Encrypt the attribute value and update the tuple.
- If the primary key class is equal to the class of the subject that executes the UPDATE statement, all tuples that have the same primary key will be deleted.

Figure 5.4 illustrates the flow chart for the update operation in the encryption-based multilevel database model.

5.3.5 The UPLEVEL Statement

The UPLEVEL statement executed by a user with security class level L has the following general form:

```
UPLEVEL R GET [A₁,A₂,...,Aₙ] FROM [C₁,C₂,...,Cₙ]
WHERE P
```

where R is the relation name; $A_1, A_2, \ldots, A_n$ are data attribute names; $C_1, C_2, \ldots, C_n$ are values of classification levels for $A_1, A_2, \ldots, A_n$, respectively; and P is a predicate expression that may include conditions involving the classification attributes and tuple-class attributes, in addition to the usual data attributes. Only tuples $t \in r$ with $t[TC] \leq L$ will be decrypted by key according to the classification level of the tuple $Key[TC]$ and will be taken into the calculation of P.

For decrypted tuples that have at least one tuple $t' \in r$ that satisfies the predicate P, an L-tuple, t, is constructed as follows:

- Create a temporary tuple for decrypted data to store the deleted tuple during the execution of the UPLEVEL statement.
- If A_i is in the GET clause, encrypt the data in the tuple with class equal to the security class level in the FROM clause.
- If A_i is not in the GET clause, set the data value to null.

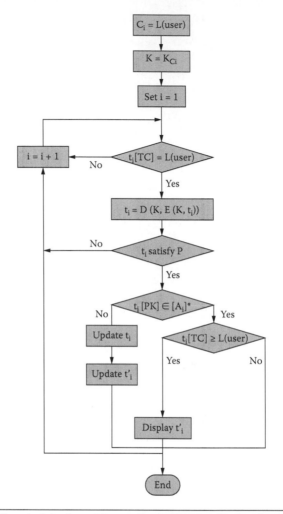

Figure 5.4 Flow chart for the update operation in the encryption-based multilevel database model. (N. Kaur, R. Singh, and H. S. Saini. 2009. *Proceedings of IEEE International Advance Computing Conference* (IACC 2009) Patiala, India, 1400–1404.)

After tuple t is constructed, the following procedure will be applied:

- If there is a tuple that has a primary key equal to the primary key of the constructed tuple and its security class level is equal to the security class level of the user who executes the UPLEVEL statement, this tuple will be replaced by the constructed tuple; otherwise, the tuple will be added to the relation.

Figure 5.5 illustrates the flow chart for the uplevel operation in the encryption-based multilevel database model.

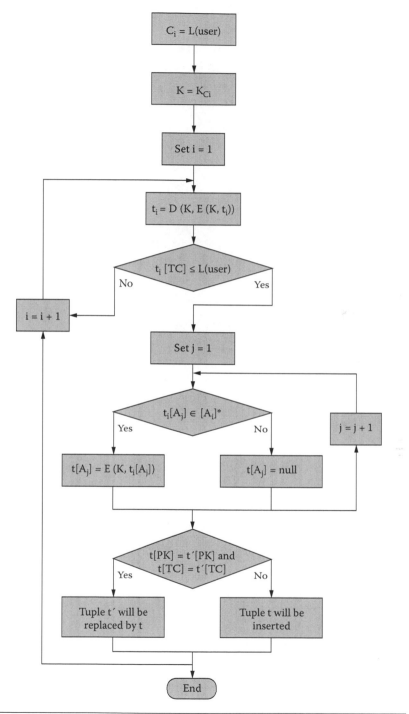

Figure 5.5 Flow chart for the uplevel operation in the encryption-based multilevel database model. (R. Haraty and N. Bekaii. 2006. *Journal of Computer Science* 2 (1): 19–28.)

5.4 Performance Study

This section describes the performance study of multilevel relational database security models such as SeaView, Jajodia–Sandhu, Smith–Winslett, MLR, and belief-consistent models and the encryption-based multilevel database and illustrates the impact of changing the size and schema of the relational database on the performance of these models.

The machine that is used for the implementation consists of CPU speed of 2.2 GHz, physical RAM size of 3 GB, and hard disk size of 320 GB. The software used in the implementation is a Microsoft SQL server 2008 R2 and the experiments' measurements were captured at the machine using a monitoring tool provided by the Microsoft SQL server.

Also, a prototype is implemented to determine the impact of the encryption algorithms on a multilevel database and to find the suitable algorithm to be used in the new encryption system. From Figure 5.6, we observe that the suitable encryption algorithm is the AES_128 algorithm that supports encryption with good performance and is cost effective.

5.4.1 Experimental Database Structure

The timesheet database consists of four relations and was created and populated to facilitate our performance study. Timesheet system relations used in the implementation are described as follows:

- The employee relation provides information about employees:
  - Employee(EMPID, Code, Name, Department, Type, Contract, Shift, Religion, Job, Position, Address, City).
- The departure relation is used to store the departure notice of each employee when he leaves the site of the work:
  - Departure(EMPID, DepartureDate, ReturnDate, DepartureType)
- The timesheet relation is used to store the timesheet of each employee every day:
  - TimeSheet(EMPID, Date, TimeSheet, OverTime, Remarks)
- The annual rights relation is used to store the rights of each employee every year:
  - AnnualRights(EMPID, Year, Description, Inc, ADays, GDays)

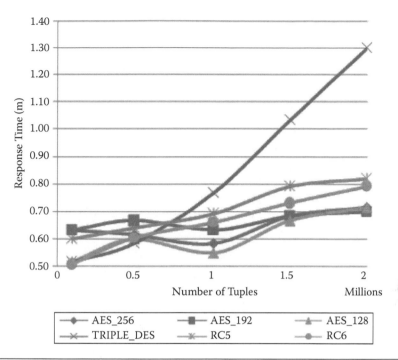

Figure 5.6 The impact of changing the number of tuples on the performance of the encryption algorithms in a multilevel database in the selection query. (P. Dave. 2008. Available at http://dotnet-slackers.com/articles/sql/IntroductionToSQLServerEncryptionAndSymmetricKeyEncryptionTutorial. aspx, accessed May 2011.)

Figure 5.7 shows the ER diagram for the timesheet system used in the implementation of the prototype to facilitate our performance study.

The experiments investigate the impact of changing the number of tuples, the number of attributes, and the number of security levels on the performance of the relational multilevel database models. These experiments use the CPU response time (in minutes) as a metric. For each query, the monitoring tool observes the time that the system takes to retrieve the result of the user query.

The queries were run several times and take the average response time for executing the query. Also, we distribute the number of the tuples of the relation in the database to be equal for all the security classification levels.

We assume that the base value for the number of tuples is 1,000,000, the base number of attributes is three, and the base number of security levels is four.

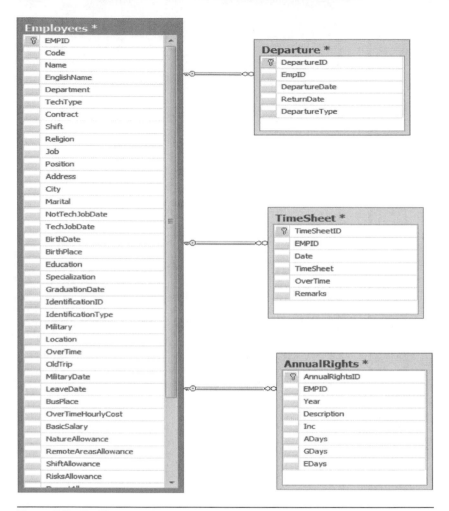

Figure 5.7 The ER diagram for the timesheet system used in the implementation.

5.4.2 SELECT Query

The following experiments define the impact of changing the number of tuples, the number of attributes, and the number of security levels on the performance of the multilevel relational database security models and the encryption-based multilevel database model when executing the selection query. The overhead of the decryption is included in the evaluation of the performance of the multilevel data retrieval. The where clause in the SELECT query is taken into consideration when we evaluate the performance of the multilevel database security models and the encryption-based multilevel database model when executing the selection query.

The SELECT statement that is used in the following experiments is described as follows:

```
Select * from Employee where department = 'Sales.'
```

5.4.2.1 Impact of Varying the Number of Tuples This experiment is used to measure the impact of changing the number of tuples on the performance of the multilevel relational database models. The number of tuples is varied to 100,000, 500,000, 1,000,000, 1,500,000 and 2,000,000. Fix the number of attributes at three; fix the number of security levels at four. From Figure 5.8 the response times grow for all models as the number of tuples is increased.

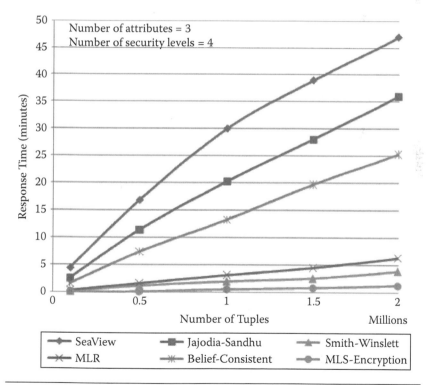

Figure 5.8 Impact of changing the number of tuples in the selection query. (M. Garuba. 2003. PhD thesis, Department of Mathematics, Royal Holloway, University of London, Egham, Surrey. Available at http://digirep.rhul.ac.uk/items/f076f347-2036-6bd0-98c8-e1d2dc9cf4ab/1/, accessed April 2011.)

Also, supporting encryption in the encryption-based multilevel database model improves the performance of the multilevel relational database because database size is decreased due to removing the extra attributes used for the class levels.

5.4.2.2 Impact of Varying the Number of Attributes This experiment is used to measure the impact of changing the number of attributes on the performance of the multilevel relational database models. The number of attributes varies from two to three, four, five, and six. Fix the number of tuples at 1,000,000; fix the number of security levels at four. From Figure 5.9 the response times grow for all models as the number of attributes is increased. Also, supporting encryption in the encryption-based multilevel database model improves the performance of the multilevel relational database because the database size is decreased due to removing the extra attributes used for the class levels.

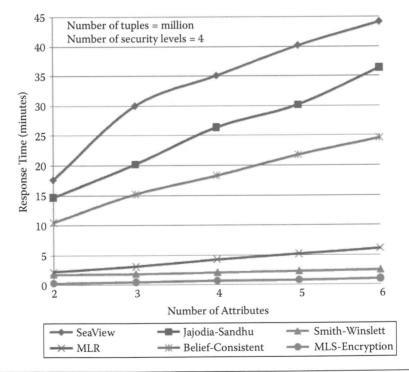

Figure 5.9 Impact of changing the number of attributes in the selection query. (M. Garuba, E. Appiah, and L. Burge. 2004. *Proceedings of the International Conference on Information Technology: Coding and Computing* (ITCC'04), 566–570.)

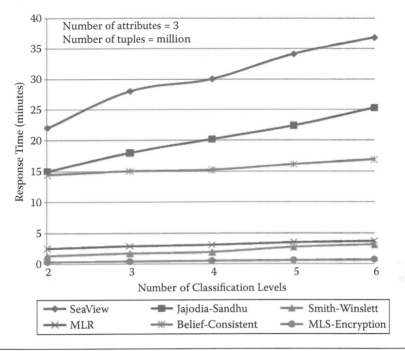

Figure 5.10   Impact of changing the number of security levels in the selection query. (Z. Rashid, A. Basit, and Z. Anwar. 2010. *Proceedings of 6th International Conference on Emerging Technologies* (ICET), 337–342.)

5.4.2.3 Impact of Varying the Number of Security Levels   This experiment is used to measure the impact of changing the numbers of security levels on the performance of the multilevel relational database models. The number of security levels varies from two to three, four, five, and six. Fix the number of tuples at 1,000,000; fix the number of attributes at four. From Figure 5.10 the response times grow for all models as the number of security levels is increased. Also, supporting encryption in the encryption-based multilevel database model improves the performance of a multilevel database because the database size is decreased due to removing the extra attributes used for the class levels.

5.4.3 JOIN Query

The following experiments define the impact of changing the number of tuples, the number of attributes, and the number of security levels on the performance of the multilevel relational database security models and the encryption-based multilevel database model when executing the JOIN query. The overhead of the decryption is included in the evaluation of the performance of the multilevel data retrieval. The where clause in the JOIN query will be taken into consideration when we evaluate the performance of the multilevel database security models and the encryption-based multilevel database model when executing the JOIN query. The JOIN operation involves two tables: the employee table and the departure table. The JOIN statement that is used in the following experiments is described as follows:

```
Select * from Employee join Departure
on Employee.Name = Departure.Name where Employee.
    department = 'Sales'
```

5.4.3.1 Impact of Varying the Number of Tuples The number of tuples is varied from 100,000 to 500,000, 1,000,000, 1,500,000, and 2,000,000. Fix the number of attributes at three; fix the number of security levels at four. From Figure 5.11 the response times grow

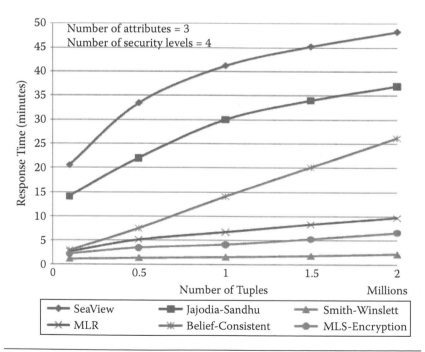

Figure 5.11 Impact of changing the number of tuples in a join query. (V. M. Doshi et al. 1996. *Proceedings of IEEE Transactions on Knowledge and Data Engineering* 8 (1): 46–55.)

for all models as the number of tuples is increased. Also, supporting encryption in the encryption-based multilevel database model improves the performance of a multilevel database because the database size is decreased due to removing the extra attributes used for the class levels.

5.4.3.2 Impact of Varying the Number of Attributes The number of attributes in each table is varied from two to three, four, five, and six. Fix the number of tuples at 1,000,000; fix the number of security levels at four. From Figure 5.12 the response times grow for all models as the number of attributes is increased. Also, supporting encryption in the encryption-based multilevel database model improves the performance of a multilevel database because the database size is decreased due to removing the extra attributes used for the class levels.

5.4.3.3 Impact of Varying the Number of Security Levels The number of security levels is varied from two to three, four, five, and six. Fix the number of tuples at 1,000,000; fix the number of attributes at four.

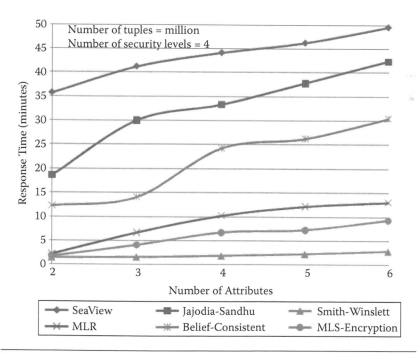

Figure 5.12 Impact of changing the number of attributes in a join query. (L. Pan. 2008. *Proceedings of International Symposium on Electronic Commerce and Security,* 518–522.)

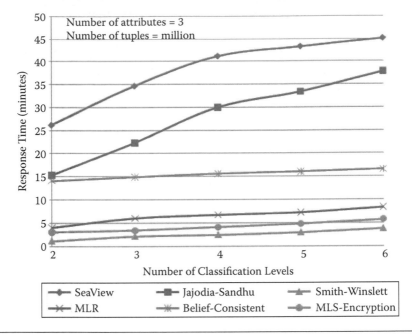

Figure 5.13 Impact of varying the number of security levels in a join query. (L. Pan. 2008. *Proceedings of International Symposium on Electronic Commerce and Security*, 518–522.)

From Figure 5.13 the response times grow for all models as the number of the security levels is increased. Also, supporting encryption in the encryption-based multilevel database model improves the performance of a multilevel database because the database size is decreased due to removing the extra attributes used for the class levels.

5.4.4 UPDATE Query

The number of the updated tuples is varied from 100,000 to 500,000, 750,000, and 1,000,000. Fix the number of attributes at three; fix the number of security levels at four. From Figure 5.14 the response times grow for all models as the number of tuples is increased. Also, supporting encryption in the encryption-based multilevel database model decreases the performance of a multilevel database because, during the execution of the update statement, the encryption and decryption mechanisms will be included together in the update procedure.

The where clause in the UPDATE query will be taken into consideration when we evaluate the performance of the multilevel database

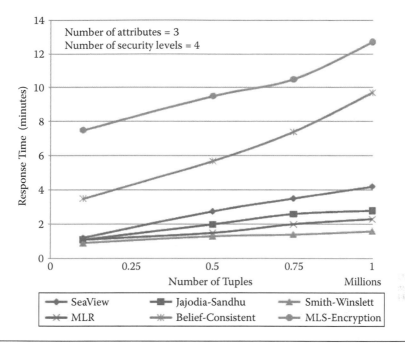

Figure 5.14   Impact of varying the number of tuples in an update query. (L. Pan. 2008. *Proceedings of International Symposium on Electronic Commerce and Security,* 518–522.)

security models and the proposed encryption-based multilevel security (MLS) model when executing the UPDATE query. The UPDATE statement that is used in the following experiments is described as follows:

```
Update Employee set salary = salary+100 where
    department = 'Sales'
```

5.5 Analysis of Experimental Results

The performance of the Smith–Winslett model is the best because it does not support the security classification at the level of each single attribute; the access classes can be assigned only to key attributes and to tuples as a whole. The MLR model offers less performance than the Smith–Winslett model because it supports the security classification at the level of each single attribute. The belief-consistent model has less performance than the MLR model because it supports a combination of the security classification levels for each single attribute to enable the user to assert his beliefs of lower level users' information.

The Jajodia–Sandhu model has bad performance because of the impact of union operation between single-level relations in the recovery algorithm. The SeaView model has very bad performance because of the impact of the JOIN operation between vertical single-level relations and union operation between horizontal single-level relations in the recovery algorithm.

From the experimental results in the previous section, the encryption-based multilevel database model, which is a combination of the MLR model and encryption algorithm, has performance better than the performance of the MLR model in retrieving data from the multilevel database. This improvement in performance is due to the reduction of the multilevel database size, removing the attributes classification columns, and encrypting the records by an encryption key according to its security level. Also, by adding an encryption algorithm, the overhead in the MLR model of checking the security class level hierarchy for each data element when retrieving data is reduced. Instead of checking the security class level hierarchy when getting data in the encryption-based multilevel database model, the encryption keys belong to the subject to encrypt each data element that is used when retrieving data. The performance of the encryption-based multilevel database model is less than the performance of the MLR model in updating data because the overhead of supporting the encryption algorithm in the update query is executed. Table 5.4 shows the reduction in database size in the encryption-based multilevel database model compared to the original MLR model and the other MLS models.

Table 5.4   Reduction in Database Size in Proposed Model Compared to Original MLR Model and Other MLS Models

MODEL/ CRITERIA	ORIGINAL MLR	SEAVIEW	JAJODIA– SANDHU	SMITH– WINSLETT	BELIEF- CONSISTENT MLS	ENCRYPTION- BASED MULTILEVEL DATABASE
Actual database size in megabytes	106	129	116	98	110	91
Reduction in database size in our proposed model	Reduced by 15%	Reduced by 30%	Reduced by 22%	Reduced by 8%	Reduced by 18%	

Table 5.5 Comparative Study between Encryption-Based Multilevel Database and Other Multilevel Database Security Models

MODEL/ CRITERIA	SEAVIEW	JAJODIA– SANDHU	SMITH– WINSLETT	MLR	BELIEF-CONSISTENT MLS	ENCRYPTION-BASED MULTILEVEL DATABASE
Performance in minutes	47	35	3	6	25	2
Encryption	Not supported	Not supported	Not supported	Not supported	Not supported	Supported

Table 5.5 gives a comparative study between the proposed encryption-based multilevel database model and the other multilevel database security models.

5.6 Summary

The encryption-based multilevel database model is implemented by adding an encryption system as an additional layer of security over the MLR model in multilevel relational database security. A working multilevel secure database prototype was implemented in a Microsoft SQL server database to measure the performance experiments that were instrumented using the system. Also, this chapter measured the impact of supporting encryption in the multilevel relational database; the overhead of the encryption of data insertion and decryption of data retrieval are included in the performance study.

Supporting encryption in multilevel relational databases improves the performance of the retrieving of data in the SELECT and JOIN queries. This improvement in the performance due to the relational database size is decreased because the extra attributes used for the class levels are replaced by supporting the encryption in the multilevel relational database. Also, the multilevel relational database design is easier because there is no change in the structure of the base table. Supporting encryption in the multilevel relational database has a bad performance because of the extra CPU processing results from supporting the encryption algorithm in an MLS database. When supporting the encryption algorithm in the UPDATE query is executed, we decrypt the data, ensure the condition of the update statement, execute the update statement, and encrypt the data again.

6

FORMAL ANALYSIS FOR ENCRYPTION-BASED MULTILEVEL MODEL FOR DBMS

6.1 Introduction

This chapter will present the formal analysis for data manipulation language (DML) operations like SELECT, INSERT, UPDATE, and DELETE for the encryption-based multilevel model for relational database management systems. Also, this chapter will give the soundness, completeness, and the security mathematical proof for the DML operations of the encryption-based multilevel database model. The mathematical proofs show that the DML operations transform any database in the correct state to another database in the correct state, which indicates the power of the encryption-based multilevel database model [75].

This model achieves good quality because it satisfies integrity properties such as entity integrity, polyinstantiation integrity, data borrow integrity, foreign key integrity, and referential integrity of the multilevel database.

The work presented in this chapter offers two major contributions to the field:

- Redefining the mathematical model for the DML operations for the encryption-based multilevel model
- Proving the soundness, completeness, and security of the DML operations for the encryption-based multilevel model

6.2 The Encryption-Based Multilevel Model for DBMS Definition

6.2.1 MLR Model Definition

Definition 6.2.1.1: A multilevel relational database scheme is defined in the following form [76]:

- $R(A_1, C_1, A_2, C_2, ..., A_n, C_n, TC)$, where A_i is the attribute that stores the data, C_i is the attribute that stores the security classification level of the attribute A_i, and TC is the attribute that stores the security classification level of the tuple. The domain of the value of the attribute C_i is defined by a set $\{L_i, ..., H_i\}$ where the L_i is the lowest security classification level and the H_i is the highest security classification level. The domain of the TC is defined as $U_{i=1}^{n}(\{L_i, ..., H_i\})$, where U stands for the set of union.

Definition 6.2.1.2: The multilevel relational database instance is defined in the following form [76]:

- $r(A_1, C_1, A_2, C_2, ..., A_n, C_n, TC)$, where r is a group of some tuples that have the values $(a_1, c_1, a_2, c_2, ..., a_n, c_n, tc)$, where the value of $a_i \in D_i$ and the value of $c_i \in \{L_i, ..., H_i\}$, or a_1 = *null* and $c_i \in \{L_i, ..., H_i\}$ U *null*, and $tc \geq$ lub $\{c_i | c_i \neq null$: $i = 1...,n\}$; lub stands for the least upper bound.

Definition 6.2.1.3: The relational database is a set of related relations and the database state is a set of all the relation instances of the relational database at a specific time [76].

- The instance $r(A_1, C_1, A_2, C_2, ..., A_n, C_n, TC)$ has some definitions that will be described as follows:
  - The primary key A_1 and its security classification level attribute C_1:
    - $t[A_1, C_1]$ defines the tuple in the relation instance r and also defines the security classification level of the tuple.
    - $t[C_1] = c_1$ means that the tuple is inserted into the relational database by a user with c_1 security classification level.

- Tuple classification attribute (TC):
    - $t[TC] = tc$ with $t[C_1] = c_1$ means a tuple t is inserted by a user with tc security classification level. Tuple t can only be displayed by users with security classification level $c' \geq tc$. The tuple t can be modified by a user with tc security classification level. $t[TC] = t[C_1]$ means that tuple t is the base tuple and all tuples $t' \in r$ such that $t'[A_1, C_1] = t[A_1, C_1]$ depend on tuple t.
- Data A_i and its security classification level attribute $C_i (2 \leq i \leq n)$:
    - $t[A_i, C_i]$ with $t[C_i] = c_i$ and $t[TC] = tc[c_i \leq tc]$ defines which data $t[A_i]$ can be altered by users with tc security classification level. $t[A_i, C_i]$ can be modified by users with tc or c_i security classification levels. When $t[C_i] < t[TC]$, $t[A_i] \neq null$ is defined and a tuple that is borrowed from the $t'[A_i]$ of t' that has $t'[A_1, C_1] = t[A_1, C_1] \wedge t'[TC] = t'[c_i] = t[c_i]$.
- Null value:
    - $t[A_i, C_i] = [null, c_i]$, $[c_i < tc]$ means that for each data attribute A_i, there are users with tc security classification levels that expect to borrow data owned by users with c_i security classification levels. Both $t[A_i, C_i] = [null, null]$ and $t[A_i, C_i] = [null, tc]$ mean that there are no data available in the data attribute A_i. The [null, null] case applies when tc $\notin \{L_i,...,H_j\}$; the [null, tc] case applies otherwise.

6.2.2 Encryption-Based Multilevel Model for DBMS Definition

The encryption-based multilevel model uses an encryption system with secure certificates and keys. This model encrypts each tuple with an encryption key according to its security classification level (tuple classification).

Definition 6.2.2.1: A multilevel relational database scheme is defined in the following form:

- $R(E_{C_1}(A_1), E_{C_2}(A_2),..., E_{C_n}(A_n), TC)$, where A_i is the attribute that stores the data, C_i is the attribute that stores the security classification level of the attribute A_i, and TC is the attribute that stores the security classification level of the tuple. The domain of the value of the attribute C_i is defined by a set $\{L_i,...H_i\}$ where the L_i is the lowest security classification level and the H_i is the highest security classification level. $E_{C_i}(A_i)$ is the encryption function of a data attribute. The domain of the TC is defined as $U_{i=1}^{n}(\{L_i,...,H_i\})$, where U stands for the set of union.

Definition 6.2.2.2: The multilevel relational database instance is defined in the following form:

- $r(E_{C_1}(A_1), E_{C_2}(A_2),..., E_{C_n}(A_n), TC)$, where r is a group of some tuples that have the form $r(E_{c_1}(a_1), E_{c_2}(a_2),...., E_{c_n}(a_n), tc)$, where the value of $a_i \in D_i$ and the value of $c_i \in \{L_i, ..., H_i\}$ or $a_i = $ null and $c_i \in \{L_i, ..., H_i\} \cup$ null, and $tc \geq$ lub $\{c_i \mid c_i \neq$ null: $i = 1...,n\}$; lub stands for the least upper bound.

Definition 6.2.2.3: The relational database is a set of related relations and the database state is a set of all the relation instances of the relational database at a specific time.

The instance $r(E_{C_1}(A_1), E_{C_2}(A_2),..., E_{C_n}(A_n), TC)$ has some definitions that will be described as follows:

- The primary key $E_{C_1}(A_1)$:
  - $t[E_{C_1}(A_1)]$ defines the tuple in the relation instance r and also defines the security classification level of the tuple.
  - $Key(E_{C_1}(A_1)) = c_1$ means that the tuple is inserted into the relational database by a user with c_1 security classification level.
- Tuple-class attribute TC:
  - $t[TC] = tc$ with $t[C_1] = c_1$ means that tuple t is inserted by a user with tc security classification level. Tuple t can only be displayed by users with security classification level $c' \geq tc$. The tuple t can be modified by a user with tc security classification level. $t[TC] = t[C_1]$ means that tuple t is the base tuple and all tuples $t' \in r$ such that $t'[A_1, C_1] = t[A_1, C_1]$ depend on tuple t.

- Data attribute A_i and security classification level attribute $C_i (2 \leq i \leq n)$:

  - $t[E_{C_i}(A_i)]$ with $Key(t[E_{C_i}(A_i)]) = c_i$ defines that the data $t[A_1]$ can be altered by users with tc security classification level. $t[E_{C_i}(A_i)]$ can be modified by users with tc or c_i security classification levels. When $t[C_i] < t[TC]$, $t[A_i] \neq$ null is defined as a tuple borrowed from the $t'[A_i]$ of t' that has $t'[A_1, C_1] = t[A_1, C_1] \wedge t'[TC] = t'[c_i] = t[c_i]$.

- Null value:

  - $t[A_i, C_i] = [\text{null}, c_i]$, $(c_i < tc)$ means that for each data attribute A_i, there are users with tc security classification level that expect to borrow data owned by users with c_i security classification level. Both $t[A_i, C_i] = [\text{null}, \text{null}]$ and $t[A_i, C_i] = [\text{null}, tc]$ mean that there are no data available in the data attribute A_i. The [null, null] case applies when $tc \notin \{L_i, \ldots, H_i\}$; the [null, tc] case applies otherwise.

6.3 Integrity Properties

6.3.1 Entity Integrity

In the entity integrity (EI) properties, a multilevel relational database instance r satisfies the entity integrity if the following requirement exists [77]:

For each tuple $t \in r$:

$$A_i \in AK \Rightarrow t[A_i] \neq \text{null};$$

$$A_i, A_j \in AK \Rightarrow t[C_i] = t[C_j];$$

and

$$A_i \in AK \Rightarrow t[C_i] \geq t[C_{AK}].$$

The first requirement ensures that no tuple $t \in r$ has a null value for any attribute in the primary key attributes AK. The second requirement ensures that all the primary key attributes AK should have the same security classification level in the tuple $t \in r$. The third requirement states that the security classification level of the nonprimary key attributes must be greater than or equal to the security classification level of the primary key attributes.

6.3.2 Polyinstantiation Integrity

In polyinstantiation integrity (PI), a multilevel relational database instance r satisfies the polyinstantiation integrity if the following requirement exists [78]:

For $1 \leq i \leq n$:

$$A_1, TC \rightarrow C_i;$$

and

$$A_1, C_1, C_i \rightarrow A_i;$$

This property ensures that the primary key attribute A_1, in conjunction with the security classification level attributes C_1 and C_i, functionally determines the value of the A_i attribute.

6.3.3 Data-Borrow Integrity

In data-borrow integrity (DBI), a multilevel relational database instance r satisfies the data borrow if the following requirement exists [79]:

For $1 \leq i \leq n$, all the nonprimary key attributes in tuple $t \in r$ that have data encrypted by key according to security classification levels lower than the tuple classification level, there exists polyinstantiated tuple t' that has

$$t'[A_1] = t[A_1] \wedge t'[TC] = t'[c_i] = t[c_i] \wedge t'[A_i] = t[A_i].$$

6.3.4 Foreign Key Integrity

In foreign key integrity (FKI), let FK be a foreign key of the referencing relation R. A multilevel relational database instance r satisfies the foreign key if the following requirement exists [79]:

For each tuple $t \in r$:

$$(\forall A_i \in FK), t[A_i] \neq \text{null}$$

and

$$A_i, A_i \in FK \Rightarrow t[C_i] = t[C_i]$$

The first requirement of this property ensures that no foreign key attribute in the referencing relation has a null data value. The second requirement ensures that all the foreign key attributes FK should have the same security classification level in the tuple $t \in r$.

6.3.5 Referential Integrity

In referential integrity (RI), suppose that *FK1* is defined for a foreign key in the referencing relation R_1 that has a primary key AK_1. Suppose that R_2 is defined for the referenced relation that has a primary key AK_2 [80]. Multilevel relational database instances r_1, r_2 satisfy the referential integrity if the following requirement exists:
For all

$$t_{11} \in r_1$$

such that

$$t_{11}[FK_1] \neq \text{null},$$

there exists

$$t_{21} \in r_2$$

such that

$$t_{11}[FK_1] = t_{21}[AK_2] \wedge t_{11}[TC] = t_{21}[TC] \wedge t_{11}[C_{FK_1}] \geq t_{21}[C_{AK_2}],$$

and for all

$$t_{11}, t_{12} \in r_1$$

and

$$t_{21}, t_{22} \in r_2,$$

if

$$t_{11}[AK_1] = t_{12}[AK_1] \wedge t_{11}[TC] = t_{21}[TC] \wedge t_{12}[TC] = t_{22}[TC]$$

$$= t_{11}[C_{FK_1}] = t_{12}[C_{FK_1}] \wedge t_{11}[FK_1] = t_{21}[AK_2]$$

$$= t_{22}[AK_2], \text{then } t_{21}[AK_2] = t_{22}[AK_2].$$

6.4 Manipulation

This section presents the data manipulation statements for the encryption-based multilevel database model.

6.4.1 *The INSERT Statement*

The INSERT statement executed by a user with security level L (user) has the following general form [81]:

```
INSERT INTO R [A₁, A₂, ...,Aₙ]
VALUES [a₁, a₂, ..., aₙ]
```

R is the relation name and $[A_1, A_2, ..., A_n]$ are the attribute names. K_{Ci} is the symmetric encryption key associated to the security level of the user. $E(K, a_i)$ is the encryption of data value a_i by an encryption key. Each INSERT data manipulation can insert, at most, one tuple into the relation R. The inserted tuple t is constructed as follows:

```
For 1≤i≤n
If (Aᵢ ∈ R[Aᵢ]*)
{
Ci = L(user)
K = KCi
t[Aᵢ] = E(K,aᵢ)
}
Else
{
t[Aᵢ] = null
}
t[TC] = L
i = i+1
```

Insert new tuple t into the multilevel relational database.

The insertion is permitted if the database state satisfies the entity integrity, the foreign key integrity, and the referential integrity properties.

6.4.2 *The DELETE Statement*

The DELETE statement executed by a user with security class level L has the following general form [82]:

```
DELETE FROM R
WHERE P
```

where R is the relation name, assuming that relation R has attributes $[A_1, A_2, ..., A_n]$, r is the database relation instance, and P is a predicate expression that may include conditions involving classification attributes. $t_{i(temp)}$ is a temporary tuple for the decrypted data during the execution of the delete statement. $D(K,E(K,t_i))$ is the decryption of the encrypted data value in the tuple t_i by a symmetric encryption key.

```
Cᵢ = L(user)
K = KCi
For 1≤i≤n
IF (tᵢ[TC]= L(user)
{
tᵢ(temp) = D(K, E(K, tᵢ))
If (tᵢ(temp) = p)
{
Delete ti
}
i = i +1
}
Else IF (tᵢ[TC] > L(user))
{
Mark to be deleted by high user.
i = i+1
}
Else
{
i = i+1
}
```

The DELETE statement is permitted if the database state satisfies the entity integrity, the foreign key integrity, and the referential integrity properties.

6.4.3 The SELECT Statement

The SELECT statement executed by a user with security class level L has the following general form [82]:

```
SELECT [A₁,A₂, ...,Aₙ] FROM R
WHERE P
```

where R is the relation name, $[A_1, A_2, \ldots, A_n]$ are the attributes names, and P is a predicate expression that may include conditions involving the security classification attributes. $ti_{(temp)}$ is a temporary tuple for the decrypted data during the execution of the DELETE statement. $D(K,E(K,t_i))$ is the decryption of the encrypted data value in the tuple t_i by a symmetric encryption key.

```
C_i = L(user)
K = KCi
For 1≤i≤n
IF (t_i[TC] = L(user))
{
t_i(temp) = D(K,E(K,t_i))
If (t_i(temp) = p)
{
Display ti
}
i = i+1
}
Else
{
i = i+1
}
```

6.4.4 The UPDATE Statement

The UPDATE statement executed by a subject with security class level L has the following general form [82]:

```
UPDATE R SET [A₁=a₁,A₂=a₂, ..., Aₙ=aₙ]
WHERE P
```

where R is the relation name, $[A_1, A_2, \ldots, A_n]$ are the attribute names, and P is a predicate expression that may include conditions involving classification attributes. $t_{i(temp)}$ is a temporary tuple for the decrypted data during the execution of the delete statement. $D(K,E(K,t_i))$ is the decryption of the encrypted data value in the tuple t_i by a symmetric encryption key.

```
C_i = L(user)
K = KCi
For 1≤i≤n
IF (t_i[TC] = L(user))
{
t_i(temp) = D(K, E(K, t_i))
```

```
If (t_i(temp) = p)
{
IF (t_i[TC]>L(user))
{
Mark to be deleted by high user.
i = i+1
}
Else
{
t_i[A_i] = E(K, a_i)
Update ti
}
i = i +1
}
Else
{
i = i+1
}
```

The UPDATE statement is permitted if the database state satisfies the entity integrity, the foreign key integrity, and the referential integrity properties.

6.4.5 *The UPLEVEL Statement*

The UPLEVEL statement executed by a user with security class level L has the following general form [82]:

```
UPLEVEL R GET [A_1, A_2, ..., A_n] FROM [C_1, C_2, ..., C_n]
WHERE P
```

where R is the relation, $A_1, A_2, ..., A_n$ are the data attributes, $C_1, C_2, ..., C_n$ are the security classification levels for $A_1, A_2, ..., A_n$, and P is a predicate that may include conditions that define the tuples that should be upleveled.

```
C_i = L(user)
K = KCi
For 1≤i≤n
IF (t_i[TC] = L(user))
{
t_i(temp) = D(K, E(K, t_i))
```

```
For 1≤j≤n
{
IF  (t_{i(temp)} [A_j] ∈ [A_j]*)
{
t_i[A_j] =E(K,t_{i(temp)} [A_j])
}
Else
{
t_i[A_j] = null
}
j = j +1
}
Tuple t will be inserted
}
Else
{
i = i+1
}
```

The UPLEVEL statement is permitted if the database state satisfies the entity integrity, the foreign key integrity, and the referential integrity properties.

6.5 Soundness

The soundness of the encryption-based multilevel database model will be proven in this section. The following two definitions will clarify the meaning of the soundness in the encryption-based multilevel database model [83].

Definition 6.5.1: If all the multilevel relational instances satisfy the integrity properties, the multilevel relational database will be in a legal state. ∎

Definition 6.5.2: If the sequences of the data manipulation operational statements transform any legal database state to another legal database state, the multilevel relational database will be sound. ∎

To prove the soundness of the encryption-based multilevel database model, four cases should be proven.

6.5.1 Case 1: In the INSERT Operation

The entity integrity, the foreign key integrity, and the referential integrity properties should be satisfied in the INSERT operation.

Polyinstantiation integrity is satisfied because of the following:

- There is no polyinstantiated tuple t'' in the original relation instance r with $t''[E_{C_1}(A_1)] = t[E_{C_1}(A_1)] \wedge t''[TC] = L$, since inserting the tuple t is permitted only if there is no $t' \in r$ such that $t'[A_1] = t[A_1] \wedge t'[TC] = L$.
- There is no polyinstantiated tuple t'' in the original relation instance r with $t''[E_{C_1}(A_1)] = t[E_{C_1}(A_1)] \wedge t''[TC] > L$.

Data-borrow integrity is satisfied because of the following:

- There is no data attribute $t[A_i](1 \le i \le n)$ in the tuple t with $t[C_i] < t[TC]$.

6.5.2 Case 2: In the DELETE Operation

The referential integrity properties should be satisfied in the DELETE operation.

Entity integrity is satisfied because of the following:

- There is no tuple polyinstantiated tuple t'' in the original relation instance r with $t''[E_{C_1}(A_1)]$.

Polyinstantiation integrity is satisfied because of the following:

- There is no polyinstantiated tuple t' in the original relation instance r with $t'[E_{C_1}(A_1)] = t[E_{C_1}(A_1)] \wedge t'[TC] > L \wedge t'[C_i] = L(2 \le i \le n)$.
- There is no polyinstantiated tuple t'' with $t''[E_{C_1}(A_1)] = t[E_{C_1}(A_1)] \wedge t''[TC] < L \wedge t''[C_i] = L(2 \le i \le n)$.

Data-borrow integrity is satisfied because of the following:

- There is no polyinstantiated tuple t' in the original relation instance r with $t'[E_{C_1}(A_1)] = t[E_{C_1}(A_1)] \wedge t'[TC] > L \wedge t'[C_i] = L(2 \le i \le n)$.

Foreign key integrity is satisfied because of the following:

- There is no polyinstantiated tuple t' in the original relation instance r with $t'[E_{C_1}(A_1)] = t[E_{C_1}(A_1)] \wedge t'[TC] > L \wedge t'[C_{FK}] = L$.

6.5.3 *Case 3: In the UPDATE Operation*

The entity integrity, the foreign key integrity, and the referential integrity properties should be satisfied in the UPDATE operation.

Polyinstantiation integrity is satisfied because of the following:

- There is no polyinstantiated tuple t' in the original relation instance r with $t'[E_{C_1}(A_1)] = t[E_{C_1}(A_1)] \wedge t'[TC] > L \wedge t'[C_i] = L (2 \leq i \leq n)$.
- There is no polyinstantiated tuple t'' with $t'' [E_{C_1}(A_1)] = t[E_{C_1}(A_1)] \wedge t''[TC] > L \wedge t''[C_i] = L (2 \leq i \leq n)$.

Data-borrow integrity is satisfied because of the following:

- There is no polyinstantiated tuple t' in the original relation instance r with $t'[E_{C_1}(A_1)] = t[E_{C_1}(A_1)] \wedge t'[TC] > L \wedge t'[C_i] = L (2 \leq i \leq n)$.

6.5.4 *Case 4: In the UPLEVEL Operation*

The polyinstantiation integrity, the foreign key integrity, and the referential integrity properties should be satisfied in the UPDATE operation.

Entity integrity is satisfied because of the following:

- There is no tuple polyinstantiated tuple t' in the original relation instance r with $t'[E_{C_1}(A_1)] = t[E_{C_1}(A_1)]$.

Data-borrow integrity is satisfied because of the following:

- There is no polyinstantiated tuple t' in the original relation instance r with $t'[E_{C_1}(A_1)] = t[E_{C_1}(A_1)] \wedge t'[TC] > L \wedge t'[C_i] = L (2 \leq i \leq n)$.

6.6 Completeness

The completeness of the encryption-based multilevel database model will be proven in this section. The following definitions will clarify the meaning of the completeness in the encryption-based multilevel database model [83].

Definition 6.6.1: If the sequences of the data manipulation operations transform any legal database state to another legal database state, the multilevel relational database will be complete.   ■

Theorem 6.6.1: The encryption-based multilevel model is complete. ■

To prove the completeness of the encryption-based multilevel model, the following lemmas should be proven.

Lemma 6.6.1: The sequences of the data manipulation operations transform any legal database state to an empty database state. ■

Proof: In the DELETE operation, the following steps can be performed:

- If the base tuple is deleted, any entity will be deleted totally. In the DELETE operation, if the values of $t[E_{C_1}(A_1)]$ are given in the WHERE clause, only the referencing tuples will be deleted. This will ensure the referential integrity property.
- The empty database state can exist by deleting all entities in all multilevel relational instances.

Lemma 6.6.2: The sequences of the data manipulation operation transform any empty database to any legal database state. ■

Proof: In the INSERT operation, the following steps can be performed:

- The referencing tuples will be inserted before inserting the referenced tuples.
- Each tuple is inserted by a user with a security classification level equal to the tuple classification value as follows:
- The base tuple t is inserted by a user using an INSERT statement with all A_i that have $t_1[A_i] \neq null$ listed in the INTO clause, and $t_1[A_i]$ in the VALUES clause.

In the UPLEVEL operation, inserting any additional tuple t_m is done by the following step:

- All $t_m[E_{C_1}(A_1)]$ with $t_m[C_i] < t_m[TC]$ are included in the USE clause of the UPLEVEL statement.

The legal database state can exist by using INSERT, UPLEVEL, and UPDATE for inserting all entities in all multilevel relational instances. This legal database state should satisfy the entity integrity, the polyinstantiation integrity, the foreign key integrity, the data-borrow integrity, and the referential integrity properties.

Proof of Theorem 6.6.1: From Lemmas 6.6.1 and 6.6.2, the sequences of the data manipulation operational statements transform any legal database state to another legal database state.   ∎

6.7 Security

Security is the basic issue of the encryption-based multilevel model and is the advantage of this model over the traditional database and the multilevel security database models. So, the security of the encryption-based multilevel model is considered to be proved [83].

In this section, the following notation will be used:

S: all users with security classification levels

T: all tuples with security classification levels in a database state
   Given any access level L,

   $SV(L)$: the group of the users with security classification
      levels lower than or equal to L

   $SH(L)$: S − $SV(L)$

   $TV(L)$: the group of tuples with security classification
      levels lower than or equal to L

   $TH(L)$: T − $TV(L)$

It is known that, for any security classification level L, $S = SV(L) \cup SH(L)$ and $SV(L) \cap SH(L) = \varphi$, while $T = TV(L) \cup TH(L)$ and $TV(L) \cap TH(L) = \varphi$.

The following definitions will clarify the security requirement that should be satisfied in the encryption-based multilevel database model.

Definition 6.7.1: A secure multilevel database model should ensure that there is no interference when modifying the relations in the multilevel database. For example, changing any input from user $S_1 \in SH(L)$ cannot affect the output to any user $S_2 \in SV(L)$.   ∎

As shown in Figure 6.1, the input to the encryption-based multilevel database model is a sequence of the data manipulation operational statements (such as INSERT, DELETE, SELECT, UPDATE, and

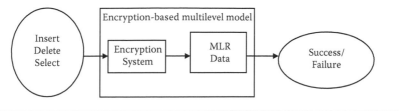

Figure 6.1 The interface of the encryption-based multilevel model.

UPLEVEL statements) from users with varying security classification levels. The outputs from the encryption-based multilevel database model are the results retrieved by the users that include the following:

- Group of the retrieved tuples for the SELECT statement
- SUCCESS or FAILURE status for the INSERT, DELETE, UPDATE, or UPLEVEL statements

Theorem 6.7.1: The encryption-based multilevel model is secure. To prove this theorem, the following lemmas should be proven. ■

Lemma 6.7.1: For security classification level L, changing $TH(L)$ cannot affect the output to the user $S \in SV(L)$. ■

Proof of Lemma 6.7.1: If a SELECT statement is executed by a user that has security classification level L', where $S \in SV(L)(L' \leq L)$, no tuples in $TH(L')$ will be taken into the calculation of P. Since $L' \leq L$ includes that $TH(L') \supseteq TH(L)$, modifying $TH(L)$ cannot affect the tuples' output to $S \in SV(L)$. ■

By the INSERT, DELETE, UPDATE, and UPLEVEL operations for a user that has security classification level L', where $S \in SV(L)(L' \leq L)$:

The INSERT operation executed by a user, s, could be rejected if:

- There is a tuple $t' \in r$ with $t'[A_1] = a_1 \wedge t'[TC] = L'$.
- The tuple t that is inserted violates the entity integrity, the foreign key integrity, or the referential integrity properties.

The DELETE operation executed by a user, s, could be rejected if:

- The tuple with security classification level L that is deleted is referenced by some tuples that have security classification level L' where $(L' \leq L)$.

The UPDATE operation executed by a user, s, could be rejected if:

- There is a tuple $t' \in r$ with $t'[A_1] = t[A_1] \wedge t'[TC] = L'$.
- The tuple t that is updated violates the entity integrity, foreign key integrity, or referential integrity properties.

The UPLEVEL operation executed by a user, s, could be rejected if:

- There is a tuple $t' \in r$ with $t'[A_1] = t[A_1] \wedge t'[C_1] = t[C_1] \wedge t'[TC] = L'$.
- The tuple t that is updated violates the entity integrity, the foreign key integrity, or the referential integrity properties.

Since $t, t' \notin TH(L') \supseteq TH(L)$, modifying $TH(L)$ cannot affect the S/F information output to $S \in SV(L)$; therefore, modifying $TH(L)$ cannot affect the output to $S \in SV(L)$.

Lemma 6.7.2: For security classification level L, deleting any input from user $S \in SH(L)$ cannot change $TV(L)$. ∎

Proof of Lemma 6.7.2: The user can change the database states by an INSERT, DELETE, UPDATE, or UPLEVEL operation. ∎

The INSERT operation is executed by a user, s, that has security classification level L', where $S \in SH(L) (L' > L)$ can only generate the L'-tuple t' since $L' > L$, $t' \notin TV(L)$.

The DELETE operation is executed by a user, s, that has security classification level L', where $S \in SH(L) (L' > L)$ can only delete L'-tuples t', and may change the polyinstantiation tuple t'' at levels $L''(L'' > L')$.

The UPDATE operation is executed by a user, s, that has security classification level L', where $S \in SH(L) (L' > L)$ can only change L'-tuples t' and may change the polyinstantiation tuple t'' at levels $L''(L'' > L')$.

The UPLEVEL operation is executed by a user, s, that has security classification level L', where $S \in SH(L) (L' > L)$ can only change L'-tuples t' and may change the polyinstantiation tuple t'' at levels $L''(L'' > L')$.

From the previous paragraphs, deleting any input from a subject $S \in SH(L)$ cannot change $TV(L)$.

Proof of Theorem 6.7.1: From Lemma 6.7.1 and Lemma 6.7.2, for any security classification level L, since $S = SV(L) \cup SH(L)$, $SV(L) \cap$

$SH(L) = \varphi$; while $T = TV(L) \cup TH(L)$ and $TV(L) \cap TH(L) = \varphi$, deleting any input from user $S_1 \in SH(L)$ cannot affect the output to $S_2 \in SH(L)$. ∎

6.8 Summary

This chapter presented the concept of the encryption-based multilevel database model, which improved the performance of the multilevel relational database by decreasing the database size and enhancing the response time for retrieving the data from the multilevel relational database. The mathematical forms for the data manipulation operations such as SELECT, INSERT, UPDATE, and DELETE of the multilevel relational database were refined to match the effect of adding the encryption algorithm to the multilevel relational database model. The mathematical proof of the soundness, the completeness, and the security was introduced to demonstrate that the encryption-based multilevel database model is robust against database attacks and free from covert channel problems. The mathematical model for multilevel integrity properties such as entity integrity, polyinstantiation integrity, data borrow integrity, foreign key integrity, and referential integrity was introduced to characterize the verification of the encryption-based multilevel database model.

7

CONCURRENCY CONTROL IN MULTILEVEL RELATIONAL DATABASES

7.1 Introduction

Most of the multilevel relational databases use the mandatory access control mechanism that is based on the Bell–LaPadula model [84]. This model depends on the terms of the subjects and the data. The data may be a relation, a tuple, or an attribute within a tuple. The subject is the active process that needs to access some data. Every datum can be associated with a classification level (such as U = unclassified, C = confidential, S = secret, and TS = top secret). Every subject also is associated with a classification level (such as U = unclassified, C = confidential, S = secret, and TS = top secret). Classification levels are partially ordered. The access control in multilevel security is based on the Bell–LaPadula model, which has the following properties:

- Simple security property: The subject can have a read access to data only if his classification level is identical to or higher than the classification level of the data.
- The *-property: The subject can have a write access to data only if his classification level is identical to or lower than the classification level of the data.
- The strong *-property: The subject can have a write access to data only if his classification level is identical to the classification level of the data.

In multilevel relational databases, concurrency control manages the concurrent execution of data manipulation language operations (such as SELECT, INSERT, UPDATE, and DELETE) that are performed by different users on the same data at the same time [85]. There are many concurrency control models that are implemented to produce serializable executions of the data manipulation language operations. The most common concurrency control models are two-phase-locking, timestamp-ordering, and optimistic concurrency control models.

In the two-phase-locking (2PL) model, the data manipulation language operation should need to have a write/read lock before it writes or reads a data item [86].

In the timestamp-ordering model, a unique timestamp is assigned to every data manipulation language operation and implements a read timestamp and a write timestamp for each data item [87]. When a data manipulation language operation is issued to read or write on the data item, this operation is allowed only if the read or the write timestamp of the data item is lower than the timestamp of the data manipulation language operation; otherwise, the operation will be rejected.

In the traditional optimistic model, data manipulation language operations are allowed to read and write on the data item without any restriction.

Concurrency control is important for the multilevel relational database because the covert channel problem can be found through the overlap of the multilevel security operations [88]. In the multilevel relational database, the concurrency control model should ensure that the covert channel does not exist during the executions of the operations at different levels of security. The covert channel problem happens when a low classification level data manipulation language operation is delayed or aborted by another high classification level operation due to the need to access shared data items. So, by delaying low classification level operations, high classification level information can be indirectly known to the lower security level.

In the multilevel relational database, the following conflicts may occur:

- Read-down conflict among different classification levels
- Read–write conflict at the same classification levels
- Write–write conflict at the same classification levels

Read-down conflict needs to be treated differently from the conflict in relational multilevel security database systems because a relational multilevel security database operation can read data in its classification level and the classification level lower than it but can write data only in its classification level.

Common concurrency control models like the two-phase-locking and the timestamp-ordering models are not suitable for the relational multilevel security database because they establish the covert channel problem between operations having different classification levels that need access to the shared data item in the relational database. Many models have been implemented for solving concurrency control in the relational multilevel security database, such as secure locking, secure timestamp-ordering and multiversion timestamp-ordering (MVTO) models [89].

In the secure locking model, a high classification level data manipulation operation should remove its lock on data when a low classification level data manipulation operation needs a write lock on the same data at the same time. When a read lock raised by a high classification level data manipulation operation is aborted, it should be removed. Because a low classification level data manipulation operation is not blocked by a high classification level data manipulation operation, many low classification level data manipulation operations may cause a high classification level data manipulation operation to be broken repeatedly, resulting in starvation [90].

In the secure timestamp-ordering model, if a high classification level data manipulation operation needs to read low classification level data, it will not start until all low classification level data manipulation operations earlier in the timestamp are finished. A change of this model gives the ability to the high classification level data manipulation operation to read the low classification level data when it needs to, but it cannot complete changes until all the low classification level data manipulation operations have been completed [91].

Multilevel secure concurrency control models use an MVTO model to eliminate both covert channels and starvation. When a low classification level data manipulation operation needs to write a datum A while a high classification level data manipulation operation already needs a read lock on A, the low classification level data manipulation operation creates a new version of A. A problem of inconsistent versions of the data is given to the read of the high classification level data manipulation operation, which is called a retrieval anomaly. To solve the problem of the retrieval anomaly for the multilevel data manipulation operations, the one-copy serializability algorithm is presented. If a high classification level needs to read data that are being updated by a low classification level data manipulation operation, the high security level transaction will be reexecuted starting from reading that blocked data to present a one-copy serializable schedule [92].

The work presented in this chapter offers several major contributions to the field:

- Implementing a secure multiversion concurrency control model by modifying the Rajwinder Singh model [93] by dividing the write set of the transaction into two parts, which decreases the blocking time of high classification level transactions and improves the response time
- Implementing a prototype to measure the performance cost for dividing write set of the transaction into two parts in the secure multiversion concurrency control model
- Proofing the correctness of the secure multiversion concurrency control model by using the criteria of security, serializability, fairness, selection of correct data version, and fast version selection

7.2 Related Work

Kim and Sohn presented a multiversion secure concurrency control model that satisfies the integrity and security rules [94]. This model used the information of the conflict transaction set and the lock and made the scheduler decide if a new version could be accessed to a high classification level data manipulation operation. This model is free from the problem of the starvation of high classification level data manipulation operations by presenting the conflict transaction set, the invisible area, and the t-lock. Also, this model can improve the availability of the relational multilevel database security system by adding the concept of version management, which uses the t-locks and write timestamps. Kim and Sohn present the following definitions:

- Definition 1: A read/write set of a transaction T_i is defined as $R\text{-set}T_i/W\text{-set}T_i$. It contains the data that will be read/written by the transaction T_i. When the transaction T_i is entered to the scheduler, the scheduler gets $R\text{-set}T_i$ and $W\text{-set}T_i$.
- Definition 2: The period between the times of the high classification level transaction, T_H, is blocked by another low

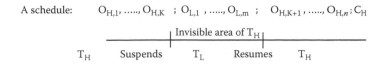

Figure 7.1   The notion of the invisible area.

transaction, T_L; the time when T_H executes again is called the invisible area to T_H. Defining the invisible area prevents the high classification level transaction, T_H, from reading new versions created by the low transaction, T_L, running within this area; otherwise, T_H may have the problem of the retrieval anomaly.

- Figure 7.1 presents the definition of the invisible area with the execution of the high classification level transactions, T_H; the low classification level transactions, T_L; the high classification level operations, O_H; the low classification level transactions, O_L; and the high classification level transactions commit, C_H.

- Definition 3: A conflict transaction set of the high transaction T_H is defined as $C\text{-set}T_H$ and contains the transactions that enter an invisible area of T_H. Suppose that T_L is entered to the scheduler. If $R\text{-set}T_H \cap W\text{-set}T_L \neq \varphi$, then $T_L \in C\text{-set}T_H$.

- Definition 4: The transaction identifier (TID) is attached to low transaction T_L. The term "t-lock" will be used for the attachment and detachment of a TID. When T_L exists in the invisible area of T_H, its TID will be in the $C\text{-set}T_H$ of the blocked high transaction T_H.

Rajwinder Singh [95] adds a transaction into $T_L \in C\text{-set}T_H$. Singh's model reads the recent version by the high classification level transaction T_H and shows that the size of $C\text{-set}T_H$ can be decreased by increasing the condition without effect on the security of the multilevel relational database. Singh divided $R\text{-set}T_H$ into two parts: $R\text{-set}_{\text{done}}T_H$ and $R\text{-set}_{\text{remaining}}T_H$:

$$R\text{-set}_{\text{done}}T_H \cup R\text{-set}_{\text{remaining}}T_H = R\text{-set}T_H.$$

$R\text{-set}_{\text{done}}T_H$ consists of the data read by T_H.

$R\text{-set}_{\text{remaining}}T_H$ consists of the data to be read by T_H.

7.3 Enhanced Secure Multiversion Concurrency Control Model

The enhanced secure multiversion concurrency control model is based on the Rajwinder Singh proposed model to prevent creating the covert channel without retrieval anomaly and to be free of the starvation of the high-level transaction for multilevel relational database transactions. The enhanced model improves on the Rajwinder Singh model by splitting the write set of the low-level transactions that conflict with the read set of the high-level transactions into "done" and "remaining." This modification reduces the size of C-setT_H by relaxing the condition used in the Rajwinder Singh model without affecting the security of the database.

The enhanced secure multiversion concurrency control model divided W-setT_L into two parts: W-set$_{done}T_L$ and W-set$_{remaining}T_L$.

$$W\text{-set}_{done}T_L \cup W\text{-set}_{remaining}T_L = W\text{-set}T_L.$$

W-set$_{done}T_L$ contains data written by T_L and W-set$_{remaining}T_L$ contains data to be written by T_L.

The enhanced secure multiversion concurrency control model also used an infinite timestamp instead of using t-lock to solve the problem of the retrieval anomaly. When a transaction T is inserted into the concurrency control manager, it will be assigned to a unique timestamp, defined asts(T). If a transaction T creates the ith versions of the data item A, an infinite write timestamp defined as $W_{ts}(A_i)$ will be assigned. Then it will be updated with ts(T) when T commits. So, the read operation during its execution will get the version of data item A in which its write timestamp is the recent timestamp and is lower than or equal to its timestamp.

The enhanced secure multiversion concurrency control model assumes that there is one scheduler that manages all the multilevel transactions.

The enhanced secure multiversion concurrency control model contains the following six steps:

- Step 1: When transaction T_i is entered to the scheduler, R-setT_i and W-setT_i will be received.
- Step 2: If no transaction exists in the execution phase, the scheduler runs and the scheduler will perform step 6.

- Step 3: If a transaction T_j exists in the execution phase, the scheduler has three cases:
  - Case 1: $L(T_i) > L(T_j)$. Step 4 is done, where $L(T_i)$, $L(T_j)$ are the classification levels of the transactions T_i, T_j.
  - Case 2: $L(T_i) = L(T_j)$. Step 5 is ruined.
  - Case 3: $L(T_i) < L(T_j)$.
    - The scheduler denies T_j.
    - Set T_i is in the invisible area of T_j.
    - Create a new version of the data and an infinite write timestamp is defined to it.
    - The transaction T_i will be executed immediately to overcome the covert channel problem.
    - If $(R\text{-set}_{\text{done}}T_j \cap W\text{-set}_{\text{remaining}}T_i \neq \varphi)|(R\text{-set}_{\text{done}}T_j \cap R\text{-set}_{\text{remaining}}T_i \neq \varphi)$, then T_i is added into $C\text{-set}T_j$.
    - Perform step 6.
- Step 4: If the low transaction T_j is in the execution phase, the scheduler will make the high classification level transaction T_i wait until T_j commits and will perform step 6.
- Step 5: If the two transactions have the same classification level, the scheduler will execute them at the same time.
  - If $(W\text{-set}_{\text{remaining}}T_j \cap R\text{-set}_{\text{done}}T_i \neq \phi)$ & $(W\text{-set}_{\text{remaining}}T_j \cap W\text{-set}_{\text{remaining}}T_i \neq \phi)$, then T_i will enter an invisible area of T_j for the time of the creation of a new version of conflicted data. After each of T_i and T_j are committed, step 6 will be performed.
- Step 6: If the transaction T is the only transaction that is run at step 2, the scheduler will wait for other transactions to be submitted. Otherwise, the scheduler will execute the transaction, say T_K, that has the lowest classification level among the waiting transactions. The infinite write timestamp is assigned to the new versions in the invisible areas of T_K. Figure 7.2 shows the flow chart for the enhanced secure multiversion concurrency control model.

7.4 Performance Evaluation

The performance of the enhanced secure multiversion concurrency control model will be evaluated using two classification levels (high and low) in the simulation.

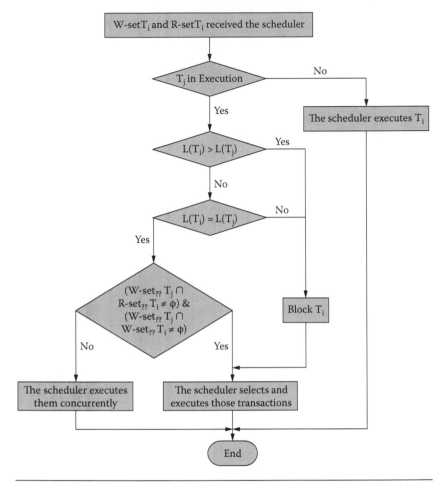

Figure 7.2   The flow chart for the enhanced secure multiversion concurrency control model.

7.4.1 Workload Model

The workload defines the transactions according to their classification levels and their data. Table 7.1 presents the main parameters of the workload.

7.4.2 System Model

The machine that is used in the implementation consists of CPU speed of 2.2 GHz, physical RAM size of 3 GB, and hard-disk size of 320 GB. The software used in the implementation is a Microsoft SQL server 2008 R2 and the experiments' measurements were

Table 7.1 Workload Parameter

PARAMETER	DESCRIPTION	VALUE
Arrival rate	The arrival rate of the transaction	From 0 to 100
Clear levels	Number of classification levels	2
Transaction size	The average size of the transaction	10

captured at the machine using a monitoring tool provided by the Microsoft SQL server.

An experimental database, the timesheet database, consisting of four relations was created and populated to facilitate our performance study. Timesheet system relations used in the implementation are described as follows:

The employee relation provides information about employees:
Employees(EMPID, Code, Name, Department, Type, Contract, Shift, Religion, Job, Position, Address, City)

The departure relation is used to store the departure notice of each employee when he leaves the site of the work:
Departure(EmpID, DepartureDate, ReturnDate, DepartureType)

The timesheet relation is used to store the timesheet of each employee every day:
TimeSheet(EMPID, Date, Timesheet, OverTime, Remarks)

The annual rights relation is used to store the rights of each employee every year:
AnnualRights(EMPID, Year, Description, Inc, ADays, GDays)

Figure 7.3 shows an ER diagram for the timesheet system used in the implementation of the prototype to facilitate our performance study. The experiment investigates the average response times of transactions at every security level for varying arrival rates. This experiment uses the CPU response time (in milliseconds) as the metric.

7.4.3 Experiments and Results

In Figure 7.4, the response times of an enhanced secure multiversion concurrency control model and the Rajwinder Singh model are defined by using various arrival rates. In this figure, the response time of the enhanced secure multiversion concurrency control model and

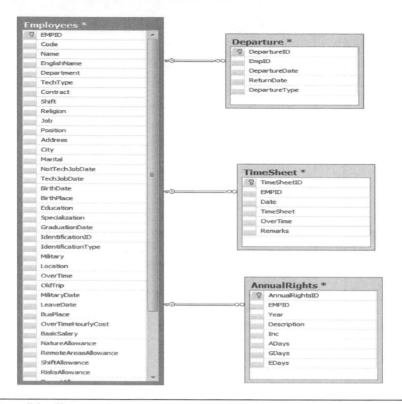

Figure 7.3   ER diagram for the timesheet system used in the implementation.

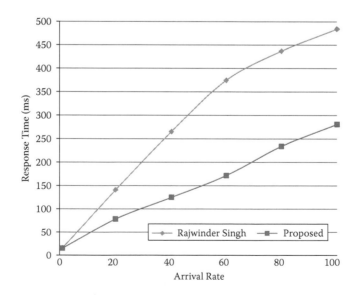

Figure 7.4   The impact of varying the arrival rates on the response times of the enhanced secure multiversion concurrency control model and the Rajwinder Singh model.

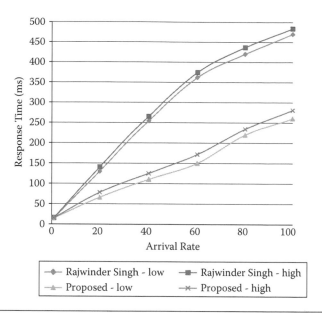

Figure 7.5 The impact of varying the arrival rates on the response times of the enhanced secure multiversion concurrency control model and the Rajwinder Singh model per security level.

the Rajwinder Singh model is the same at the low arrival rates. This is because the conflict area is low. As the arrival rate increases, the enhanced secure multiversion concurrency control model has better performance than the performance of the Rajwinder Singh model. This improvement in the performance is due to the reduction of the denying time of high classification level transactions and improves their response time.

In Figure 7.5, the response times of the enhanced secure multiversion concurrency control model and the Rajwinder Singh model are measured by calculating the response times at each classification level by using various arrival rates.

7.5 Correctness of the Enhanced Secure Multiversion Concurrency Control Model

The retrieval anomaly problem has a bad effect on the availability of the multilevel relational database and it leads high transactions to be aborted many times [96]. So, there is a great need for a secure concurrency control model that meets the integrity, security, and availability requirements for the multilevel relational database. The covert channels and the starvation of the high transaction problems should be prevented. In this section, the criteria for the correctness of the enhanced secure multiversion concurrency control model will be described as follows:

- Preventing the creation of the covert channel problem: The low classification level transactions should not be delayed when the high classification level transaction is in the execution phase.
- Preventing the starvation of the high transaction problem: If the low classification level transactions need to be executed when the high classification level transactions are executing, the high transactions must not suffer from the repeated aborts problem.
- Producing the serializable schedule for multilevel transactions: Because of maintaining the consistency of the multilevel relational database, the serializable schedule should be presented for multilevel transactions.
- Preventing the retrieval anomaly problem when multiversion data are run: The high security class level transactions should read the right versions of the data, although there is a creation of a new data version by the low security class level transactions.
- The fast selection of the data version through more than one version when multiversion data are run: While there are many data versions in the multilevel relational database, the data version selection needs to be fast.

7.5.1 Proof of Correctness

The enhanced secure multiversion concurrency control model should not violate security requirement issues. This section will verify the correctness of this model according to the criteria presented in the previous section.

The covert channel is blocked by requiring the low security class level transaction to be run when it is entered into the scheduler, and by preventing the high security class level transactions when the low transaction is executing [97].

The starvation of the high security class level transactions can be prevented by disallowing them to be reexecuted to read the new versions generated by the low security class level transactions to save the consistency of the data when existing in the invisible area.

A serializable schedule can be presented for the multilevel transactions by making the scheduler a one-copy serializable and one-copy serial. The high classification level transaction will resume reading the data that have been stored in the database.

The proof of the one-copy serializability of the enhanced secure multiversion concurrency control model will be described as follows:

- Definition 1: a multiversion history H on T and a datum X. A version order for X is a total order for all versions of X in H. We define the version order by $<$ and write $X_i < X_j$ if the version X_i precedes X_j in the version order. $H = \{\Sigma_T, <_T\}$ where:
  1. $\Sigma_T = U_i \Sigma_i$ for $i = 1,\ldots\ldots,n$.
  2. $<_T = U_i <_i$ for $i = 1,\ldots\ldots,n$.
  3. For any conflicting operations O_i, O_j in Σ_T, either $O_i <_T O_j|$ $O_j <_T O_i$.
- Definition 2: H is a multiversion history on T and there is some version order e for each item X. A multiversion serialization graph MVSG(H) for a multiversion history H over T is a directed graph such that
  - Nodes of MVSG(H) are transactions in T.
  - There is a (directed) edge, $T_i \rightarrow T_j$, $i \neq j$, in MVSG(H) whenever $R_j[X_i] \in H$.
  - MVSG(H) also contains version order edges: For each $R_k[X_j]$ and $W_i[X_i]$ in H, there is an edge $T_i \rightarrow T_j$ if $X_i < X_j$; otherwise, there is an edge $T_K \rightarrow T_i$.

The retrieval anomaly problem can be prevented by assigning an infinite write timestamp to the new data versions that are created by the low transaction so that they are invisible to a high transaction.

The fast version selection can be performed by giving the read operation the recent versions of the data that are not assigned to infinite write timestamp because the data versions with infinite write timestamp are visible to the transaction when the transaction resumes at the end of its invisible area.

7.6 Summary

In this chapter, the secure multiversion concurrency control model based on the Rajwinder Singh model was implemented to solve the problem of covert channel, retrieval anomaly, and starvation of high security level transactions by maintaining multiple data versions. The model divided $W\text{--set}T_j$ into two parts—$W\text{--set}_{done}T_j$ and $W\text{--set}_{remaining}T_j$—and used an infinite timestamp instead of using t-lock to prevent the creation of retrieval anomaly problems and to ensure serializability of transaction. These modifications reduced the conflict area between high- and low-level transactions and reduced the blocking time of high-level transactions, resulting in improvement of their response time. Also, this chapter implements a working multilevel secure database prototype in a Microsoft SQL server database to measure the performance experiments that were instrumented using the system. Additionally, this chapter investigated the performance of the proposed secure multiversion concurrency control model by varying the transaction arrival rate. Finally, the correctness of a secure multiversion concurrency control model by using the criteria of security, serializability, fairness, selection of correct data version, and fast version selection was proven.

8

THE INSTANCE-BASED MULTILEVEL SECURITY MODEL

8.1 Introduction

Most multilevel relational databases use the mandatory access control mechanism that is based on the Bell–LaPadula model [98]. This model depends on the terms of the subjects and the objects. The object may be a relation, a tuple, or an attribute within a tuple. The subject is the active process that needs to access some objects. Every object can be associated with a classification level such as U (unclassified), C (confidential), S (secret), or TS (top secret). Every subject also is associated with a classification level (unclassified, confidential, secret, or top secret). Classification levels are partially ordered.

There are many challenges that face multilevel relational database systems. The multilevel relational database system is restricted by the security requirements in the Bell–LaPadula model, which prevent covert channels [99] among the different classification levels. When applying the security requirements in the multilevel relational database, security should be ensured. As a result, some problems will be raised and will be described as follows:

- The redundancy of the data: The SeaView model defines a rule called the entity polyinstantiation integrity [100], which provides the multilevel relational database system to save the same tuple with various classification levels to protect the higher classification level data.

Table 8.1 illustrates an example for the entity polyinstantiation in the multilevel relational database. The primary key of the multilevel relation is the employee attribute and the classification levels are defined to the data. The tuple classification is the security level for all the tuples in the relation.

In Table 8.1, the three tuples present the same data but the polyinstantiation integrity policy divides the information according to the various classification levels. Thus, this model stores more data in the multilevel relational database, resulting in data redundancy.

The MLR security model [100] presents the "data borrow" concept and stores pointers in the higher level data (not the real data) to overcome the data redundancy problem. There is another problem: We still need to save three tuples to present the single real datum.

The BCMLS model [100] prevents the data redundancy problem if the data redundancy of the attributes has the same classification level, as shown in Table 8.1. The tuples can be saved as in Table 8.2 in BCMLS. If we have data as in Table 8.3, the BCMLS model will need to save three tuples and the data redundancy cannot be decreased.

- The problem of the null value inference: The inference when dealing with the data is the second problem that faces the multilevel security model. For example, if we have some of the data as shown in Table 8.4(a), if the user with U classification level needs to execute select query, the result may be null values, as described in Table 8.4(b). The null values could cause some inference risks [101].

Table 8.1   Entity Polyinstantiation Integrity

EMPLOYEE	DEPARTMENT	SALARY	TC
Ahmed U	Sales U	7,000 U	U
Ahmed U	Sales U	7,000 U	S
Ahmed U	Sales U	7,000 U	TS

Table 8.2   Data Redundancy of Attributes of the Same Classification Level

EMPLOYEE	DEPARTMENT	SALARY	TC
Ahmed U S TS	Accounting U S TS	7,000 U S TS	U S TS

Table 8.3 Three Tuples Belong to Three Levels in BCMLS

EMPLOYEE	DEPARTMENT	SALARY	TC
Ahmed U S TS	Accounting U -S -TS	7,000 U S -TS	-U S TS
Ahmed U S TS	Sales -U S TS	7,000 -U -S -TS	S -TS
Ahmed U S TS	Sales U -S TS	7,000 S TS	S TS

Table 8.4(a)   The Inference Problem

EMPLOYEE	DEPARTMENT	SALARY
Ahmed U	Sales U	7,000 U
Ahmed U	Account S	8,000 U

Table 8.4(b)   The Inference Problem

EMPLOYEE	DEPARTMENT	SALARY
Ahmed U	Sales U	7,000 U
Ahmed U	Null	8,000 U

- The problem of the sensitive key value: The polyinstantiation integrity rule in the multilevel relational security models is intended to ensure the security of the data from the lower classification level users by allowing only nonkey attributes to access various values at various classification levels [101]. Since the multilevel relational database model uses the key attributes to define the tuples, the polyinstantiation integrity policy should be disallowed and then cannot prevent the risk on the data.

Table 8.5 presents the problem of the sensitive key value. In the employee table, the attribute employee is the primary key attribute. Three tuples have various classification levels. The first contains the value "Ahmed" in the employee attribute, which has the unclassified classification level (U). The second tuple still has the value Ahmed for classification level (S). In the third tuple, the value for the employee attribute has been modified to "Ali" and has the top classification level (T).

Suppose that the three tuples represent the same thing. The highest classification level user with the classification level (TS) will access all three tuples as in Table 8.5 and will not know that the first two tuples are used to protect the third tuple from the lower classification level users.

Table 8.5   The Sensitive Key Value Problem

EMPLOYEE	DEPARTMENT	SALARY	TC
Ahmed U	Accounting U	7,000 U	U
Ahmed S	Sales S	8,000 U	S
Ali TS	Sales S	10,000 TS	TS

8.2 The Instance-Based Multilevel Security Model (IBMSM)

The instance-based model presents a two-layered model to the data; every layer represents a different domain (Figure 8.1) [102]. Every layer saves data and performs operations as follows:

- The instance layer contains the instances with its properties of the model in a specific domain. The instance layer can create and manipulate data for the domain of instances.
- The class layer contains the classes that define the similarities of the instances that belong to the instance layer. The class layer can create and manipulate the classes in the class layer.

The users can define an object with its properties by the classification levels in the multilevel relational database. The IBMSM contains the following parts: the instance, the class, and the control models and will be described as follows:

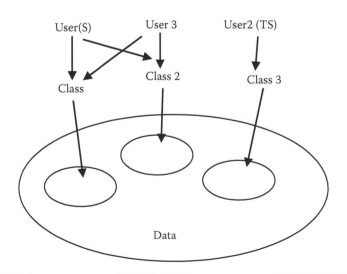

Figure 8.1   Two layers in IBMSM.

8.2.1 Definition 1: The Property View [102]

The instance at a classification level L_j is defined by $i\{(P_i, L_j) \mid P_{i_*} \in P,$ $L_j \in L\}$ where i is defined as the instance identifier, P_i is defined as the property view on the group of the properties (P), and L_j is defined as the classification level on the classification levels. A pair (P_i, L_j) presents the property's view that belongs to the classification level L_j.

For example, in instance1{(FirstName Ahmed, U), (Salary 100, S), (Salary 100, U), (Address Tanta, TS), (Address Cairo, S)}, the S level can access the following view:

```
Instance1{(FirstName Ahmed, U), (Salary 100, S),
(Salary 100, U), (Address Cairo, S)}.
```

The U level will access the following view:

```
Instance1{(FirstName Ahmed, U), (Salary 100, U)}.
```

Since the user with a lower classification level cannot read the higher classification level data, the instance view at the U classification level contains less data than the view at the S classification level.

8.2.2 Definition 2: The Class View [102]

The class is defined as Class_ID({P_j}, {u_j}) where Class_ID is defined as the class identifier, {P_j} is defined as the group of properties, and {u_j} is defined as the group of users defined on the system.

The class can define which instances will be involved in the class and can include the data of which users have the ability to access this class. For example, if a class is defined as Class1({FirstName, Salary, Address}, {user1, user2}), an instance of the class will be defined as follows: Instance1{(FirstName Ahmed), (Salary 110), (Address Tanta)} of the class. An instance Instance2{(FirstName Mohammed), (Salary 110)} does not belong to the class.

8.2.3 Definition 3: The Instance View at Classification Level L_j [102]

The instance view at classification level L_j, which is $i\{(P_i, L_q) \mid P_i \in P,$ $L_q \leq L_j$ and $L_q L_j \in L\}$ is related to the Class({P_K}, {u_j}) if the property {P_K} is a subgroup of the property {P_i}. A user with U classification level can access Class({P_K}, {u_j}) if the user $U \in \{u_j\}$.

Rule 1: A user U with classification level L has the ability to read the property of an instance with the classification level L_j if $L \geq L_j$.

8.3 The advant address of IBMSM

- Preventing the null value inference problem: If the user cannot see the instance's property at specific classification level, this property should not be found at this classification level [103]. The absence of the property does not mean that this property is rejected. For example, the null value may be used if the value of the instance's property does not exist or if the instance cannot access this property. Thus, the meaning of the null value is not clear.
- Preventing the data redundancy problem: In the IBMSM, a datum could have many views in different classification levels [103]. It is possible that several tuples (as different classification levels) could refer to one object. However, in the IBMSM, any object is defined by its instance identifier.

8.4 The Select Operation Procedure of the IBMSM

The SQL-like command for the select operation has the following form:

```
SELECT [A_i]*
FROM R
WHERE P
```

The selection operation is implemented as follows:

Step 1: get the classification level of the user that executes the select operation L(User).

Step 2: get the class views that belong to this user.

Step 3: get all the instance views that belong to the class views of the user and satisfy the select condition P.

Step 4: for each instance, in the instance views, display the property that has a class level lower than or equal to the classification level of the user.

Figure 8.2 illustrates the SELECT operation procedure in the IBMSM.

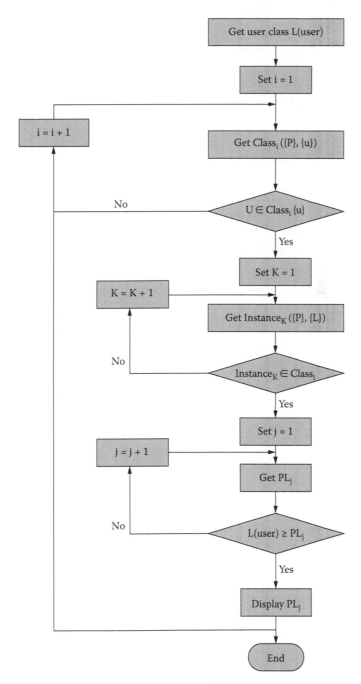

Figure 8.2 The SELECT operation procedure in IBMSM. (E. Fernandez, E. Gudes, and H. Song. 1989. *Proceedings of the IEEE Symposium on Security and Privacy,* 110–115.)

8.5 Insert Operation Procedure of the IBMSM

The SQL-like command for the insert operation has the following form:

```
INSERT
INTO R [A_i]*
VALUES [a_i]*
```

The insertion operation is implemented as follows:

Step 1: get the classification level of the user that executes the insert operation L(User).

Step 2: get the class views that belong to this user.

Step 3: if the attribute is included in the attributes list in the insert statement, this attribute will be set to its value from the values list in the insert statement; otherwise, the value of this attribute will be null.

Step 4: insert the new instance with properties of the attributes' values and the class level of the user into the multilevel relation.

Figure 8.3 illustrates the INSERT operation procedure in IBMSM.

8.6 The Update Operation Procedure of the IBMSM

The SQL-like command for the update operation has the following form:

```
UPDATE R
SET A_i = a_i, [A_i=a_i] *
WHERE P
```

The update operation is implemented as follows:

Step 1: get the classification level of the user that executes the update operation L(User).

Step 2: get the class views that belong to this user.

Step 3: get all the instance views that belong to the class views of the user and satisfy the update condition P.

Step 4: for each instance, in the instance views, update the property that has class level equal to the class level of the user.

Figure 8.4 illustrates the UPDATE operation procedure in IBMSM.

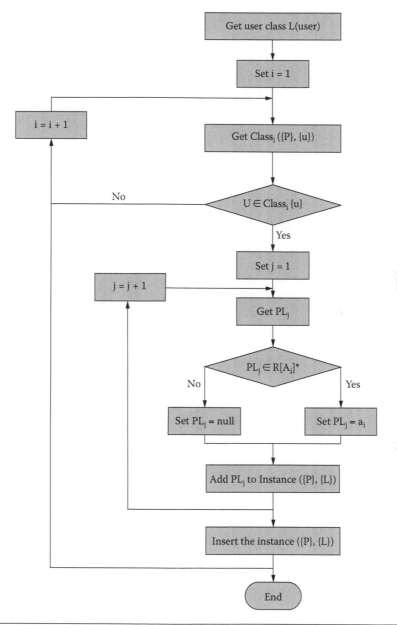

Figure 8.3   The INSERT operation procedure in IBMSM. (E. Fernandez, E. Gudes, and H. Song. 1994. *International Journal of IEEE Transactions on Knowledge and Data Engineering* 6 (2): 275–292.)

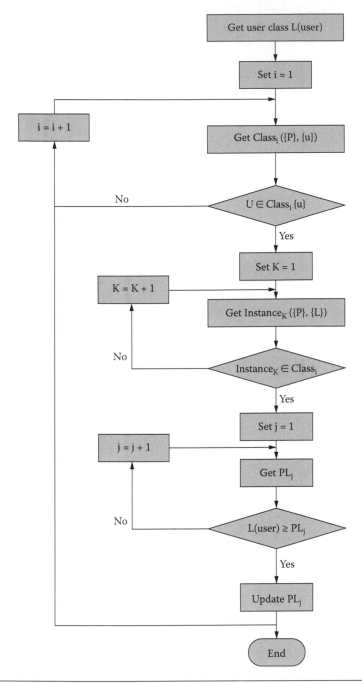

Figure 8.4 The UPDATE operation procedure in IBMSM. (E. Fernandez et al. 1994. *International Journal of IEEE Transactions on Knowledge and Data Engineering* 6 (2): 275–292.)

8.7 The Delete Operation Procedure of the IBMSM

The SQL-like command for the delete operation has the following form:

```
DELETE
FROM R
WHERE P
```

where R is an MLS relation and P is a delete condition that identifies tuples that are to be deleted.

Step 1: get the classification level of the user that executes the delete operation L(User).

Step 2: get the class views that belong to this user.

Step 3: get all the instance views that belong to the class views of the user and satisfy the update condition P.

Step 4: for each instance, in the instance views, delete the property that has class level equal to the class level of the user.

Figure 8.5 illustrates the DELETE operation procedure in IBMSM.

8.8 Comparative Study for Polyinstantiation Models

Table 8.6 illustrates the strengths and weaknesses of each model in the last section. This table explains that earlier MLS database models did not consider semantics as important as implementation. Over time, the importance of semantics was properly recognized and the Smith–Winslett model introduced simple semantics concepts. That simplicity is paid for with restricting the scope of an update to a single entity during the update procedure. The MLR model removed that restriction (among other things), but it cannot assert disbelief into the tuple. The belief-consistent model has the most complete semantics but it has never been fully implemented within a software application because it is very complex. The IBMSM provides the ability to save one instance [107]. So, the IBMSM provides multilevel security and maximizes sharing of data at various classification levels.

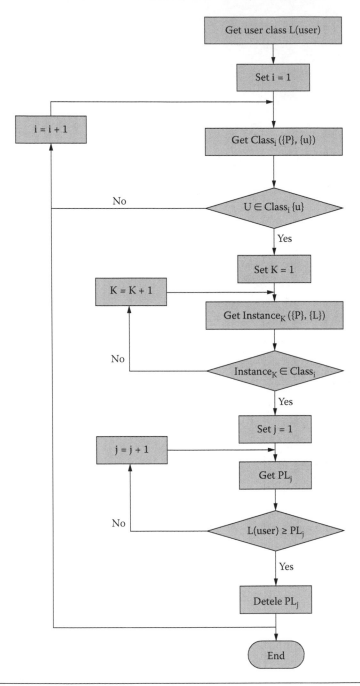

Figure 8.5   The DELETE operation procedure in IBMSM. (J. Parsons and J. Su. 2006. *Proceedings of Design Science Research in Information Systems and Technology (DESRIST),* Claremont, CA, 107–130.)

Table 8.6 Comparative Study for Polyinstantiation Models

PROBLEM MODEL	DATA REDUNDANCY	NULL VALUE INFERENCE	RESTRICTION OF THE SCOPE OF AN UPDATE	DISBELIEF IN A TUPLE	SIMPLICITY
SeaView	Not solved	Not solved	Solved	Not solved	Very simple
Jajodia–Sandhu	Solved	Not solved	Solved	Not solved	Simple
Smith–Winslett	Solved	Not solved	Not solved	Not solved	Simple
MLR	Solved	Not solved	Solved	Not solved	Complex
Belief- consistent multilevel secure relational data	Solved	Not solved	Solved	Solved	Very complex
IBMSM	Solved	Solved	Solved	Solved	Simple

8.9 Summary

The IBMSM data model is a simple, unambiguous, and powerful model for supporting multilevel security databases. The advantage of the IBMSM is that it eliminates null value inference and data redundancy problems in other multilevel security database models. In this chapter, we implemented the DML operations for the IBMSM. We also explained the pseudocode and the flow charts for SELECT, INSERT, UPDATE, and DELETE operations of the IBMSM. In this chapter, we introduced a comparative study between the IBMSM and other multilevel security database models to ensure that the IBMSM solved most of the problems in the previous models. Also in this chapter, we presented an overview of the multilevel relational database security models and introduced the problems of each model.

9

THE SOURCE CODE

9.1 Introduction

This chapter will present the source code of the prototype that was used throughout this book. The tools that are used in the implementation of the prototype are described as follows:

- Microsoft SQL server 2008 R2. SQL server is a relational database management system (RDBMS) from Microsoft that is designed for the enterprise environment. SQL Server runs on T-SQL (Transact-SQL), a set of programming extensions from Sybase and Microsoft that add several features to standard SQL, including transaction control, exception and error handling, row processing, and declared variables.
- Microsoft Visual Studio C#. Microsoft Visual Studio is an integrated development environment (IDE) from Microsoft. It is used to develop console and graphical user interface applications. The C# language is a simple, modern, general-purpose, object-oriented programming language.

This chapter will present the screen shots of the prototype and the source code of the Microsoft SQL server 2008 R2 and the Microsoft Visual Studio C# that were used in the implementation of the prototype.

9.2 Screen Shots of the Prototype

The screen in Figure 9.1 is used for making the user log in to the database by selecting the SQL server and entering his user name and his password. At this screen the prototype will verify the credentials of the user and will determine the user's security classification level (Figure 9.2).

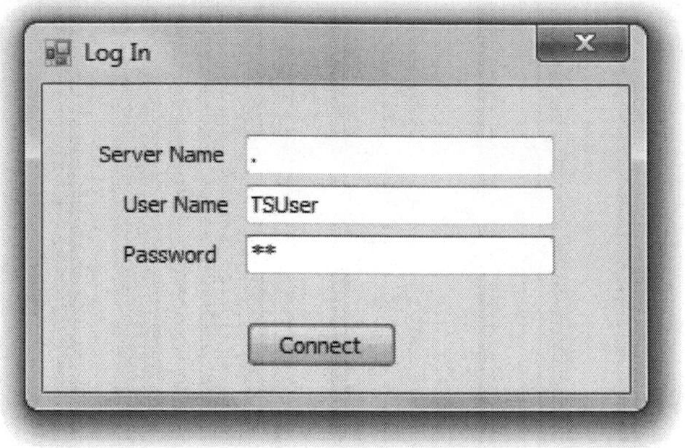

Figure 9.1 The login form.

name	CName	Department	Salary	CDept	CSalary	TC
Ahmed	U	it	3000.0000	C	C	TS
Ahmed	U	it	4000.0000	C	S	TS
Ahmed	U	it	6000.0000	C	TS	TS
Ahmed	U	it	7000.0000	C	U	TS
Ahmed	U	Production	3000.0000	TS	C	TS
Ahmed	U	Production	4000.0000	TS	S	TS
Ahmed	U	Production	6000.0000	TS	TS	TS
Ahmed	U	Production	7000.0000	TS	U	TS
Ahmed	U	Sales	3000.0000	U	C	TS
Ahmed	U	Sales	4000.0000	U	S	TS
Ahmed	U	Sales	6000.0000	U	TS	TS
Ahmed	U	Sales	7000.0000	U	U	TS

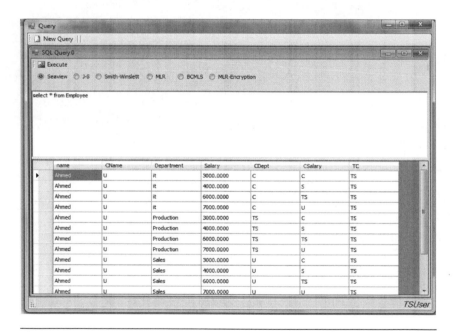

Figure 9.2 The query form.

After successfully logging in, the user will get the query form. This screen is used to help the user in executing his SQL query statement and it contains the following:

- Execution button: used for executing the SQL query statement
- Selective radio button: used for selecting the multilevel database security model

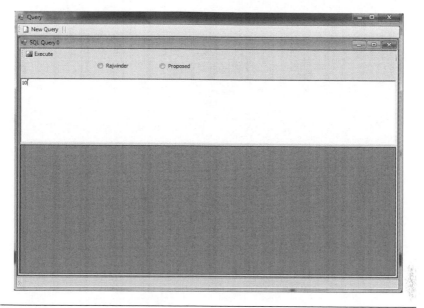

Figure 9.3   The concurrency control form.

- Text box: used for writing the SQL query statement
- Data grid: used for viewing the result of the SQL query statement (Figure 9.3)

This screen helps the user in executing the SQL query statement and in simulating the concurrency control in the multilevel database security. This form contains the following:

- Execution button: used for simulating the concurrency control in the multilevel database security
- Selective radio button: used for selecting concurrency control models in the multilevel database security model
- Text box: used for writing the number of the concurrent transaction in the same time

9.3 Source Code of the Microsoft SQL Server

The source code of the Microsoft SQL server will be divided into four parts:

- Create some tables that define the security classification levels of the data in the multilevel relational database.

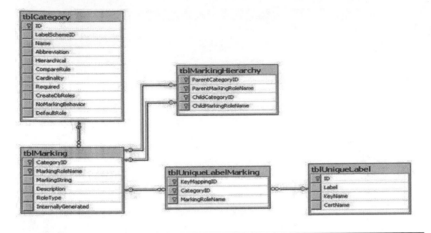

Figure 9.4 The entity relationship diagram of the data security classification levels tables.

- Create roles that define the security classification levels of the users in the multilevel relational database.
- Make some modifications to the base table.
- Define the view for each model of the multilevel relational database models.

9.3.1 Source Code of the Data Security Classification Level Tables (Figure 9.4)

```
CREATE TABLE [dbo].[tblCategory](
        [ID] [int] IDENTITY(1,1) NOT NULL,
        [LableSchemeID] [int] NULL,
        [Name] [nvarchar](50) NULL,
        [Abbreviation] [nvarchar](50) NULL,
        [Hierarichical] [nchar](10) NULL,
        [CompareRule] [nvarchar](50) NULL,
        [Cardinality] [nvarchar](50) NULL,
        [Required] [nchar](1) NULL,
        [CreateDbRoles] [nchar](1) NULL,
        [NoMarkingBehavior] [nvarchar](50) NULL,
        [DefaultRole] [nvarchar](50) NULL,
CONSTRAINT [PK_tblCategory] PRIMARY KEY CLUSTERED
(
        [ID] ASC
)WITH (PAD_INDEX = OFF, STATISTICS_NORECOMPUTE = OFF,
    IGNORE_DUP_KEY = OFF, ALLOW_ROW_LOCKS = ON, ALLOW_
    PAGE_LOCKS = ON) ON [PRIMARY]
) ON [PRIMARY]
```

```
GO
CREATE TABLE [dbo].[tblMarking](
       [CategoryID] [int] NOT NULL,
       [MarkingRoleName] [nvarchar](50) NOT NULL,
       [MarkingString] [nvarchar](50) NULL,
       [Description] [nvarchar](50) NULL,
       [RoleType] [nvarchar](50) NULL,
       [InternallyGenerated] [nvarchar](50) NULL,
CONSTRAINT [PK_tblMarking] PRIMARY KEY CLUSTERED
(
       [CategoryID] ASC,
       [MarkingRoleName] ASC
)WITH (PAD_INDEX = OFF, STATISTICS_NORECOMPUTE = OFF,
   IGNORE_DUP_KEY = OFF, ALLOW_ROW_LOCKS = ON, ALLOW_
   PAGE_LOCKS = ON) ON [PRIMARY]
) ON [PRIMARY]
GO
CREATE TABLE [dbo].[tblMarkingHierarchy](
       [ParentCategoryID] [int] NOT NULL,
       [ParentMarkingRoleName] [nvarchar](50) NOT NULL,
       [ChildCategoryID] [int] NOT NULL,
       [ChildMarkingRoleName] [nvarchar](50) NOT NULL,
CONSTRAINT [PK_tblMarkingHierarchy] PRIMARY KEY
   CLUSTERED
(
       [ParentCategoryID] ASC,
       [ParentMarkingRoleName] ASC,
       [ChildCategoryID] ASC,
       [ChildMarkingRoleName] ASC
)WITH (PAD_INDEX = OFF, STATISTICS_NORECOMPUTE = OFF,
   IGNORE_DUP_KEY = OFF, ALLOW_ROW_LOCKS = ON, ALLOW_
   PAGE_LOCKS = ON) ON [PRIMARY]
) ON [PRIMARY]
GO
CREATE TABLE [dbo].[tblUniqueLabel](
       [ID] [int] NOT NULL,
       [Label] [nvarchar](50) NULL,
       [KeyName] [nvarchar](50) NULL,
       [CertName] [nvarchar](50) NULL,
CONSTRAINT [PK_tblUniqueLabel] PRIMARY KEY CLUSTERED
(
       [ID] ASC
)WITH (PAD_INDEX = OFF, STATISTICS_NORECOMPUTE = OFF,
   IGNORE_DUP_KEY = OFF, ALLOW_ROW_LOCKS = ON, ALLOW_
   PAGE_LOCKS = ON) ON [PRIMARY]
```

```
) ON [PRIMARY]
GO
CREATE TABLE [dbo].[tblUniquelabelMarking](
      [KeyMappingID] [int] NOT NULL,
      [CategoryID] [int] NOT NULL,
      [MarkingRoleName] [nvarchar](50) NOT NULL,
CONSTRAINT [PK_tblUniquelabelMarking] PRIMARY KEY
   CLUSTERED
(
      [KeyMappingID] ASC,
      [CategoryID] ASC,
      [MarkingRoleName] ASC
)WITH (PAD_INDEX = OFF, STATISTICS_NORECOMPUTE = OFF,
   IGNORE_DUP_KEY = OFF, ALLOW_ROW_LOCKS = ON, ALLOW_
   PAGE_LOCKS = ON) ON [PRIMARY]
) ON [PRIMARY]
GO
```

9.3.2 *Source Code of the User Security Classification Levels*

```
CREATE LOGIN [UUser] WITH PASSWORD = N'U', DEFAULT_
   DATABASE = [master], DEFAULT_LANGUAGE = [us_
   english], CHECK_EXPIRATION = OFF, CHECK_POLICY = OFF
GO
CREATE LOGIN [CUser] WITH PASSWORD = N'C', DEFAULT_
   DATABASE = [master], DEFAULT_LANGUAGE = [us_
   english], CHECK_EXPIRATION = OFF, CHECK_POLICY = OFF
GO
CREATE LOGIN [SUser] WITH PASSWORD = N'S', DEFAULT_
   DATABASE = [master], DEFAULT_LANGUAGE = [us_
   english], CHECK_EXPIRATION = OFF, CHECK_POLICY = OFF
GO
CREATE LOGIN [TSUser] WITH PASSWORD = N'TS', DEFAULT_
   DATABASE = [master], DEFAULT_LANGUAGE = [us_
   english], CHECK_EXPIRATION = OFF, CHECK_POLICY = OFF
GO
USE [MLSDB]
CREATE USER [UUser] FOR LOGIN [UUser] WITH DEFAULT_
   SCHEMA = [dbo]
GO
USE [MLSDB]
CREATE USER [CUser] FOR LOGIN [CUser] WITH DEFAULT_
   SCHEMA = [dbo]
GO
```

```
USE [MLSDB]
CREATE USER [SUser] FOR LOGIN [SUser] WITH DEFAULT_
    SCHEMA = [dbo]
GO
USE [MLSDB]
CREATE USER [TSUser] FOR LOGIN [TSUser] WITH DEFAULT_
    SCHEMA = [dbo]
GO
USE [MLSDB]
CREATE ROLE [U] AUTHORIZATION [dbo]
GO
USE [MLSDB]
CREATE ROLE [C] AUTHORIZATION [dbo]
GO
USE [MLSDB]
CREATE ROLE [S] AUTHORIZATION [dbo]
GO
USE [MLSDB]
CREATE ROLE [TS] AUTHORIZATION [dbo]
GO
```

Figures 9.5–9.8 will introduce the properties of the roles that define the security classification levels of the users in the multilevel relational database.

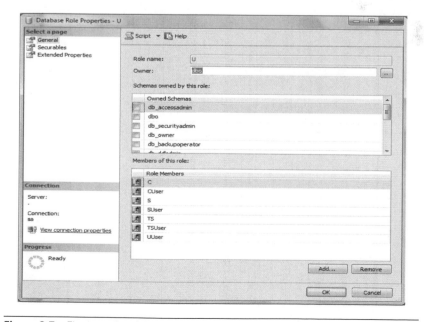

Figure 9.5 The properties of the U role in the database.

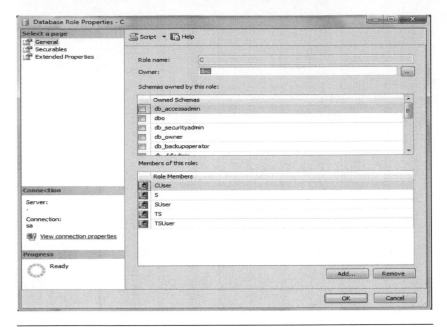

Figure 9.6   The properties of the C role in the database.

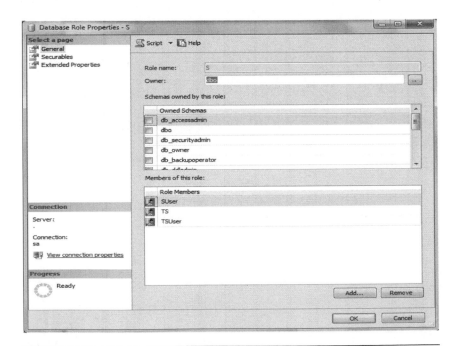

Figure 9.7   The properties of the S role in the database.

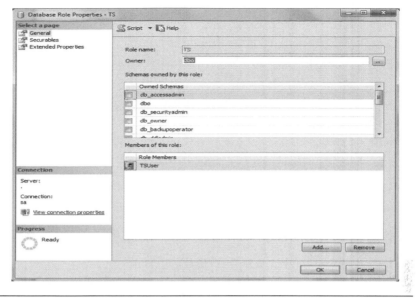

Figure 9.8 The properties of the TS role in the database.

9.3.3 Source Code of the Modifications to the Base Table

The base table is called Employee and its source code for the creation is described as follows:

```
CREATE TABLE [dbo].[Emp](
      [Name] [nvarchar](50) NOT NULL,
      [Department] [nvarchar](50) NULL,
      [Salary] [smallmoney] NULL,
CONSTRAINT [PK_Employee_1] PRIMARY KEY CLUSTERED
(
      [Name] ASC,
)WITH (PAD_INDEX = OFF, STATISTICS_NORECOMPUTE = OFF,
   IGNORE_DUP_KEY = OFF, ALLOW_ROW_LOCKS = ON, ALLOW_
   PAGE_LOCKS = ON) ON [PRIMARY]
) ON [PRIMARY]
GO
```

The modifications to the base table to form the SeaView model are described as follows:

```
CREATE TABLE [dbo].[D1-u](
      [Name] [nvarchar](50) NULL,
      [CName] [int] NOT NULL
```

```
) ON [PRIMARY]
GO
CREATE TABLE [dbo].[D2-c](
        [Name] [nvarchar](50) NULL,
        [CName] [int] NOT NULL,
        [Department] [nvarchar](50) NULL,
        [CDept] [int] NOT NULL
) ON [PRIMARY]
GO
CREATE TABLE [dbo].[D2-s](
        [Name] [nvarchar](50) NULL,
        [CName] [int] NOT NULL,
        [Department] [nvarchar](50) NULL,
        [CDept] [int] NOT NULL
) ON [PRIMARY]
GO
CREATE TABLE [dbo].[D2-ts](
        [Name] [nvarchar](50) NULL,
        [CName] [int] NOT NULL,
        [Department] [nvarchar](50) NULL,
        [CDept] [int] NOT NULL
) ON [PRIMARY]
GO
CREATE TABLE [dbo].[D2-u](
        [Name] [nvarchar](50) NULL,
        [CName] [int] NOT NULL,
        [Department] [nvarchar](50) NULL,
        [CDept] [int] NOT NULL
) ON [PRIMARY]
GO
CREATE TABLE [dbo].[D3-c](
        [Name] [nvarchar](50) NULL,
        [CName] [int] NOT NULL,
        [Salary] [smallmoney] NULL,
        [CSalary] [int] NOT NULL
) ON [PRIMARY]
GO
CREATE TABLE [dbo].[D3-s](
        [Name] [nvarchar](50) NULL,
        [CName] [int] NOT NULL,
        [Salary] [smallmoney] NULL,
        [CSalary] [int] NOT NULL
) ON [PRIMARY]
GO
```

```
CREATE TABLE [dbo].[D3-ts](
      [Name] [nvarchar](50) NULL,
      [CName] [int] NOT NULL,
      [Salary] [smallmoney] NULL,
      [CSalary] [int] NOT NULL
) ON [PRIMARY]
GO
CREATE TABLE [dbo].[D3-u](
      [Name] [nvarchar](50) NULL,
      [CName] [int] NOT NULL,
      [Salary] [smallmoney] NULL,
      [CSalary] [int] NOT NULL
) ON [PRIMARY]
GO
```

The modifications to the base table to form the Jajodia–Sandhu model are described as follows:

```
CREATE TABLE [dbo].[Du](
      [Name] [nvarchar](50) NULL,
      [CName] [int] NOT NULL,
      [Department] [nvarchar](50) NULL,
      [CDept] [int] NOT NULL,
      [Salary] [smallmoney] NULL,
      [CSalary] [int] NOT NULL
) ON [PRIMARY]
GO
CREATE TABLE [dbo].[Dc](
      [Name] [nvarchar](50) NULL,
      [CName] [int] NOT NULL,
      [Department] [nvarchar](50) NULL,
      [CDept] [int] NOT NULL,
      [Salary] [smallmoney] NULL,
      [CSalary] [int] NOT NULL
) ON [PRIMARY]
GO
CREATE TABLE [dbo].[Ds](
      [Name] [nvarchar](50) NULL,
      [CName] [int] NOT NULL,
      [Department] [nvarchar](50) NULL,
      [CDept] [int] NOT NULL,
      [Salary] [smallmoney] NULL,
      [CSalary] [int] NOT NULL
) ON [PRIMARY]
GO
```

```
CREATE TABLE [dbo].[Dts](
       [Name] [nvarchar](50) NULL,
       [CName] [int] NOT NULL,
       [Department] [nvarchar](50) NULL,
       [CDept] [int] NOT NULL,
       [Salary] [smallmoney] NULL,
       [CSalary] [int] NOT NULL
) ON [PRIMARY]
GO
```

The modifications to the base table to form the Smith–Winslett model are described as follows:

```
CREATE TABLE [dbo].[Smith-Employee](
       [Name] [nvarchar](50) NOT NULL,
       [CName] [int] NOT NULL,
       [Department] [nvarchar](50) NULL,
       [Salary] [smallmoney] NULL,
       [TC] [int] NOT NULL,
CONSTRAINT [PK_Smith-Employee] PRIMARY KEY CLUSTERED
(
       [Name] ASC,
       [CName] ASC
)WITH (PAD_INDEX = OFF, STATISTICS_NORECOMPUTE = OFF,
   IGNORE_DUP_KEY = OFF, ALLOW_ROW_LOCKS = ON, ALLOW_
   PAGE_LOCKS = ON) ON [PRIMARY]
) ON [PRIMARY]
GO
```

The modifications to the base table to form the MLR model are described as follows:

```
CREATE TABLE [dbo].[Employee](
       [Name] [nvarchar](50) NOT NULL,
       [CName] [int] NOT NULL,
       [Department] [nvarchar](50) NULL,
       [CDept] [int] NOT NULL,
       [Salary] [smallmoney] NULL,
       [CSalary] [int] NOT NULL,
       [TC] [int] NOT NULL,
CONSTRAINT [PK_Employee_1] PRIMARY KEY CLUSTERED
(
       [Name] ASC,
```

```
        [CName] ASC,
        [CDept] ASC,
        [CSalary] ASC,
        [TC] ASC
)WITH (PAD_INDEX = OFF, STATISTICS_NORECOMPUTE = OFF,
    IGNORE_DUP_KEY = OFF, ALLOW_ROW_LOCKS = ON, ALLOW_
    PAGE_LOCKS = ON) ON [PRIMARY]
) ON [PRIMARY]
GO
```

The modifications to the base table to form the belief-consistent model are described as follows:

```
CREATE TABLE [dbo].[BCEmployee](
        [Name] [nvarchar](50) NOT NULL,
        [CName] [int] NOT NULL,
        [Department] [nvarchar](50) NULL,
        [CDept] [int] NULL,
        [Salary] [smallmoney] NULL,
        [CSalary] [int] NULL,
        [TC] [int] NULL,
        [flag] [int] NULL,
CONSTRAINT [PK_BCEmployee] PRIMARY KEY CLUSTERED
(
        [Name] ASC,
        [CName] ASC
)WITH (PAD_INDEX = OFF, STATISTICS_NORECOMPUTE = OFF,
    IGNORE_DUP_KEY = OFF, ALLOW_ROW_LOCKS = ON, ALLOW_
    PAGE_LOCKS = ON) ON [PRIMARY]
) ON [PRIMARY]
GO
```

The modifications to the base table to form the encryption-based multilevel database security model are described as follows:

```
CREATE TABLE [dbo].[Employee-Encryption](
        [Name] [nvarchar](max) NOT NULL,
        [Department] [nvarchar](max) NULL,
        [Salary] [nvarchar](max) NULL,
        [TC] [int] NOT NULL
) ON [PRIMARY]
GO
```

*9.3.4 Source Code of the View for Each Model of the
          Multilevel Relational Database Models*

The following SQL functions are used in the views of each model of
the multilevel relational database models:

```
CREATE FUNCTION [dbo].[SortLabels]()
RETURNS @Labels TABLE
(
Sort int,
LabelID int,
Label nvarchar(50)
)
AS
BEGIN
with RecursionCTE (Sort,Label)
as
(
select 0,ChildMarkingRoleName
from dbo.tblMarkingHierarchy
where ParentMarkingRoleName = '0'
union all
select R2.Sort+1,ChildMarkingRoleName
from dbo.tblMarkingHierarchy as R1
join RecursionCTE as R2 on R1.ParentMarkingRoleName =
    R2.Label
)
insert into @Labels select RecursionCTE.Sort,dbo.
tblUniqueLabel.ID,RecursionCTE.Label from
RecursionCTE inner join dbo.tblUniqueLabel on
RecursionCTE.Label = dbo.tblUniqueLabel.Label
RETURN
END
GO
create FUNCTION [dbo].[GetUserLabel]()
RETURNS nvarchar(10)
AS
BEGIN
declare @Label nvarchar(10)
        select @Label = g.name
                        from sys.database_principals u,
                          sys.database_principals g,
                          sys.database_role_members m
                        where g.principal_id = m.role_
                          principal_id
```

```
                              and u.principal_id = m.
                                  member_principal_id
                    and u.name = CURRENT_USER
return @Label
END
GO
Create FUNCTION [dbo].[GetTCLabel](@CID int,@CName
    int,@CDept int,@CSalary int)
RETURNS int
AS
BEGIN
declare @TC int
select @TC = LabelID from dbo.SortLabels()
where Sort in (select min(Sort) from dbo.SortLabels()
    where LabelID in (@CID,@CName,@CDept,@CSalary))
return @TC
END
GO
CREATE FUNCTION [dbo].[Get1BCLabe](@label int)
RETURNS nvarchar(10)
AS
BEGIN
declare @NewLabel nvarchar(10)
declare @ULabel nvarchar(1)
declare @CLabel nvarchar(1)
declare @SLabel nvarchar(1)
declare @TLabel nvarchar(1)
set @NewLabel = ''
set @ULabel = ''
set @CLabel = ''
set @SLabel = ''
set @TLabel = ''
set @ULabel = Cast(@label% 4 as nvarchar(1))
set @label = @label/4
set @CLabel = Cast(@label% 4 as nvarchar(1))
set @label = @label/4
set @SLabel = Cast(@label% 4 as nvarchar(1))
set @label = @label/4
set @TLabel = Cast(@label% 4 as nvarchar(1))
if @ULabel = '1'
set @NewLabel = @NewLabel+'-U'
else if @ULabel = '2'
set @NewLabel = @NewLabel+'U'
if @CLabel = '1'
set @NewLabel = @NewLabel+'-C'
```

```
else if @CLabel = '2'
set @NewLabel = @NewLabel+'C'
if @SLabel = '1'
set @NewLabel = @NewLabel+'-S'
else if @SLabel = '2'
set @NewLabel = @NewLabel+'S'
if @TLabel = '1'
set @NewLabel = @NewLabel+'-T'
else if @TLabel = '2'
set @NewLabel = @NewLabel+'T'
return @NewLabel
END
GO
CREATE FUNCTION [dbo].[GetLabelID](@Label nvarchar(10))
RETURNS int
AS
BEGIN
declare @LabelID int
      SELECT @LabelID = KeyMappingID FROM
tblUniqueLabelMarking WITH (NOLOCK)
WHERE CategoryID = 1 AND
MarkingRoleName = @Label
return @LabelID
END
GO
CREATE FUNCTION [dbo].[GetColumnLabel](@ID int)
RETURNS nvarchar(10)
AS
BEGIN
declare @Label nvarchar(10)
      select @Label = Label from dbo.vwVisibleLabels
where ID = @ID
if @Label is null
begin
return dbo.GetUserLabel()
end
return @Label
END
GO
CREATE FUNCTION [dbo].[GetColumnData](@ColumnData
   nvarchar(50),@ColumnLabel int)
RETURNS nvarchar(50)
AS
BEGIN
declare @Data nvarchar(50)
```

```sql
declare @Label nvarchar(10)
      select @Label = Label from dbo.vwVisibleLabels
where ID = @ColumnLabel
if @Label is null
begin
set @Data = 'NULL'
end
else
begin
set @Data = @ColumnData
end
return @Data
END
GO
Create FUNCTION [dbo].[GetCLabel](@ID int)
RETURNS nvarchar(10)
AS
BEGIN
declare @Label nvarchar(10)
      select @Label = Label from [dbo].[tblUniqueLabel]
where ID = @ID
return @Label
END
GO
CREATE FUNCTION [dbo].[GetBCUserView](@label int)
RETURNS nvarchar(10)
AS
BEGIN
declare @NewLabel nvarchar(10)
declare @ViewLabel nvarchar(10)
declare @BreakedLabel nvarchar(10)
declare @UserLabelID int
declare @NumericLabel int
declare @Counter int
set @NumericLabel = 0
set @Counter = 1
set @NewLabel = ''
select @UserLabelID = [dbo].GetLabelID([dbo].
   [GetUserLabel]())
select @BreakedLabel = [dbo].BreaklLabe(@label)
WHILE (@Counter < = @UserLabelID)
BEGIN
set @NumericLabel = @NumericLabel+(POWER(4, @Counter-1)
   *CAST(SUBSTRING(@BreakedLabel,@Counter,1) AS int))
```

```
– set @ViewLabel = @ViewLabel+SUBSTRING(@BreakedLabel,
    @Counter,1)
SET @Counter = @Counter + 1
END
set @NewLabel = dbo.Get1BCLabe(@NumericLabel)
return @NewLabel
END
GO
create FUNCTION [dbo].[BreaklLabe](@label int)
RETURNS nvarchar(10)
AS
BEGIN
declare @NewLabel nvarchar(10)
declare @ULabel int
declare @CLabel int
declare @SLabel int
declare @TLabel int
set @ULabel = @label% 4
set @label = @label/4
set @CLabel = @label% 4
set @label = @label/4
set @SLabel = @label% 4
set @label = @label/4
set @TLabel = @label% 4
set @NewLabel = Cast(@ULabel As nvarchar(1))
    +Cast(@CLabel As nvarchar(1)) +Cast(@SLabel As
    nvarchar(1))+Cast(@TLabel As nvarchar(1))
return @NewLabel
END
GO
```

The source code of the view for each model of the multilevel relational database models is described as follows:

```
CREATE VIEW [dbo].[vwVisibleLabels]
AS
SELECT ID, Label
FROM tblUniqueLabel WITH (NOLOCK)
WHERE
ID IN– Classification
(SELECT KeyMappingID FROM
tblUniqueLabelMarking WITH (NOLOCK)
WHERE CategoryID = 1 AND
IS_MEMBER(MarkingRoleName) = 1)
```

```
GO
CREATE VIEW [dbo].[vwEmployee]
AS
SELECT dbo.GetColumnData(dbo.Employee.Name, dbo.
    Employee.CName) AS Name, dbo.GetColumnLabel
    (dbo.Employee.CName) AS ClassName,
              dbo.GetColumnData(dbo.Employee.Department,
dbo.Employee.CDept) AS Department, dbo.
GetColumnLabel(dbo.Employee.CDept) AS ClassDept,
              dbo.GetColumnData(dbo.Employee.Salary,
                  dbo.Employee.CSalary) AS Salary, dbo.
                  GetColumnLabel(dbo.Employee.CSalary) AS
                  ClassSalary,
              dbo.GetColumnLabel(dbo.Employee.TC) AS TC
FROM    dbo.Employee INNER JOIN
              dbo.vwVisibleLabels ON dbo.Employee.TC
                  = dbo.vwVisibleLabels.ID
GO
CREATE VIEW [dbo].[VBCEmployee]
AS
SELECT Name, dbo.GetBCUserView(CName) AS C _ Name,
    Department, dbo.GetBCUserView(CDept) AS C _ Department,
    Salary, dbo.GetBCUserView(CSalary) AS C _ Salary,
              dbo.GetBCUserView(TC) AS C_Tuple
FROM    dbo.BCEmployee
WHERE (dbo.GetBCUserView(TC) <> '')
GO
CREATE VIEW [dbo].[UserVisibleSmithEmployee]
AS
SELECT dbo.SmithEmployee.name, dbo.SmithEmployee.
    CName, dbo.SmithEmployee.Department, dbo.
    SmithEmployee.Salary, dbo.SmithEmployee.TC
FROM    dbo.SmithEmployee INNER JOIN
              dbo.vwVisibleLabels ON dbo.GetLabelID
                  (dbo.SmithEmployee.TC) = dbo.
                  vwVisibleLabels.ID
GO
CREATE VIEW [dbo].[UserVisibleSeaViewEmployee]
AS
SELECT dbo.SeaViewEmployee.name, dbo.SeaViewEmployee.
    CName, dbo.SeaViewEmployee.Department, dbo.
    SeaViewEmployee.CDept, dbo.SeaViewEmployee.Salary,
              dbo.SeaViewEmployee.CSalary, dbo.
                  SeaViewEmployee.TC
FROM    dbo.SeaViewEmployee INNER JOIN
```

```
                         dbo.vwVisibleLabels ON dbo.GetLabelID
                            (dbo.SeaViewEmployee.TC) = dbo.
                            vwVisibleLabels.ID
GO
CREATE VIEW [dbo].[UserVisibleJSEmployee]
AS
SELECT dbo.JSEmployee.name, dbo.JSEmployee.CName, dbo.
   JSEmployee.Department, dbo.JSEmployee.Salary, dbo.
   JSEmployee.TC
FROM   dbo.JSEmployee INNER JOIN
               dbo.vwVisibleLabels ON dbo.GetLabelID(dbo.
   JSEmployee.TC) = dbo.vwVisibleLabels.ID
GO
CREATE VIEW [dbo].[SmithEmployee]
AS
SELECT name, dbo.[GetCLabel](CName) CName, Department,
   Salary,dbo.[GetCLabel](CName) TC
FROM dbo.[Smith-Employee]
GO
CREATE VIEW [dbo].[SeaViewEmployee]
AS
SELECT dbo.[D2-u].name, dbo.[GetCLabel](dbo.[D2-u].CName)
   CName, dbo.[D2-u].Department, dbo.[GetCLabel]
   (dbo.[D2-u].CDept) CDept, dbo.[D3-u].Salary,
               dbo.[GetCLabel](dbo.[D3-u].CSalary)
                  CSalary, dbo.[GetCLabel]([dbo].
                  [GetTCLabel](4, dbo.[D2-u].CName, dbo.
                  [D2-u].CDept, dbo.[D3-u].CSalary)) TC
FROM   dbo.[D2-u] JOIN
               dbo.[D3-u] ON dbo.[D2-u].Name = dbo.
                  [D3-u].Name
UNION
SELECT dbo.[D2-u].name, dbo.[GetCLabel](dbo.[D2-u].CName)
   CName, dbo.[D2-u].Department, dbo.[GetCLabel](dbo.
   [D2-u].CDept) CDept, dbo.[D3-c].Salary,
               dbo.[GetCLabel](dbo.[D3-c].CSalary)
                  CSalary, dbo.[GetCLabel]([dbo].
                  [GetTCLabel](4, dbo.[D2-u].CName, dbo.
                  [D2-u].CDept, dbo.[D3-c].CSalary)) TC
FROM   dbo.[D2-u] JOIN
               dbo.[D3-c] ON dbo.[D2-u].Name = dbo.[D3-c].Name
UNION
SELECT dbo.[D2-u].name, dbo.[GetCLabel](dbo.[D2-u].CName)
   CName, dbo.[D2-u].Department, dbo.[GetCLabel]
   (dbo.[D2-u].CDept) CDept, dbo.[D3-s].Salary,
```

```
                    dbo.[GetCLabel](dbo.[D3-s].CSalary)
                         CSalary, dbo.[GetCLabel]([dbo].
                         [GetTCLabel](4, dbo.[D2-u].CName, dbo.
                         [D2-u].CDept, dbo.[D3-s].CSalary)) TC
FROM    dbo.[D2-u] JOIN
                    dbo.[D3-s] ON dbo.[D2-u].Name = dbo.[D3-s].Name
UNION
SELECT dbo.[D2-u].name, dbo.[GetCLabel](dbo.[D2-u].CName)
    CName, dbo.[D2-u].Department, dbo.[GetCLabel](dbo.
    [D2-u].CDept) CDept, dbo.[D3-ts].Salary,
                    dbo.[GetCLabel](dbo.[D3-ts].CSalary)
                         CSalary, dbo.[GetCLabel]([dbo].
                         [GetTCLabel](4, dbo.[D2-u].CName, dbo.
                         [D2-u].CDept, dbo.[D3-ts].CSalary)) TC
FROM    dbo.[D2-u] JOIN
                    dbo.[D3-ts] ON dbo.[D2-u].Name = dbo.
                         [D3-ts].Name
UNION
SELECT dbo.[D2-c].name, dbo.[GetCLabel](dbo.[D2-c].CName)
    CName, dbo.[D2-c].Department, dbo.[GetCLabel](dbo.
    [D2-c].CDept) CDept, dbo.[D3-u].Salary,
                    dbo.[GetCLabel](dbo.[D3-u].CSalary)
                         CSalary, dbo.[GetCLabel]([dbo].
                         [GetTCLabel](4, dbo.[D2-c].CName, dbo.
                         [D2-c].CDept, dbo.[D3-u].CSalary)) TC
FROM    dbo.[D2-c] JOIN
                    dbo.[D3-u] ON dbo.[D2-c].Name = dbo.
                         [D3-u].Name
UNION
SELECT dbo.[D2-c].name, dbo.[GetCLabel](dbo.[D2-c].CName)
    CName, dbo.[D2-c].Department, dbo.[GetCLabel](dbo.
    [D2-c].CDept) CDept, dbo.[D3-c].Salary,
                    dbo.[GetCLabel](dbo.[D3-c].CSalary)
                         CSalary, dbo.[GetCLabel]([dbo].
                         [GetTCLabel](4, dbo.[D2-c].CName, dbo.
                         [D2-c].CDept, dbo.[D3-c].CSalary)) TC
FROM    dbo.[D2-c] JOIN
                    dbo.[D3-c] ON dbo.[D2-c].Name = dbo.
                         [D3-c].Name
UNION
SELECT dbo.[D2-c].name, dbo.[GetCLabel](dbo.[D2-c].CName)
    CName, dbo.[D2-c].Department, dbo.[GetCLabel]
    (dbo.[D2-c].CDept) CDept, dbo.[D3-s].Salary,
                    dbo.[GetCLabel](dbo.[D3-s].CSalary)
                         CSalary, dbo.[GetCLabel]([dbo].
```

```
                   [GetTCLabel](4, dbo.[D2-c].CName, dbo.
                   [D2-c].CDept, dbo.[D3-s].CSalary)) TC
FROM   dbo.[D2-c] JOIN
               dbo.[D3-s] ON dbo.[D2-c].Name = dbo.[D3-s].Name
UNION
SELECT dbo.[D2-c].name, dbo.[GetCLabel](dbo.[D2-c].CName)
   CName, dbo.[D2-c].Department, dbo.[GetCLabel](dbo.
   [D2-c].CDept) CDept, dbo.[D3-ts].Salary,
               dbo.[GetCLabel](dbo.[D3-ts].CSalary)
                   CSalary, dbo.[GetCLabel]([dbo].
                   [GetTCLabel](4, dbo.[D2-c].CName, dbo.
                   [D2-c].CDept, dbo.[D3-ts].CSalary)) TC
FROM   dbo.[D2-c] JOIN
               dbo.[D3-ts] ON dbo.[D2-c].Name = dbo.
                   [D3-ts].Name
UNION
SELECT dbo.[D2-s].name, dbo.[GetCLabel](dbo.[D2-s].CName)
   CName, dbo.[D2-s].Department, dbo.[GetCLabel](dbo.
   [D2-s].CDept) CDept, dbo.[D3-u].Salary,
               dbo.[GetCLabel](dbo.[D3-u].CSalary)
                   CSalary, dbo.[GetCLabel]([dbo].
                   [GetTCLabel](4, dbo.[D2-s].CName, dbo.
                   [D2-s].CDept, dbo.[D3-u].CSalary)) TC
FROM   dbo.[D2-s] JOIN
               dbo.[D3-u] ON dbo.[D2-s].Name = dbo.[D3-u].Name
UNION
SELECT dbo.[D2-s].name, dbo.[GetCLabel](dbo.[D2-s].CName)
   CName, dbo.[D2-s].Department, dbo.[GetCLabel](dbo.
   [D2-s].CDept) CDept, dbo.[D3-c].Salary,
               dbo.[GetCLabel](dbo.[D3-c].CSalary)
                   CSalary, dbo.[GetCLabel]([dbo].
                   [GetTCLabel](4, dbo.[D2-s].CName, dbo.
                   [D2-s].CDept, dbo.[D3-c].CSalary)) TC
FROM   dbo.[D2-s] JOIN
               dbo.[D3-c] ON dbo.[D2-s].Name = dbo.[D3-c].Name
UNION
SELECT dbo.[D2-s].name, dbo.[GetCLabel](dbo.[D2-s].CName)
   CName, dbo.[D2-s].Department, dbo.[GetCLabel](dbo.
   [D2-s].CDept) CDept, dbo.[D3-s].Salary,
               dbo.[GetCLabel](dbo.[D3-s].CSalary)
                   CSalary, dbo.[GetCLabel]([dbo].
                   [GetTCLabel](4, dbo.[D2-s].CName, dbo.
                   [D2-s].CDept, dbo.[D3-s].CSalary)) TC
FROM   dbo.[D2-s] JOIN
               dbo.[D3-s] ON dbo.[D2-s].Name = dbo.[D3-s].Name
```

```
UNION
SELECT dbo.[D2-s].name, dbo.[GetCLabel](dbo.[D2-s].CName)
   CName, dbo.[D2-s].Department, dbo.[GetCLabel](dbo.
   [D2-s].CDept) CDept, dbo.[D3-ts].Salary,
               dbo.[GetCLabel](dbo.[D3-ts].CSalary)
                  CSalary, dbo.[GetCLabel]([dbo].
                  [GetTCLabel](4, dbo.[D2-s].CName, dbo.
                  [D2-s].CDept, dbo.[D3-ts].CSalary)) TC
FROM   dbo.[D2-s] JOIN
               dbo.[D3-ts] ON dbo.[D2-s].Name = dbo.
                  [D3-ts].Name
UNION
SELECT dbo.[D2-ts].name, dbo.[GetCLabel](dbo.[D2-ts].CName)
   CName, dbo.[D2-ts].Department, dbo.[GetCLabel](dbo.
   [D2-ts].CDept) CDept, dbo.[D3-u].Salary,
               dbo.[GetCLabel](dbo.[D3-u].CSalary)
                  CSalary, dbo.[GetCLabel]([dbo].
                  [GetTCLabel](4, dbo.[D2-ts].CName, dbo.
                  [D2-ts].CDept, dbo.[D3-u].CSalary)) TC
FROM   dbo.[D2-ts] JOIN
               dbo.[D3-u] ON dbo.[D2-ts].Name = dbo.
                  [D3-u].Name
UNION
SELECT dbo.[D2-ts].name, dbo.[GetCLabel](dbo.[D2-ts].CName)
   CName, dbo.[D2-ts].Department, dbo.[GetCLabel](dbo.
   [D2-ts].CDept) CDept, dbo.[D3-c].Salary,
               dbo.[GetCLabel](dbo.[D3-c].CSalary)
                  CSalary, dbo.[GetCLabel]([dbo].
                  [GetTCLabel](4, dbo.[D2-ts].CName, dbo.
                  [D2-ts].CDept, dbo.[D3-c].CSalary)) TC
FROM   dbo.[D2-ts] JOIN
               dbo.[D3-c] ON dbo.[D2-ts].Name = dbo.
                  [D3-c].Name
UNION
SELECT dbo.[D2-ts].name, dbo.[GetCLabel](dbo.[D2-ts].CName)
   CName, dbo.[D2-ts].Department, dbo.[GetCLabel](dbo.
   [D2-ts].CDept) CDept, dbo.[D3-s].Salary,
               dbo.[GetCLabel](dbo.[D3-s].CSalary) CSalary,
                  dbo.[GetCLabel]([dbo].[GetTCLabel](4, dbo.
                  [D2-ts].CName, dbo.[D2-ts].CDept, dbo.
                  [D3-s].CSalary)) TC
FROM   dbo.[D2-ts] JOIN
               dbo.[D3-s] ON dbo.[D2-ts].Name = dbo.
                  [D3-s].Name
```

```
UNION
SELECT dbo.[D2-ts].name, dbo.[GetCLabel](dbo.[D2-ts].CName)
    CName, dbo.[D2-ts].Department, dbo.[GetCLabel](dbo.
    [D2-ts].CDept) CDept, dbo.[D3-ts].Salary,
              dbo.[GetCLabel](dbo.[D3-ts].CSalary)
                  CSalary, dbo.[GetCLabel]([dbo].
                  [GetTCLabel](4, dbo.[D2-ts].CName, dbo.
                  [D2-ts].CDept, dbo.[D3-ts].CSalary)) TC
FROM   dbo.[D2-ts] JOIN
              dbo.[D3-ts] ON dbo.[D2-ts].Name = dbo.
                  [D3-ts].Name
GO
CREATE VIEW [dbo].[JSEmployee]
AS
SELECT name, dbo.[GetCLabel](CName) CName, Department,
    dbo.[GetCLabel](CDept) CDept, Salary,
              dbo.[GetCLabel](CSalary) CSalary, dbo.
                  [GetCLabel]([dbo].[GetTCLabel](4,
                  CName, CDept, CSalary)) TC
FROM   dbo.Du
UNION
SELECT name, dbo.[GetCLabel](CName) CName, Department,
    dbo.[GetCLabel](CDept) CDept, Salary,
              dbo.[GetCLabel](CSalary) CSalary, dbo.
                  [GetCLabel]([dbo].[GetTCLabel]
                  (4, CName, CDept, CSalary)) TC
FROM   dbo.Dc
UNION
SELECT name, dbo.[GetCLabel](CName) CName, Department,
    dbo.[GetCLabel](CDept) CDept, Salary,
              dbo.[GetCLabel](CSalary) CSalary, dbo.
                  [GetCLabel]([dbo].[GetTCLabel](4,
                  CName, CDept, CSalary)) TC
FROM   dbo.Ds
UNION
SELECT name, dbo.[GetCLabel](CName) CName, Department,
    dbo.[GetCLabel](CDept) CDept, Salary,
              dbo.[GetCLabel](CSalary) CSalary, dbo.
                  [GetCLabel]([dbo].[GetTCLabel](4,
                  CName, CDept, CSalary)) TC
FROM   dbo.Dts
GO
CREATE VIEW [dbo].[VwEmployee-Encryption]
```

```
AS
SELECT CONVERT(nvarchar(MAX), DecryptByKey(dbo.
    [Employee-Encryption].Name)) AS Name,
    CONVERT(nvarchar(MAX), DecryptByKey(dbo.[Employee-
    Encryption].Department)) AS Department,
            CONVERT(nvarchar(MAX), DecryptByKey(dbo.
                [Employee-Encryption].Salary)) AS
                Salary, dbo.[Employee-Encryption].TC
FROM   dbo.[Employee-Encryption]  INNER JOIN
            dbo.vwVisibleLabels ON dbo.[Employee-
                Encryption].TC = dbo.vwVisibleLabels.ID
```

9.4 Source Code of the Microsoft Visual Studio C#

The source code of the Microsoft visual studio C# will be divided into five parts:

- Create classes that help the window forms in performing the database operations and parsing the SQL query statement.
- Create login form to authenticate the user and to identify his security classification level.
- Create queries form to generate multiple query forms inside at the same session.
- Create query form to be used in writing the SQL query statement for each model from the multilevel database security models.
- Create concurrency control form to be used in simulating the concurrency control in the multilevel database security models.

9.4.1 Source Code of the Classes

- DBOperations class

```
using System;
using System.Data;
using System.Data.SqlClient;
///<summary>
///Summary description for Class1
///</summary>
```

```
namespace GlobalClasses
{
public class DBOperations
{
        public DBOperations()
        {
}
//
//Date:6/4/2008
//purpose:to Check user name and password of user
        public static void SqlConn(string Server, string
            User, string Pass) {globals.ServerConnStr
            = "Data Source = " + Server + ";Initial
            Catalog = MLSDB;User Id = " + User +
            ";Password = " + Pass + ";";}
//
//Date:25/10/2008
//purpose:to get data from database by excuting SQL
   satment.
        public static DataSet GetData(string SqlStr)
        {
        DataSet ds = new DataSet();
        string SqlConnStr = globals.ServerConnStr;
        SqlConnection SqlConn = new
           SqlConnection(SqlConnStr);
        SqlConn.Open();
        SqlCommand SqlCmd = new SqlCommand(SqlStr,
           SqlConn);
        SqlDataAdapter Adpt = new SqlDataAdapter(SqlCmd);
        Adpt.Fill(ds);
        SqlConn.Close();
        return ds;
}
//
//Date:21/7/2009
//purpose:to fill data table in dataset by excuting
   SQL statement.
        public static void FillDataSet(ref DataSet DS,
           string DT, string SqlStr)
        {
        string SqlConnStr = globals.ServerConnStr;
        SqlConnection SqlConn = new
           SqlConnection(SqlConnStr);
        SqlConn.Open();
```

```
      SqlCommand SqlCmd = new SqlCommand(SqlStr,
         SqlConn);
      SqlDataAdapter Adpt = new SqlDataAdapter(SqlCmd);
      Adpt.Fill(DS, DT);
      SqlConn.Close();
      }
      public static string DateFormate(string Date)
      {
      string [] dateMDY = Date.Split('/');
      string DateDMY = dateMDY[1] + '/' + dateMDY[0]
         + '/' + dateMDY[2];
      return DateDMY;
}
//
//Date:7/7/2009
//purpose:to convert from string to nullable int.
      public static int? StringToNullableInt32(string s)
      {int i;
      if (Int32.TryParse(s, out i)) return i;
      return null;
}
//
//Date:25/10/2008
//purpose:to Set data from database by excuting SQL
   satment.
      public static void SetData(string SqlStr)
      {
      string SqlConnStr = globals.ServerConnStr;
      SqlConnection SqlConn = new
         SqlConnection(SqlConnStr);
      SqlConn.Open();
      SqlCommand SqlCmd = new SqlCommand(SqlStr,
         SqlConn);
      SqlCmd.ExecuteNonQuery();
      SqlConn.Close();
}
}
}
```

- Globals class

```
using System;
using System.Configuration ;
using System.Collections ;
```

```csharp
using System.IO;
using GlobalClasses;
///Summary description for Class1
///</summary>
namespace GlobalClasses
{
public class globals
{
        public static string ServerName;
        public static string Password;
        public static string UserName;
        public static string ServerConnStr;
        public static string UserLabel;
        public static int UserLabelID;
        public static string Scrub(string text)
{return text.Replace(" ", "");}
        public static string[] KeyWords = new
            string[8];//"select", "insert",
            "update","Delete", "Where", "from", "Set",
            "Values"
        public enum SqlStatment
{
select,
Insert,
update,
Delete
}
}
}
```

- MLSDB class

```csharp
using System;
using System.Collections.Generic;
using System.Linq;
using System.Text;
using System.Collections;
namespace GlobalClasses
{
public class MLSDB
{
        public static string DMLSTR(String SQLSTR)
        {
```

```
string DML = "";
if (SQLSTR.ToUpper().Contains("SELECT"))
{
        if (SQLSTR.ToUpper().Contains("WHERE"))
        {
        DML = SQLSTR.Substring(SQLSTR.ToUpper().
            IndexOf("FROM") + 4, SQLSTR.
            ToUpper().IndexOf("WHERE") - (SQLSTR.
            ToUpper().IndexOf("FROM") + 4));
}
        else
        {
        DML = SQLSTR.Substring(SQLSTR.
            ToUpper().IndexOf("FROM") + 4);
}
}
else if (SQLSTR.ToUpper().Contains("UPDATE"))
{
        DML = SQLSTR.Substring(SQLSTR.ToUpper().
            IndexOf("UPDATE") + 6, SQLSTR.
            ToUpper().IndexOf("SET") - (SQLSTR.
            ToUpper().IndexOf("UPDATE") + 6));
}
else if (SQLSTR.ToUpper().Contains("INSERT"))
{
        DML = SQLSTR.Substring(SQLSTR.
            ToUpper().IndexOf("INSERT") + 6,
            SQLSTR.ToUpper().IndexOf("VALUES")
            - (SQLSTR.ToUpper().
            IndexOf("INSERT") + 6));
}
        else if
(SQLSTR.ToUpper().Contains("UPLEVEL"))
        {
        DML = SQLSTR.Substring(SQLSTR.ToUpper().
            IndexOf("UPLEVEL") + 7, SQLSTR.
            ToUpper().IndexOf("GET") - (SQLSTR.
            ToUpper().IndexOf("UPLEVEL") + 7));
}
else if (SQLSTR.ToUpper().Contains("VERIFY"))
{
        if(SQLSTR.ToUpper().Contains("TRUE"))
        {
        DML = SQLSTR.Substring(SQLSTR.ToUpper().
            IndexOf("TRUE") + 4, SQLSTR.
```

```
                            ToUpper().IndexOf("WHERE") - (SQLSTR.
                            ToUpper().IndexOf("TRUE") + 4));
                }
                else if(SQLSTR.ToUpper().
                    Contains("FALSE"))
                {
                DML = SQLSTR.Substring(SQLSTR.ToUpper().
                    IndexOf("FALSE") + 5, SQLSTR.
                    ToUpper().IndexOf("WHERE") - (SQLSTR.
                    ToUpper().IndexOf("FALSE") + 5));
                }
                }
                else if (SQLSTR.ToUpper().Contains("DELETE"))
                {
                        if (SQLSTR.ToUpper().Contains("WHERE"))
                        {
                        DML = SQLSTR.Substring(SQLSTR.ToUpper().
                            IndexOf("FROM") + 4, SQLSTR.
                            ToUpper().IndexOf("WHERE") - (SQLSTR.
                            ToUpper().IndexOf("FROM") + 4));
                }
                        else
                        {
                        DML = SQLSTR.Substring(SQLSTR.
                            ToUpper().IndexOf("FROM") + 4);
                }
                }
                return DML;
        }

        public static string AttributeSTR(String
            SQLSTR)
        {
        string DML = "";
        if (SQLSTR.ToUpper().Contains("SELECT"))
        {
                DML = SQLSTR.Substring(SQLSTR.
                    ToUpper().IndexOf("SELECT") + 6,
                    SQLSTR.ToUpper().IndexOf("FROM")
                    - (SQLSTR.ToUpper().
                    IndexOf("SELECT") + 6));
        }
        else if (SQLSTR.ToUpper().Contains("UPDATE"))
        {
                if (SQLSTR.ToUpper().
                    Contains("WHERE"))
```

```
        {
        DML = SQLSTR.Substring(SQLSTR.ToUpper().
            IndexOf("SET") + 3, SQLSTR.ToUpper().
            IndexOf("WHERE") - (SQLSTR.ToUpper().
            IndexOf("SET") + 3));
    }
        else
        {
        DML = SQLSTR.Substring(SQLSTR.
            ToUpper().IndexOf("SET") + 3);
    }
    }
else if (SQLSTR.ToUpper().
    Contains("UPLEVEL"))
{
        if (SQLSTR.ToUpper().Contains("WHERE"))
        {
        DML = SQLSTR.Substring(SQLSTR.ToUpper().
            IndexOf("GET") + 3, SQLSTR.ToUpper().
            IndexOf("WHERE") - (SQLSTR.ToUpper().
            IndexOf("GET") + 3));
    }
        else
        {
        DML = SQLSTR.Substring(SQLSTR.
            ToUpper().IndexOf("SET") + 3);
    }
    }
else if (SQLSTR.ToUpper().Contains("VERIFY"))
{
        if (SQLSTR.ToUpper().Contains("TRUE"))
        {
        DML = "TRUE";
    }
        else
        {
        DML = "FALSE";
    }
    }
else if (SQLSTR.ToUpper().Contains("INSERT"))
{
        DML = SQLSTR.Substring(SQLSTR.
            ToUpper().IndexOf("VALUES") + 6);
    }
else if (SQLSTR.ToUpper().Contains("DELETE"))
```

```
        {
                if (SQLSTR.ToUpper().Contains("WHERE"))
                {
                DML = SQLSTR.Substring(SQLSTR.
                    ToUpper().IndexOf("WHERE") + 5);
        }
                else
                {
                DML = "";
        }
        }
        return DML;
}

        public static string PredicateSTR(String SQLSTR)
        {
        string DML = "";
        if (SQLSTR.ToUpper().Contains("WHERE"))
                {
                DML = SQLSTR.Substring(SQLSTR.
                    ToUpper().IndexOf("WHERE") + 5);
        }
                else
                {
                DML = "";
        }
        return DML;
}

        public static int GetUserLabelID()
        {
        int UserLabel = 0;
        string SqlStr = "select [dbo].
            GetLabelID([dbo].[GetUserLabel]()) ";
        UserLabel = int.Parse(DBOperations.
            GetData(SqlStr).Tables 0].Rows[0][0].
            ToString());
        return UserLabel;
}

        public static string GetUserLabel()
        {
        string UserLabel = "";
        string SqlStr = "select [dbo].[GetUserLabel]() ";
        UserLabel = DBOperations.GetData(SqlStr).
            Tables 0].Rows[0][0].ToString();
        return UserLabel;
}
```

```
public static int GetLabelID(string UserLabel)
{
int UserLabelID = 0;
string SqlStr = "select [dbo].GetLabelID('" +
   UserLabel + "') ";
UserLabelID = int.Parse(DBOperations.
   GetData(SqlStr).Tables 0].Rows[0][0].ToString());
return UserLabelID;
}

public static string GetBCLabel(int UserLabelID)
{
string UserLabel = "";
string UChar = "";
string CChar = "";
string SChar = "";
string TSChar = "";
UChar = (UserLabelID% 4).ToString();
UserLabelID = UserLabelID/4;
CChar = (UserLabelID% 4).ToString();
UserLabelID = UserLabelID/4;
SChar = (UserLabelID% 4).ToString();
UserLabelID = UserLabelID/4;
TSChar = (UserLabelID% 4).ToString();
if (UChar = = "1")
{
        UserLabel = UserLabel + "-U";
}
else if (UChar = = "2")
{
        UserLabel = UserLabel + "U" ;
}
if (CChar = = "1")
{
        UserLabel = UserLabel + "-C" ;
}
else if (CChar = = "2")
{
        UserLabel = UserLabel + "C";
}
if (SChar = = "1")
{
        UserLabel = UserLabel + "-S";
}
else if (SChar = = "2")
```

```
        {
                UserLabel = UserLabel + "S";
        }
        if (TSChar = = "1")
        {
                UserLabel = UserLabel + "-T";
        }
        else if (TSChar = = "2")
        {
                UserLabel = UserLabel + "T";
        }
        return UserLabel;
}

public static int GetBCLabelNumeric(string
   UserLabel)
{
int UserLabelID = 0 ;
UserLabel = BreakBCLabel(UserLabel);
UserLabelID = int.Parse(UserLabel.Substring
   (0, 1)) + (int.Parse(UserLabel.Substring
   (1, 1)) * 4) + (int.Parse(UserLabel.
   Substring(2, 1)) * 16) + (int.
   Parse(UserLabel.Substring(3, 1)) * 64);
return UserLabelID;
}

public static string GetBCUserView(string Label)
{
string labelView = "";
int NumericLabel = 0;
Label = BreakBCLabel(Label);
int UserLabelID = globals.UserLabelID ;
for (int i = 0; i < UserLabelID; i++)
{
        NumericLabel = NumericLabel +
           (int.Parse(Label.Substring(i, 1)) *
           Convert.ToInt32 (Math.Pow(4, i)));
}
labelView = GetBCLabel(NumericLabel);
return labelView;
}

public static string BreakBCLabel(string
   UserLabel)
{
string UserLabelID = "0";
string Unumric = "0";
```

```
string Cnumric = "0";
string Snumric = "0";
string TSnumric = "0";
if(UserLabel.Contains('U'))
{
        if (UserLabel.IndexOf('U') = = 0)
        {
        Unumric = "2";
}

        else
        {
        if (UserLabel.Substring(UserLabel.
           IndexOf('U') - 1, 1) = = "-")
        {
                Unumric = "1";
        }
        else
        {
                Unumric = "2";
        }
}
}
if (UserLabel.Contains('C'))
{
        if (UserLabel.IndexOf('C') = = 0)
        {
        Cnumric = "2";
}

        else
        {
        if (UserLabel.Substring(UserLabel.
           IndexOf('C') - 1, 1) = = "-")
        {
                Cnumric = "1";
        }
        else
        {
                Cnumric = "2";
        }
}
}
if (UserLabel.Contains('S'))
{
        if (UserLabel.IndexOf('S') = = 0)
```

```
            {
            Snumric = "2";
      }
            else
            {
            if (UserLabel.Substring(UserLabel.
               IndexOf('S') - 1, 1) = = "-")
            {
                    Snumric = "1";
            }
            else
            {
                    Snumric = "2";
            }
      }
      }
      if (UserLabel.Contains('T'))
      {
            if (UserLabel.IndexOf('T') = = 0)
            {
            TSnumric = "2";
      }
            else
            {
            if (UserLabel.Substring
               (UserLabel.IndexOf('T') - 1, 1)
               = = "-")
            {
                    TSnumric = "1";
            }
            else
            {
                    TSnumric = "2";
            }
      }
      }
      UserLabelID = Unumric + Cnumric + Snumric +
         TSnumric;
      return UserLabelID;
}

      public static string GetBCprimarylevel
         (int NumericLabel)
      {
      string Label = GetBCLabel(NumericLabel);
```

```
        return Label.Substring(0, 1);
}

        public static string GetBCSecondarylevel
            (int NumericLabel)
        {
        string Label = GetBCLabel(NumericLabel);
        return Label.Remove(Label.IndexOf(GetBCprimar
            ylevel(NumericLabel)), 1);
}

        public static string GetBCUserbelief
            (string Label)
        {
        int NumericLabel = GetBCLabelNumeric(Label);
        int belief = 0;
        string retvalue = "";
        int UserLabelID = globals.UserLabelID;
        string UserLabel = globals.UserLabel;
        for (int i = 0; i < UserLabelID; i++)
        {
                belief = NumericLabel% 4;
                NumericLabel = NumericLabel/4;
        }
        if (belief = = 1)
        {
                retvalue = "-" + UserLabel;
        }
        else if (belief = = 2)
        {
                retvalue = UserLabel;
        }
        return retvalue;
}

        public static int UnverifyBCUserbelief
            (int NumericLabel)
        {
        string Label = GetBCLabel(NumericLabel);
        string UserLabel = globals.UserLabel;
        Label = Label.Remove(Label.
            IndexOf(UserLabel), 1); ;
        return GetBCLabelNumeric(Label);
}

        public static int VerifyBCUserbelief
            (int NumericLabel,bool belief)
        {
        string Label = GetBCLabel(NumericLabel);
```

```
        string UserLabel = globals.UserLabel;
        int UserLabelID = globals.UserLabelID;
        if (belief)
        {
                Label = Label.Insert(UserLabelID - 1,
                    globals.UserLabel);
        }
        else
        {
                Label = Label.Insert(UserLabelID
                    - 1,"-"+ globals.UserLabel);
        }
        return GetBCLabelNumeric(Label);
}

        public static ArrayList GetAttribute(string Str)
        {
        //ArrayList ReturnARR = new ArrayList();
        ArrayList ARR = new ArrayList();
        string Attribute = "";
        string Values = "";
        if (Str.Contains(','))
        {
                ARR.AddRange(Str.Trim().Split(','));
        }
        else
                ARR.Add(Str.Trim());
        return ARR;
        }
        public static ArrayList GetInsertValue
            (string Str)
        {
        ArrayList ARR = new ArrayList();
        Str = Str.Remove(Str.IndexOf('('), 1);
        Str = Str.Remove(Str.IndexOf(')'), 1);
        if (Str.Contains(','))
        {
                ARR.AddRange(Str.Trim().Split(','));
        }
                        return ARR;
}
        }
}
```

9.4.2 Source Code of the Login Form

```
namespace MLS
{
partial class Log_In
{
///<summary>
///Required designer variable.
///</summary>
        private System.ComponentModel.IContainer
            components = null;
///<summary>
///Clean up any resources being used.
///</summary>
///<param name = "disposing">true if managed resources
   should be disposed; otherwise, false.</param>
        protected override void Dispose(bool
            disposing)
        {
        if (disposing && (components ! = null))
        {
                components.Dispose();
        }
        base.Dispose(disposing);
}
        #region Windows Form Designer generated code
///<summary>
///Required method for Designer support - do not modify
///the contents of this method with the code editor.
///</summary>
        private void InitializeComponent()
        {
        this.label1 = new System.Windows.Forms.Label();
        this.TxtServer = new System.Windows.Forms.
           TextBox();
        this.TxtUser = new System.Windows.Forms.TextBox();
        this.label2 = new System.Windows.Forms.
           Label();
        this.TxtPassword = new System.Windows.Forms.
           TextBox();
        this.label3 = new System.Windows.Forms.
           Label();
        this.button1 = new System.Windows.Forms.Button();
        this.button2 = new System.Windows.Forms.Button();
```

```
this.SuspendLayout();
//
//label1
//
this.label1.AutoSize = true;
this.label1.Location = new System.Drawing.
    Point(26, 28);
this.label1.Name = "label1";
this.label1.Size = new System.Drawing.Size(69, 13);
this.label1.TabIndex = 0;
this.label1.Text = "Server Name";
this.label1.Click + = new System.
    EventHandler(this.label1_Click);
//
//TxtServer
//
this.TxtServer.Location = new System.Drawing.
    Point(101, 25);
this.TxtServer.Name = "TxtServer";
this.TxtServer.Size = new System.Drawing.
    Size(154, 20);
this.TxtServer.TabIndex = 1;
//
//TxtUser
//
this.TxtUser.Location = new System.Drawing.
    Point(101, 50);
this.TxtUser.Name = "TxtUser";
this.TxtUser.Size = new System.Drawing.
    Size(154, 20);
this.TxtUser.TabIndex = 3;
//
//label2
//
this.label2.AutoSize = true;
this.label2.Location = new System.Drawing.
    Point(38, 53);
this.label2.Name = "label2";
this.label2.Size = new System.Drawing.
    Size(59, 13);
this.label2.TabIndex = 2;
this.label2.Text = "User Name";
//
//TxtPassword
//
```

```
this.TxtPassword.Location = new System.
   Drawing.Point(101, 75);
this.TxtPassword.Name = "TxtPassword";
this.TxtPassword.PasswordChar = '*';
this.TxtPassword.Size = new System.Drawing.
   Size(154, 20);
this.TxtPassword.TabIndex = 5;
//
//label3
//
this.label3.AutoSize = true;
this.label3.Location = new System.Drawing.
   Point(38, 78);
this.label3.Name = "label3";
this.label3.Size = new System.Drawing.
   Size(53, 13);
this.label3.TabIndex = 4;
this.label3.Text = "Password";
//
//button1
//
this.button1.Location = new System.Drawing.
   Point(101, 118);
this.button1.Name = "button1";
this.button1.Size = new System.Drawing.
   Size(75, 23);
this.button1.TabIndex = 6;
this.button1.Text = "Connect";
this.button1.UseVisualStyleBackColor = true;
this.button1.Click + = new System.
   EventHandler(this.button1_Click);
//
//button2
//
this.button2.Location = new System.Drawing.
   Point(180, 118);
this.button2.Name = "button2";
this.button2.Size = new System.Drawing.
   Size(75, 23);
this.button2.TabIndex = 7;
this.button2.Text = "button2";
this.button2.UseVisualStyleBackColor = true;
this.button2.Visible = false;
this.button2.Click + = new System.
   EventHandler(this.button2_Click);
```

```
        //
        //Log_In
        //
        this.AcceptButton = this.button1;
        this.AutoScaleDimensions = new System.Drawing.
           SizeF(6F, 13F);
        this.AutoScaleMode = System.Windows.Forms.
           AutoScaleMode.Font;
        this.ClientSize = new System.Drawing.
           Size(292, 153);
        this.Controls.Add(this.button2);
        this.Controls.Add(this.button1);
        this.Controls.Add(this.TxtPassword);
        this.Controls.Add(this.label3);
        this.Controls.Add(this.TxtUser);
        this.Controls.Add(this.label2);
        this.Controls.Add(this.TxtServer);
        this.Controls.Add(this.label1);
        this.FormBorderStyle = System.Windows.Forms.
           FormBorderStyle.Fixed3D;
        this.MaximizeBox = false;
        this.MinimizeBox = false;
        this.Name = "Log_In";
        this.StartPosition = System.Windows.Forms.
           FormStartPosition.CenterScreen;
        this.Text = "Log In";
        this.ResumeLayout(false);
        this.PerformLayout();
    }

        #endregion
        private System.Windows.Forms.Label label1;
        private System.Windows.Forms.TextBox TxtServer;
        private System.Windows.Forms.TextBox TxtUser;
        private System.Windows.Forms.Label label2;
        private System.Windows.Forms.TextBox TxtPassword;
        private System.Windows.Forms.Label label3;
        private System.Windows.Forms.Button button1;
        private System.Windows.Forms.Button button2;
    }
}
using System;
using System.Collections.Generic;
using System.ComponentModel;
```

```csharp
using System.Data;
using System.Drawing;
using System.Linq;
using System.Text;
using System.Windows.Forms;
using System.Data.SqlClient;
namespace MLS
{
public partial class Log_In : Form
{
        public Log_In()
        {
        InitializeComponent();
}

        private void label1_Click(object sender,
           EventArgs e)
        {
}

        private void button1_Click(object sender,
           EventArgs e)
        {
        GlobalClasses.globals.ServerName = TxtServer.
           Text;
        GlobalClasses.globals.UserName = TxtUser.Text;
        GlobalClasses.globals.Password = TxtPassword.
           Text;
        GlobalClasses.DBOperations.SqlConn(TxtServer.
           Text, TxtUser.Text, TxtPassword.Text);
        try
        {
                SqlConnection SqlConn = new
                   SqlConnection(GlobalClasses.
                   globals.ServerConnStr);
                SqlConn.Open();
                SqlConn.Close();
                Query FRM = new Query();
                FRM.Show();
                GlobalClasses.globals.UserLabelID
                   = GlobalClasses.MLSDB.
                   GetUserLabelID();
                GlobalClasses.globals.UserLabel
                   = GlobalClasses.MLSDB.
                   GetUserLabel();
```

```
                this.Hide();
    }
    catch (SqlException sqlEX)
    {
                MessageBox.Show(sqlEX.Message);
    }
}

    private void button2_Click(object sender,
        EventArgs e)
    {
    DataSet ds = new DataSet();
    string SqlConnStr = "Data Source =.;Initial
        Catalog = test;Integrated Security = SSPI;";
    SqlConnection SqlConn = new
        SqlConnection(SqlConnStr);
    SqlConn.Open();
    string SqlStr = "select * from Table 1";
    SqlCommand SqlCmd = new SqlCommand(SqlStr,
        SqlConn);
    SqlDataAdapter Adpt = new SqlDataAdapter(SqlCmd);
    Adpt.Fill(ds);
    SqlConn.Close();
    for (int i = 1; i < = 5; i++)
    {
                foreach (DataRow DBrow in
                    ds.Tables 0].Rows)
                {
                string SqlConnStr1 = "Data Source =.;
                    Initial Catalog = " + DBrow[0].
                    ToString() + ";Integrated Security
                    = SSPI;";
                SqlConnection mSqlConnection1 = new
                    SqlConnection(SqlConnStr1);
                //the primary key column resides at
                    index 4
                string str1 = "insert into [" +
                    DBrow[1].ToString() + "] select *
                    from
                    [" + DBrow[1].ToString() + "]";
                mSqlConnection1.Open();
                SqlCommand mSqlCommand1 = new
                    SqlCommand(str1,
                    mSqlConnection1);
                mSqlCommand1.CommandTimeout = 200;
                mSqlCommand1.ExecuteNonQuery();
```

```
            mSqlConnection1.Close();
   }
   }
   }
public void dropprimaryKey(string tableName,
   string cnnString)
{
SqlDataReader mReader;
SqlConnection mSqlConnection = new
   SqlConnection();
SqlCommand mSqlCommand = new SqlCommand();
string cnString = cnnString;
mSqlConnection = new SqlConnection(cnString);
mSqlConnection.Open();
//sp_pkeys is SQL Server default stored
   procedure
//you pass it only table Name, it will return
//primary key column
mSqlCommand = new SqlCommand("sp_pkeys",
   mSqlConnection);
mSqlCommand.CommandType = CommandType.
   StoredProcedure;
mSqlCommand.Parameters.Add("@table_name",
   SqlDbType.NVarChar).Value = tableName;
mReader = mSqlCommand.ExecuteReader();
while (mReader.Read())
{
         try
         {
         SqlConnection mSqlConnection1 = new
            SqlConnection(cnnString);
         //the primary key column resides at
            index 4
         string str1 = "ALTER TABLE [" +
            tableName + "] DROP CONSTRAINT
            [" + mReader[5].ToString() + "]";
         mSqlConnection1.Open();
         SqlCommand mSqlCommand1 = new
            SqlCommand(str1, mSqlConnection1);
         mSqlCommand1.ExecuteNonQuery();
         mSqlConnection1.Close();
}
```

```
                        catch {}
            }
}
}
}
```

9.4.3 *Source Code of the Queries Form*

```
namespace MLS
{
partial class Query
{
///<summary>
///Required designer variable.
///</summary>
        private System.ComponentModel.IContainer
            components = null;
///<summary>
///Clean up any resources being used.
///</summary>
///<param name = "disposing">true if managed resources
    should be disposed; otherwise, false.</param>
        protected override void Dispose(bool
            disposing)
        {
        if (disposing && (components ! = null))
        {
                components.Dispose();
        }
        base.Dispose(disposing);
}

        #region Windows Form Designer generated code
///<summary>
///Required method for Designer support - do not modify
///the contents of this method with the code editor.
///</summary>
        private void InitializeComponent()
        {
        this.components = new System.ComponentModel.
            Container();
        System.ComponentModel.ComponentResourceManager
            resources = new System.ComponentModel.Compo
            nentResourceManager(typeof(Query));
```

```
this.menuStrip = new System.Windows.Forms.
   MenuStrip();
this.fileMenu = new System.Windows.Forms.
   ToolStripMenuItem();
this.newToolStripMenuItem = new System.
   Windows.Forms.ToolStripMenuItem();
this.openToolStripMenuItem = new System.
   Windows.Forms.ToolStripMenuItem();
this.toolStripSeparator3 = new System.Windows.
   Forms.ToolStripSeparator();
this.saveToolStripMenuItem = new System.
   Windows.Forms.ToolStripMenuItem();
this.saveAsToolStripMenuItem = new System.
   Windows.Forms.ToolStripMenuItem();
this.toolStripSeparator4 = new System.Windows.
   Forms.ToolStripSeparator();
this.printToolStripMenuItem = new System.
   Windows.Forms.ToolStripMenuItem();
this.printPreviewToolStripMenuItem = new
   System.Windows.Forms.ToolStripMenuItem();
this.printSetupToolStripMenuItem = new System.
   Windows.Forms.ToolStripMenuItem();
this.toolStripSeparator5 = new System.Windows.
   Forms.ToolStripSeparator();
this.exitToolStripMenuItem = new System.
   Windows.Forms.ToolStripMenuItem();
this.editMenu = new System.Windows.Forms.
   ToolStripMenuItem();
this.undoToolStripMenuItem = new System.
   Windows.Forms.ToolStripMenuItem();
this.redoToolStripMenuItem = new System.
   Windows.Forms.ToolStripMenuItem();
this.toolStripSeparator6 = new System.Windows.
   Forms.ToolStripSeparator();
this.cutToolStripMenuItem = new System.
   Windows.Forms.ToolStripMenuItem();
this.copyToolStripMenuItem = new System.
   Windows.Forms.ToolStripMenuItem();
this.pasteToolStripMenuItem = new System.
   Windows.Forms.ToolStripMenuItem();
this.toolStripSeparator7 = new System.Windows.
   Forms.ToolStripSeparator();
this.selectAllToolStripMenuItem = new System.
   Windows.Forms.ToolStripMenuItem();
```

```
this.viewMenu = new System.Windows.Forms.
   ToolStripMenuItem();
this.toolBarToolStripMenuItem = new System.
   Windows.Forms.ToolStripMenuItem();
this.statusBarToolStripMenuItem = new System.
   Windows.Forms.ToolStripMenuItem();
this.toolsMenu = new System.Windows.Forms.
   ToolStripMenuItem();
this.optionsToolStripMenuItem = new System.
   Windows.Forms.ToolStripMenuItem();
this.windowsMenu = new System.Windows.Forms.
   ToolStripMenuItem();
this.newWindowToolStripMenuItem = new System.
   Windows.Forms.ToolStripMenuItem();
this.cascadeToolStripMenuItem = new System.
   Windows.Forms.ToolStripMenuItem();
this.tileVerticalToolStripMenuItem = new
   System.Windows.Forms.ToolStripMenuItem();
this.tileHorizontalToolStripMenuItem = new
   System.Windows.Forms.ToolStripMenuItem();
this.closeAllToolStripMenuItem = new System.
   Windows.Forms.ToolStripMenuItem();
this.arrangeIconsToolStripMenuItem = new
   System.Windows.Forms.ToolStripMenuItem();
this.helpMenu = new System.Windows.Forms.
   ToolStripMenuItem();
this.contentsToolStripMenuItem = new System.
   Windows.Forms.ToolStripMenuItem();
this.indexToolStripMenuItem = new System.
   Windows.Forms.ToolStripMenuItem();
this.searchToolStripMenuItem = new System.
   Windows.Forms.ToolStripMenuItem();
this.toolStripSeparator8 = new System.Windows.
   Forms.ToolStripSeparator();
this.aboutToolStripMenuItem = new System.
   Windows.Forms.ToolStripMenuItem();
this.statusStrip = new System.Windows.Forms.
   StatusStrip();
this.toolStripStatusLabel = new System.
   Windows.Forms.ToolStripStatusLabel();
this.toolTip = new System.Windows.Forms.
   ToolTip(this.components);
this.newToolStripButton = new System.Windows.
   Forms.ToolStripButton();
```

```
this.openToolStripButton = new System.Windows.
   Forms.ToolStripButton();
this.saveToolStripButton = new System.Windows.
   Forms.ToolStripButton();
this.toolStripSeparator1 = new System.Windows.
   Forms.ToolStripSeparator();
this.printToolStripButton = new System.
   Windows.Forms.ToolStripButton();
this.printPreviewToolStripButton = new System.
   Windows.Forms.ToolStripButton();
this.toolStripSeparator2 = new System.Windows.
   Forms.ToolStripSeparator();
this.helpToolStripButton = new System.Windows.
   Forms.ToolStripButton();
this.toolStrip = new System.Windows.Forms.
   ToolStrip();
this.menuStrip.SuspendLayout();
this.statusStrip.SuspendLayout();
this.toolStrip.SuspendLayout();
this.SuspendLayout();
//
//menuStrip
//
this.menuStrip.Items.AddRange(new System.
   Windows.Forms.ToolStripItem[] {
this.fileMenu,
this.editMenu,
this.viewMenu,
this.toolsMenu,
this.windowsMenu,
this.helpMenu});
this.menuStrip.Location = new System.Drawing.
   Point(0, 0);
this.menuStrip.MdiWindowListItem = this.
   windowsMenu;
this.menuStrip.Name = "menuStrip";
this.menuStrip.Size = new System.Drawing.
   Size(632, 24);
this.menuStrip.TabIndex = 0;
this.menuStrip.Text = "MenuStrip";
this.menuStrip.Visible = false;
//
//fileMenu
//
```

```
this.fileMenu.DropDownItems.AddRange(new
   System.Windows.Forms.ToolStripItem[] {
this.newToolStripMenuItem,
this.openToolStripMenuItem,
this.toolStripSeparator3,
this.saveToolStripMenuItem,
this.saveAsToolStripMenuItem,
this.toolStripSeparator4,
this.printToolStripMenuItem,
this.printPreviewToolStripMenuItem,
this.printSetupToolStripMenuItem,
this.toolStripSeparator5,
this.exitToolStripMenuItem});
this.fileMenu.ImageTransparentColor = System.
   Drawing.SystemColors.ActiveBorder;
this.fileMenu.Name = "fileMenu";
this.fileMenu.Size = new System.Drawing.
   Size(37, 20);
this.fileMenu.Text = "&File";
//
//newToolStripMenuItem
//
this.newToolStripMenuItem.Image = ((System.
   Drawing.Image)(resources.
   GetObject("newToolStripMenuItem.Image")));
this.newToolStripMenuItem.
   ImageTransparentColor = System.Drawing.
   Color.Black;
this.newToolStripMenuItem.Name =
   "newToolStripMenuItem";
this.newToolStripMenuItem.ShortcutKeys =
   ((System.Windows.Forms.Keys)((System.
   Windows.Forms.Keys.Control | System.
   Windows.Forms.Keys.N)));
this.newToolStripMenuItem.Size = new System.
   Drawing.Size(146, 22);
this.newToolStripMenuItem.Text = "&New";
this.newToolStripMenuItem.Click + = new
   System.EventHandler(this.ShowNewForm);
//
//openToolStripMenuItem
//
this.openToolStripMenuItem.Image = ((System.
   Drawing.Image)(resources.GetObject("openToo
   lStripMenuItem.Image")));
```

```
this.openToolStripMenuItem.
    ImageTransparentColor = System.Drawing.
    Color.Black;
this.openToolStripMenuItem.Name =
    "openToolStripMenuItem";
this.openToolStripMenuItem.ShortcutKeys =
    ((System.Windows.Forms.Keys)((System.
    Windows.Forms.Keys.Control | System.
    Windows.Forms.Keys.O)));
this.openToolStripMenuItem.Size = new System.
    Drawing.Size(146, 22);
this.openToolStripMenuItem.Text = "&Open";
this.openToolStripMenuItem.Click + = new
    System.EventHandler(this.OpenFile);
//
//toolStripSeparator3
//
this.toolStripSeparator3.Name =
    "toolStripSeparator3";
this.toolStripSeparator3.Size = new System.
    Drawing.Size(143, 6);
//
//saveToolStripMenuItem
//
this.saveToolStripMenuItem.Image = ((System.
    Drawing.Image)(resources.GetObject("saveToo
    lStripMenuItem.Image")));
this.saveToolStripMenuItem.
    ImageTransparentColor = System.Drawing.
    Color.Black;
this.saveToolStripMenuItem.Name =
    "saveToolStripMenuItem";
this.saveToolStripMenuItem.ShortcutKeys =
    ((System.Windows.Forms.Keys)((System.
    Windows.Forms.Keys.Control | System.
    Windows.Forms.Keys.S)));
this.saveToolStripMenuItem.Size = new System.
    Drawing.Size(146, 22);
this.saveToolStripMenuItem.Text = "&Save";
//
//saveAsToolStripMenuItem
//
this.saveAsToolStripMenuItem.Name =
    "saveAsToolStripMenuItem";
```

```
this.saveAsToolStripMenuItem.Size = new
    System.Drawing.Size(146, 22);
this.saveAsToolStripMenuItem.Text = "Save
    &As";
this.saveAsToolStripMenuItem.Click + = new
    System.EventHandler(this.
    SaveAsToolStripMenuItem_Click);
//
//toolStripSeparator4
//
this.toolStripSeparator4.Name =
    "toolStripSeparator4";
this.toolStripSeparator4.Size = new System.
    Drawing.Size(143, 6);
//
//printToolStripMenuItem
//
this.printToolStripMenuItem.Image = ((System.
    Drawing.Image)(resources.GetObject("printTo
    olStripMenuItem.Image")));
this.printToolStripMenuItem.
    ImageTransparentColor = System.Drawing.
    Color.Black;
this.printToolStripMenuItem.Name =
    "printToolStripMenuItem";
this.printToolStripMenuItem.ShortcutKeys =
    ((System.Windows.Forms.Keys)((System.
    Windows.Forms.Keys.Control |
    System.Windows.Forms.Keys.P)));
this.printToolStripMenuItem.Size = new System.
    Drawing.Size(146, 22);
this.printToolStripMenuItem.Text = "&Print";
//
//printPreviewToolStripMenuItem
//
this.printPreviewToolStripMenuItem.Image =
    ((System.Drawing.Image)(resources.GetObject
    ("printPreviewToolStripMenuItem.Image")));
this.printPreviewToolStripMenuItem.
    ImageTransparentColor = System.Drawing.
    Color.Black;
this.printPreviewToolStripMenuItem.Name =
    "printPreviewToolStripMenuItem";
```

```
this.printPreviewToolStripMenuItem.Size = new
   System.Drawing.Size(146, 22);
this.printPreviewToolStripMenuItem.Text =
   "Print Pre&view";
//
//printSetupToolStripMenuItem
//
this.printSetupToolStripMenuItem.Name =
   "printSetupToolStripMenuItem";
this.printSetupToolStripMenuItem.Size = new
   System.Drawing.Size(146, 22);
this.printSetupToolStripMenuItem.Text = "Print
   Setup";
//
//toolStripSeparator5
//
this.toolStripSeparator5.Name =
   "toolStripSeparator5";
this.toolStripSeparator5.Size = new System.
   Drawing.Size(143, 6);
//
//exitToolStripMenuItem
//
this.exitToolStripMenuItem.Name =
   "exitToolStripMenuItem";
this.exitToolStripMenuItem.Size = new System.
   Drawing.Size(146, 22);
this.exitToolStripMenuItem.Text = "E&xit";
this.exitToolStripMenuItem.Click + = new
   System.EventHandler(this.
   ExitToolsStripMenuItem_Click);
//
//editMenu
//
this.editMenu.DropDownItems.AddRange(new
   System.Windows.Forms.ToolStripItem[] {
this.undoToolStripMenuItem,
this.redoToolStripMenuItem,
this.toolStripSeparator6,
this.cutToolStripMenuItem,
this.copyToolStripMenuItem,
this.pasteToolStripMenuItem,
this.toolStripSeparator7,
this.selectAllToolStripMenuItem});
```

```
this.editMenu.Name = "editMenu";
this.editMenu.Size = new System.Drawing.
   Size(39, 20);
this.editMenu.Text = "&Edit";
//
//undoToolStripMenuItem
//
this.undoToolStripMenuItem.Image = ((System.
   Drawing.Image)(resources.GetObject("undoToo
   lStripMenuItem.Image")));
this.undoToolStripMenuItem.ImageTransparentColor
   = System.Drawing.Color.Black;
this.undoToolStripMenuItem.Name =
   "undoToolStripMenuItem";
this.undoToolStripMenuItem.ShortcutKeys
   = ((System.Windows.Forms.Keys)((System.
   Windows.Forms.Keys.Control | System.
   Windows.Forms.Keys.Z)));
this.undoToolStripMenuItem.Size = new System.
   Drawing.Size(164, 22);
this.undoToolStripMenuItem.Text = "&Undo";
this.undoToolStripMenuItem.Click + = new
   System.EventHandler(this.
   undoToolStripMenuItem_Click);
//
//redoToolStripMenuItem
//
this.redoToolStripMenuItem.Image = ((System.
   Drawing.Image)(resources.GetObject("redoToo
   lStripMenuItem.Image")));
this.redoToolStripMenuItem.ImageTransparentColor
   = System.Drawing.Color.Black;
this.redoToolStripMenuItem.Name =
   "redoToolStripMenuItem";
this.redoToolStripMenuItem.ShortcutKeys
   = ((System.Windows.Forms.Keys)((System.
   Windows.Forms.Keys.Control | System.
   Windows.Forms.Keys.Y)));
this.redoToolStripMenuItem.Size = new System.
   Drawing.Size(164, 22);
this.redoToolStripMenuItem.Text = "&Redo";
//
//toolStripSeparator6
//
```

```
this.toolStripSeparator6.Name =
    "toolStripSeparator6";
this.toolStripSeparator6.Size = new System.
    Drawing.Size(161, 6);
//
//cutToolStripMenuItem
//
this.cutToolStripMenuItem.Image = ((System.
    Drawing.Image)(resources.
    GetObject("cutToolStripMenuItem.Image")));
this.cutToolStripMenuItem.
    ImageTransparentColor = System.Drawing.
    Color.Black;
this.cutToolStripMenuItem.Name =
    "cutToolStripMenuItem";
this.cutToolStripMenuItem.ShortcutKeys =
    ((System.Windows.Forms.Keys)((System.
    Windows.Forms.Keys.Control | System.
    Windows.Forms.Keys.X)));
this.cutToolStripMenuItem.Size = new System.
    Drawing.Size(164, 22);
this.cutToolStripMenuItem.Text = "Cu&t";
this.cutToolStripMenuItem.Click + = new
    System.EventHandler(this.
    CutToolStripMenuItem_Click);
//
//copyToolStripMenuItem
//
this.copyToolStripMenuItem.Image = ((System.
    Drawing.Image)(resources.GetObject("copyToo
    lStripMenuItem.Image")));
this.copyToolStripMenuItem.
    ImageTransparentColor = System.Drawing.
    Color.Black;
this.copyToolStripMenuItem.Name =
    "copyToolStripMenuItem";
this.copyToolStripMenuItem.ShortcutKeys =
    ((System.Windows.Forms.Keys)((System.
    Windows.Forms.Keys.Control |
    System.Windows.Forms.Keys.C)));
this.copyToolStripMenuItem.Size = new System.
    Drawing.Size(164, 22);
this.copyToolStripMenuItem.Text = "&Copy";
```

```
this.copyToolStripMenuItem.Click + = new
   System.EventHandler(this.
   CopyToolStripMenuItem_Click);
//
//pasteToolStripMenuItem
//
this.pasteToolStripMenuItem.Image = ((System.
   Drawing.Image)(resources.GetObject("pasteTo
   olStripMenuItem.Image")));
this.pasteToolStripMenuItem.
   ImageTransparentColor = System.Drawing.
   Color.Black;
this.pasteToolStripMenuItem.Name =
   "pasteToolStripMenuItem";
this.pasteToolStripMenuItem.ShortcutKeys
   = ((System.Windows.Forms.Keys)((System.
   Windows.Forms.Keys.Control | System.
   Windows.Forms.Keys.V)));
this.pasteToolStripMenuItem.Size = new System.
   Drawing.Size(164, 22);
this.pasteToolStripMenuItem.Text = "&Paste";
this.pasteToolStripMenuItem.Click + = new
   System.EventHandler(this.
   PasteToolStripMenuItem_Click);
//
//toolStripSeparator7
//
this.toolStripSeparator7.Name =
   "toolStripSeparator7";
this.toolStripSeparator7.Size = new System.
   Drawing.Size(161, 6);
//
//selectAllToolStripMenuItem
//
this.selectAllToolStripMenuItem.Name =
   "selectAllToolStripMenuItem";
this.selectAllToolStripMenuItem.ShortcutKeys
   = ((System.Windows.Forms.Keys)((System.
   Windows.Forms.Keys.Control | System.
   Windows.Forms.Keys.A)));
this.selectAllToolStripMenuItem.Size = new
   System.Drawing.Size(164, 22);
this.selectAllToolStripMenuItem.Text = "Select
   &All";
```

```
//
//viewMenu
//
this.viewMenu.DropDownItems.AddRange(new
   System.Windows.Forms.ToolStripItem[] {
this.toolBarToolStripMenuItem,
this.statusBarToolStripMenuItem});
this.viewMenu.Name = "viewMenu";
this.viewMenu.Size = new System.Drawing.
   Size(44, 20);
this.viewMenu.Text = "&View";
//
//toolBarToolStripMenuItem
//
this.toolBarToolStripMenuItem.Checked = true;
this.toolBarToolStripMenuItem.CheckOnClick
   = true;
this.toolBarToolStripMenuItem.CheckState =
   System.Windows.Forms.CheckState.Checked;
this.toolBarToolStripMenuItem.Name =
   "toolBarToolStripMenuItem";
this.toolBarToolStripMenuItem.Size = new
   System.Drawing.Size(126, 22);
this.toolBarToolStripMenuItem.Text =
   "&Toolbar";
this.toolBarToolStripMenuItem.Click + = new
   System.EventHandler(this.
   ToolBarToolStripMenuItem_Click);
//
//statusBarToolStripMenuItem
//
this.statusBarToolStripMenuItem.Checked
   = true;
this.statusBarToolStripMenuItem.CheckOnClick
   = true;
this.statusBarToolStripMenuItem.CheckState =
   System.Windows.Forms.CheckState.Checked;
this.statusBarToolStripMenuItem.Name =
   "statusBarToolStripMenuItem";
this.statusBarToolStripMenuItem.Size = new
   System.Drawing.Size(126, 22);
this.statusBarToolStripMenuItem.Text
   = "&Status Bar";
```

```
this.statusBarToolStripMenuItem.Click + = new
    System.EventHandler(this.
    StatusBarToolStripMenuItem_Click);
//
//toolsMenu
//
this.toolsMenu.DropDownItems.AddRange(new
    System.Windows.Forms.ToolStripItem[] {
this.optionsToolStripMenuItem});
this.toolsMenu.Name = "toolsMenu";
this.toolsMenu.Size = new System.Drawing.
    Size(48, 20);
this.toolsMenu.Text = "&Tools";
//
//optionsToolStripMenuItem
//
this.optionsToolStripMenuItem.Name
    = "optionsToolStripMenuItem";
this.optionsToolStripMenuItem.Size = new
    System.Drawing.Size(116, 22);
this.optionsToolStripMenuItem.Text
    = "&Options";
//
//windowsMenu
//
this.windowsMenu.DropDownItems.AddRange
    (new System.Windows.Forms.ToolStripItem[] {
this.newWindowToolStripMenuItem,
this.cascadeToolStripMenuItem,
this.tileVerticalToolStripMenuItem,
this.tileHorizontalToolStripMenuItem,
this.closeAllToolStripMenuItem,
this.arrangeIconsToolStripMenuItem});
this.windowsMenu.Name = "windowsMenu";
this.windowsMenu.Size = new System.Drawing.
    Size(68, 20);
this.windowsMenu.Text = "&Windows";
//
//newWindowToolStripMenuItem
//
this.newWindowToolStripMenuItem.Name =
    "newWindowToolStripMenuItem";
this.newWindowToolStripMenuItem.Size = new
    System.Drawing.Size(151, 22);
```

```
this.newWindowToolStripMenuItem.Text = "&New
    Window";
this.newWindowToolStripMenuItem.Click + = new
    System.EventHandler(this.ShowNewForm);
//
//cascadeToolStripMenuItem
//
this.cascadeToolStripMenuItem.Name =
    "cascadeToolStripMenuItem";
this.cascadeToolStripMenuItem.Size = new
    System.Drawing.Size(151, 22);
this.cascadeToolStripMenuItem.Text =
    "&Cascade";
this.cascadeToolStripMenuItem.Click + = new
    System.EventHandler(this.
    CascadeToolStripMenuItem_Click);
//
//tileVerticalToolStripMenuItem
//
this.tileVerticalToolStripMenuItem.Name
    = "tileVerticalToolStripMenuItem";
this.tileVerticalToolStripMenuItem.Size = new
    System.Drawing.Size(151, 22);
this.tileVerticalToolStripMenuItem.Text
    = "Tile &Vertical";
this.tileVerticalToolStripMenuItem.Click +
    = new System.EventHandler(this.
    TileVerticalToolStripMenuItem_Click);
//
//tileHorizontalToolStripMenuItem
//
this.tileHorizontalToolStripMenuItem.Name
    = "tileHorizontalToolStripMenuItem";
this.tileHorizontalToolStripMenuItem.Size
    = new System.Drawing.Size(151, 22);
this.tileHorizontalToolStripMenuItem.Text
    = "Tile &Horizontal";
this.tileHorizontalToolStripMenuItem.Click +
    = new System.EventHandler
    (this.TileHorizontalToolStripMenuItem _ Click);
//
//closeAllToolStripMenuItem
//
```

```
this.closeAllToolStripMenuItem.Name
   = "closeAllToolStripMenuItem";
this.closeAllToolStripMenuItem.Size = new
   System.Drawing.Size(151, 22);
this.closeAllToolStripMenuItem.Text = "C&lose
   All";
this.closeAllToolStripMenuItem.Click + = new
   System.EventHandler(this.
   CloseAllToolStripMenuItem_Click);
//
//arrangeIconsToolStripMenuItem
//
this.arrangeIconsToolStripMenuItem.Name
   = "arrangeIconsToolStripMenuItem";
this.arrangeIconsToolStripMenuItem.Size = new
   System.Drawing.Size(151, 22);
this.arrangeIconsToolStripMenuItem.Text
   = "&Arrange Icons";
this.arrangeIconsToolStripMenuItem.Click +
   = new System.EventHandler(this.
   ArrangeIconsToolStripMenuItem_Click);
//
//helpMenu
//
this.helpMenu.DropDownItems.AddRange
   (new System.Windows.Forms.ToolStripItem[] {
this.contentsToolStripMenuItem,
this.indexToolStripMenuItem,
this.searchToolStripMenuItem,
this.toolStripSeparator8,
this.aboutToolStripMenuItem});
this.helpMenu.Name = "helpMenu";
this.helpMenu.Size = new System.Drawing.
   Size(44, 20);
this.helpMenu.Text = "&Help";
//
//contentsToolStripMenuItem
//
this.contentsToolStripMenuItem.Name =
   "contentsToolStripMenuItem";
this.contentsToolStripMenuItem.ShortcutKeys
   = ((System.Windows.Forms.Keys)((System.
   Windows.Forms.Keys.Control | System.
   Windows.Forms.Keys.F1)));
```

```
this.contentsToolStripMenuItem.Size = new
   System.Drawing.Size(168, 22);
this.contentsToolStripMenuItem.Text = "&Contents";
//
//indexToolStripMenuItem
//
this.indexToolStripMenuItem.Image = ((System.
   Drawing.Image)(resources.GetObject("indexTo
   olStripMenuItem.Image")));
this.indexToolStripMenuItem.ImageTransparentColor
   = System.Drawing.Color.Black;
this.indexToolStripMenuItem.Name
   = "indexToolStripMenuItem";
this.indexToolStripMenuItem.Size = new System.
   Drawing.Size(168, 22);
this.indexToolStripMenuItem.Text = "&Index";
//
//searchToolStripMenuItem
//
this.searchToolStripMenuItem.Image = ((System.
   Drawing.Image)(resources.GetObject("searchT
   oolStripMenuItem.Image")));
this.searchToolStripMenuItem.
   ImageTransparentColor = System.Drawing.
   Color.Black;
this.searchToolStripMenuItem.Name =
   "searchToolStripMenuItem";
this.searchToolStripMenuItem.Size = new
   System.Drawing.Size(168, 22);
this.searchToolStripMenuItem.Text = "&Search";
//
//toolStripSeparator8
//
this.toolStripSeparator8.Name =
   "toolStripSeparator8";
this.toolStripSeparator8.Size = new System.
   Drawing.Size(165, 6);
//
//aboutToolStripMenuItem
//
this.aboutToolStripMenuItem.Name =
   "aboutToolStripMenuItem";
this.aboutToolStripMenuItem.Size = new System.
   Drawing.Size(168, 22);
```

```
this.aboutToolStripMenuItem.Text
   = "&About......";
//
//statusStrip
//
this.statusStrip.Items.AddRange(new System.
   Windows.Forms.ToolStripItem[] {
this.toolStripStatusLabel});
this.statusStrip.Location = new System.
   Drawing.Point(0, 430);
this.statusStrip.Name = "statusStrip";
this.statusStrip.RightToLeft
   = System.Windows.Forms.RightToLeft.Yes;
this.statusStrip.Size = new System.Drawing.
   Size(632, 23);
this.statusStrip.TabIndex = 2;
this.statusStrip.Text = "StatusStrip";
//
//toolStripStatusLabel
//
this.toolStripStatusLabel.Font = new System.
   Drawing.Font("Arial", 12F, System.Drawing.
   FontStyle.Italic);
this.toolStripStatusLabel.Name
   = "toolStripStatusLabel";
this.toolStripStatusLabel.Size = new System.
   Drawing.Size(52, 18);
this.toolStripStatusLabel.Text = "Status";
//
//newToolStripButton
//
this.newToolStripButton.Image = ((System.
   Drawing.Image)(resources.
   GetObject("newToolStripButton.Image")));
this.newToolStripButton.ImageTransparentColor
   = System.Drawing.Color.Black;
this.newToolStripButton.Name
   = "newToolStripButton";
this.newToolStripButton.Size = new System.
   Drawing.Size(86, 22);
this.newToolStripButton.Text = "New Query";
this.newToolStripButton.Click + = new System.
   EventHandler(this.ShowNewForm);
//
//openToolStripButton
```

```
//
this.openToolStripButton.DisplayStyle
   = System.Windows.Forms.
   ToolStripItemDisplayStyle.Image;
this.openToolStripButton.Image = ((System.
   Drawing.Image)(resources.
   GetObject("openToolStripButton.Image")));
this.openToolStripButton.ImageTransparentColor
   = System.Drawing.Color.Black;
this.openToolStripButton.Name
   = "openToolStripButton";
this.openToolStripButton.Size = new System.
   Drawing.Size(23, 22);
this.openToolStripButton.Text = "Open";
this.openToolStripButton.Visible = false;
this.openToolStripButton.Click + = new System.
   EventHandler(this.OpenFile);
//
//saveToolStripButton
//
this.saveToolStripButton.DisplayStyle
   = System.Windows.Forms.
   ToolStripItemDisplayStyle.Image;
this.saveToolStripButton.Image = ((System.
   Drawing.Image)(resources.
   GetObject("saveToolStripButton.Image")));
this.saveToolStripButton.ImageTransparentColor
   = System.Drawing.Color.Black;
this.saveToolStripButton.Name
   = "saveToolStripButton";
this.saveToolStripButton.Size = new System.
   Drawing.Size(23, 22);
this.saveToolStripButton.Text = "Save";
this.saveToolStripButton.Visible = false;
this.saveToolStripButton.Click + = new System.
   EventHandler(this.saveToolStripButton _
   Click);
//
//toolStripSeparator1
//
this.toolStripSeparator1.Name =
   "toolStripSeparator1";
this.toolStripSeparator1.Size = new System.
   Drawing.Size(6, 25);
//
```

```
//printToolStripButton
//
this.printToolStripButton.DisplayStyle = System.
   Windows.Forms.ToolStripItemDisplayStyle.
   Image;
this.printToolStripButton.Image = ((System.
   Drawing.Image)(resources.
   GetObject("printToolStripButton.Image")));
this.printToolStripButton.
   ImageTransparentColor = System.Drawing.
   Color.Black;
this.printToolStripButton.Name
   = "printToolStripButton";
this.printToolStripButton.Size = new System.
   Drawing.Size(23, 22);
this.printToolStripButton.Text = "Print";
this.printToolStripButton.Visible = false;
//
//printPreviewToolStripButton
//
this.printPreviewToolStripButton.DisplayStyle
   = System.Windows.Forms.
   ToolStripItemDisplayStyle.Image;
this.printPreviewToolStripButton.Image =
   ((System.Drawing.Image)(resources.GetObject
   ("printPreviewToolStripButton.Image")));
this.printPreviewToolStripButton.
   ImageTransparentColor = System.Drawing.
   Color.Black;
this.printPreviewToolStripButton.Name
   = "printPreviewToolStripButton";
this.printPreviewToolStripButton.Size = new
   System.Drawing.Size(23, 22);
this.printPreviewToolStripButton.Text = "Print
   Preview";
this.printPreviewToolStripButton.Visible
   = false;
//
//toolStripSeparator2
//
this.toolStripSeparator2.Name =
   "toolStripSeparator2";
this.toolStripSeparator2.Size = new System.
   Drawing.Size(6, 25);
```

```
//
//helpToolStripButton
//
this.helpToolStripButton.DisplayStyle
   = System.Windows.Forms.
   ToolStripItemDisplayStyle.Image;
this.helpToolStripButton.Image = ((System.
   Drawing.Image)(resources.
   GetObject("helpToolStripButton.Image")));
this.helpToolStripButton.ImageTransparentColor
   = System.Drawing.Color.Black;
this.helpToolStripButton.Name
   = "helpToolStripButton";
this.helpToolStripButton.Size = new System.
   Drawing.Size(23, 22);
this.helpToolStripButton.Text = "Help";
this.helpToolStripButton.Visible = false;
//
//toolStrip
//
this.toolStrip.Items.AddRange(new System.
   Windows.Forms.ToolStripItem[] {
this.newToolStripButton,
this.openToolStripButton,
this.saveToolStripButton,
this.toolStripSeparator1,
this.toolStripSeparator2,
this.printToolStripButton,
this.printPreviewToolStripButton,
this.helpToolStripButton});
this.toolStrip.Location = new System.Drawing.
   Point(0, 0);
this.toolStrip.Name = "toolStrip";
this.toolStrip.Size = new System.Drawing.
   Size(632, 25);
this.toolStrip.TabIndex = 1;
this.toolStrip.Text = "ToolStrip";
//
//Query
//
this.AutoScaleDimensions = new System.Drawing.
   SizeF(6F, 13F);
this.AutoScaleMode = System.Windows.Forms.
   AutoScaleMode.Font;
```

```
this.ClientSize = new System.
   Drawing.Size(632, 453);
this.Controls.Add(this.statusStrip);
this.Controls.Add(this.toolStrip);
this.Controls.Add(this.menuStrip);
this.IsMdiContainer = true;
this.MainMenuStrip = this.menuStrip;
this.Name = "Query";
this.Text = "Query";
this.WindowState = System.Windows.Forms.
   FormWindowState.Maximized;
this.Load + = new System.EventHandler
   (this.Query_Load);
this.FormClosing + = new System.Windows.Forms.
   FormClosingEventHandler(this.Query_
   FormClosing);
this.menuStrip.ResumeLayout(false);
this.menuStrip.PerformLayout();
this.statusStrip.ResumeLayout(false);
this.statusStrip.PerformLayout();
this.toolStrip.ResumeLayout(false);
this.toolStrip.PerformLayout();
this.ResumeLayout(false);
this.PerformLayout();
}

#endregion
private System.Windows.Forms.MenuStrip
   menuStrip;
private System.Windows.Forms.StatusStrip
   statusStrip;
private System.Windows.Forms.
   ToolStripSeparator toolStripSeparator3;
private System.Windows.Forms.
   ToolStripSeparator toolStripSeparator4;
private System.Windows.Forms.
   ToolStripSeparator toolStripSeparator5;
private System.Windows.Forms.
   ToolStripSeparator toolStripSeparator6;
private System.Windows.Forms.ToolStripMenuItem
   printSetupToolStripMenuItem;
private System.Windows.Forms.
   ToolStripSeparator toolStripSeparator7;
private System.Windows.Forms.
   ToolStripSeparator toolStripSeparator8;
```

```
private System.Windows.Forms.
   ToolStripStatusLabel toolStripStatusLabel;
private System.Windows.Forms.ToolStripMenuItem
   aboutToolStripMenuItem;
private System.Windows.Forms.ToolStripMenuItem
   tileHorizontalToolStripMenuItem;
private System.Windows.Forms.ToolStripMenuItem
   fileMenu;
private System.Windows.Forms.ToolStripMenuItem
   newToolStripMenuItem;
private System.Windows.Forms.ToolStripMenuItem
   openToolStripMenuItem;
private System.Windows.Forms.ToolStripMenuItem
   saveToolStripMenuItem;
private System.Windows.Forms.ToolStripMenuItem
   saveAsToolStripMenuItem;
private System.Windows.Forms.ToolStripMenuItem
   printToolStripMenuItem;
private System.Windows.Forms.ToolStripMenuItem
   printPreviewToolStripMenuItem;
private System.Windows.Forms.ToolStripMenuItem
   exitToolStripMenuItem;
private System.Windows.Forms.ToolStripMenuItem
   editMenu;
private System.Windows.Forms.ToolStripMenuItem
   undoToolStripMenuItem;
private System.Windows.Forms.ToolStripMenuItem
   redoToolStripMenuItem;
private System.Windows.Forms.ToolStripMenuItem
   cutToolStripMenuItem;
private System.Windows.Forms.ToolStripMenuItem
   copyToolStripMenuItem;
private System.Windows.Forms.ToolStripMenuItem
   pasteToolStripMenuItem;
private System.Windows.Forms.ToolStripMenuItem
   selectAllToolStripMenuItem;
private System.Windows.Forms.ToolStripMenuItem
   viewMenu;
private System.Windows.Forms.ToolStripMenuItem
   toolBarToolStripMenuItem;
private System.Windows.Forms.ToolStripMenuItem
   statusBarToolStripMenuItem;
private System.Windows.Forms.ToolStripMenuItem
   toolsMenu;
```

```
        private System.Windows.Forms.ToolStripMenuItem
           optionsToolStripMenuItem;
        private System.Windows.Forms.ToolStripMenuItem
           windowsMenu;
        private System.Windows.Forms.ToolStripMenuItem
           newWindowToolStripMenuItem;
        private System.Windows.Forms.ToolStripMenuItem
           cascadeToolStripMenuItem;
        private System.Windows.Forms.ToolStripMenuItem
           tileVerticalToolStripMenuItem;
        private System.Windows.Forms.ToolStripMenuItem
           closeAllToolStripMenuItem;
        private System.Windows.Forms.ToolStripMenuItem
           arrangeIconsToolStripMenuItem;
        private System.Windows.Forms.ToolStripMenuItem
           helpMenu;
        private System.Windows.Forms.ToolStripMenuItem
           contentsToolStripMenuItem;
        private System.Windows.Forms.ToolStripMenuItem
           indexToolStripMenuItem;
        private System.Windows.Forms.ToolStripMenuItem
           searchToolStripMenuItem;
        private System.Windows.Forms.ToolTip toolTip;
        private System.Windows.Forms.ToolStripButton
           newToolStripButton;
        private System.Windows.Forms.ToolStripButton
           openToolStripButton;
        private System.Windows.Forms.ToolStripButton
           saveToolStripButton;
        private System.Windows.Forms.
           ToolStripSeparator toolStripSeparator1;
        private System.Windows.Forms.ToolStripButton
           printToolStripButton;
        private System.Windows.Forms.ToolStripButton
           printPreviewToolStripButton;
        private System.Windows.Forms.
           ToolStripSeparator toolStripSeparator2;
        private System.Windows.Forms.ToolStripButton
           helpToolStripButton;
        private System.Windows.Forms.ToolStrip
           toolStrip;
    }
}
using System;
```

```csharp
using System.Collections.Generic;
using System.ComponentModel;
using System.Data;
using System.Drawing;
using System.Linq;
using System.Text;
using System.Windows.Forms;
using System.Data.SqlClient;
namespace MLS
{
public partial class Query : Form
{
        private int childFormNumber = 0;
        public Query()
        {
        InitializeComponent();
}

        private void ShowNewForm(object sender,
           EventArgs e)
        {
        QueryForm childForm = new QueryForm();
        childForm.MdiParent = this;
        childForm.Dock = DockStyle.Fill;
        childForm.Text = "SQL Query"
           + childFormNumber++;
        childForm.Show();
}

        private void OpenFile(object sender,
           EventArgs e)
        {
        OpenFileDialog openFileDialog = new
           OpenFileDialog();
        openFileDialog.InitialDirectory = Environment.
           GetFolderPath(Environment.SpecialFolder.
           Personal);
        openFileDialog.Filter = "Text Files (*.txt)|*.
           txt|All Files (*.*)|*.*";
        if (openFileDialog.ShowDialog(this) = =
           DialogResult.OK)
        {
                string FileName = openFileDialog.
                   FileName;
        }
}
```

```csharp
private void SaveAsToolStripMenuItem_
    Click(object sender, EventArgs e)
{
SaveFileDialog saveFileDialog = new
    SaveFileDialog();
saveFileDialog.InitialDirectory = Environment.
    GetFolderPath(Environment.SpecialFolder.
    Personal);
saveFileDialog.Filter = "Text Files (*.txt)|*.
    txt|All Files (*.*)|*.*";
if (saveFileDialog.ShowDialog(this)
    = = DialogResult.OK)
    {
            string FileName = saveFileDialog.
                FileName;
    }
}

private void ExitToolsStripMenuItem_
    Click(object sender, EventArgs e)
{
Application.Exit();
//this.Close();
}

private void CutToolStripMenuItem_Click(object
    sender, EventArgs e)
{
}

private void CopyToolStripMenuItem_
    Click(object sender, EventArgs e)
{
}

private void PasteToolStripMenuItem_
    Click(object sender, EventArgs e)
{
}

private void ToolBarToolStripMenuItem_
    Click(object sender, EventArgs e)
{
toolStrip.Visible = toolBarToolStripMenuItem.
    Checked;
}

private void StatusBarToolStripMenuItem_
    Click(object sender, EventArgs e)
{
```

```
    statusStrip.Visible =
        statusBarToolStripMenuItem.Checked;
}

    private void CascadeToolStripMenuItem_
        Click(object sender, EventArgs e)
    {
    LayoutMdi(MdiLayout.Cascade);
}

    private void TileVerticalToolStripMenuItem_
        Click(object sender, EventArgs e)
    {
    LayoutMdi(MdiLayout.TileVertical);
}

    private void TileHorizontalToolStripMenuItem_
        Click(object sender, EventArgs e)
    {
    LayoutMdi(MdiLayout.TileHorizontal);
}

    private void ArrangeIconsToolStripMenuItem_
        Click(object sender, EventArgs e)
    {
    LayoutMdi(MdiLayout.ArrangeIcons);
}

    private void CloseAllToolStripMenuItem_
        Click(object sender, EventArgs e)
    {
    foreach (Form childForm in MdiChildren)
    {
            childForm.Close();
    }
}

    private void undoToolStripMenuItem_
        Click(object sender, EventArgs e)
    {
}

    private void Query_FormClosing(object sender,
        FormClosingEventArgs e)
    {
    Application.Exit();
}

    private void Query_Load(object sender,
        EventArgs e)
    {
```

```
        toolStripStatusLabel.Text = GlobalClasses.
            globals.UserName;
}

        private void saveToolStripButton_Click(object
            sender, EventArgs e)
        {
        }
}
}
```

9.4.4 *Source Code of the Query Form*

```
namespace MLS
{
partial class QueryForm
{
///<summary>
///Required designer variable.
///</summary>
        private System.ComponentModel.IContainer
            components = null;
///<summary>
///Clean up any resources being used.
///</summary>
///<param name = "disposing">true if managed resources
    should be disposed; otherwise, false.</param>
        protected override void Dispose(bool
            disposing)
        {
        if (disposing && (components ! = null))
        {
                components.Dispose();
        }
        base.Dispose(disposing);
}

        #region Windows Form Designer generated code
///<summary>
///Required method for Designer support - do not modify
///the contents of this method with the code editor.
///</summary>
        private void InitializeComponent()
        {
```

```
System.ComponentModel.ComponentResourceManager
   resources = new System.ComponentModel.Compo
   nentResourceManager(typeof(QueryForm));
this.richTextBox1 = new System.Windows.Forms.
   RichTextBox();
this.toolStrip1 = new System.Windows.Forms.
   ToolStrip();
this.toolStripButton1 = new System.Windows.
   Forms.ToolStripButton();
this.splitContainer1 = new System.Windows.
   Forms.SplitContainer();
this.BCMLSBTN = new System.Windows.Forms.
   RadioButton();
this.MLRBTN = new System.Windows.Forms.
   RadioButton();
this.SmithBTN = new System.Windows.Forms.
   RadioButton();
this.JSBTN = new System.Windows.Forms.
   RadioButton();
this.SeaviewBTN = new System.Windows.Forms.
   RadioButton();
this.dataGridView1 = new System.Windows.Forms.
   DataGridView();
this.EncryptionBTN = new System.Windows.Forms.
   RadioButton();
this.toolStrip1.SuspendLayout();
this.splitContainer1.Panel1.SuspendLayout();
this.splitContainer1.Panel2.SuspendLayout();
this.splitContainer1.SuspendLayout();
((System.ComponentModel.ISupportInitialize)
   (this.dataGridView1)).BeginInit();
this.SuspendLayout();
//
//richTextBox1
//
this.richTextBox1.Dock
   = System.Windows.Forms.DockStyle.Bottom;
this.richTextBox1.Location = new System.
   Drawing.Point(0, 26);
this.richTextBox1.Name = "richTextBox1";
this.richTextBox1.Size = new System.Drawing.
   Size(547, 141);
this.richTextBox1.TabIndex = 0;
this.richTextBox1.Text = "";
```

```
this.richTextBox1.TextChanged + = new System.
   EventHandler(this.richTextBox1 _ TextChanged);
//
//toolStrip1
//
this.toolStrip1.BackColor = System.Drawing.
   SystemColors.Control;
this.toolStrip1.Items.AddRange(new System.
   Windows.Forms.ToolStripItem[] {
this.toolStripButton1});
this.toolStrip1.Location = new System.Drawing.
   Point(0, 0);
this.toolStrip1.Name = "toolStrip1";
this.toolStrip1.Size = new System.Drawing.
   Size(547, 25);
this.toolStrip1.TabIndex = 1;
this.toolStrip1.Text = "toolStrip1";
this.toolStrip1.ItemClicked + = new System.
   Windows.Forms.ToolStripItemClickedEventHand
   ler(this.toolStrip1_ItemClicked);
//
//toolStripButton1
//
this.toolStripButton1.Image =
   ((System.Drawing.Image)(resources.
   GetObject("toolStripButton1.Image")));
this.toolStripButton1.ImageTransparentColor
   = System.Drawing.Color.Magenta;
this.toolStripButton1.Name
   = "toolStripButton1";
this.toolStripButton1.Size = new System.
   Drawing.Size(67, 22);
this.toolStripButton1.Text = "Execute";
this.toolStripButton1.Click + = new System.
   EventHandler(this.toolStripButton1_Click);
//
//splitContainer1
//
this.splitContainer1.Dock = System.Windows.
   Forms.DockStyle.Fill;
this.splitContainer1.Location = new System.
   Drawing.Point(0, 25);
this.splitContainer1.Name = "splitContainer1";
this.splitContainer1.Orientation = System.
   Windows.Forms.Orientation.Horizontal;
```

```
//
//splitContainer1.Panel1
//
this.splitContainer1.Panel1.Controls.
   Add(this.EncryptionBTN);
this.splitContainer1.Panel1.Controls.
   Add(this.BCMLSBTN);
this.splitContainer1.Panel1.Controls.
   Add(this.MLRBTN);
this.splitContainer1.Panel1.Controls.
   Add(this.SmithBTN);
this.splitContainer1.Panel1.Controls.
   Add(this.JSBTN);
this.splitContainer1.Panel1.Controls.
   Add(this.SeaviewBTN);
this.splitContainer1.Panel1.Controls.
   Add(this.richTextBox1);
//
//splitContainer1.Panel2
//
this.splitContainer1.Panel2.Controls.
   Add(this.dataGridView1);
this.splitContainer1.Size = new System.
   Drawing.Size(547, 425);
this.splitContainer1.SplitterDistance = 167;
this.splitContainer1.TabIndex = 2;
//
//BCMLSBTN
//
this.BCMLSBTN.AutoSize = true;
this.BCMLSBTN.Location = new System.Drawing.
   Point(295, 3);
this.BCMLSBTN.Name = "BCMLSBTN";
this.BCMLSBTN.Size = new System.Drawing.
   Size(57, 17);
this.BCMLSBTN.TabIndex = 5;
this.BCMLSBTN.TabStop = true;
this.BCMLSBTN.Text = "BCMLS";
this.BCMLSBTN.UseVisualStyleBackColor = true;
//
//MLRBTN
//
this.MLRBTN.AutoSize = true;
this.MLRBTN.Location = new System.Drawing.
   Point(232, 3);
```

```
this.MLRBTN.Name = "MLRBTN";
this.MLRBTN.Size = new System.Drawing.
    Size(45, 17);
this.MLRBTN.TabIndex = 4;
this.MLRBTN.TabStop = true;
this.MLRBTN.Text = "MLR";
this.MLRBTN.UseVisualStyleBackColor = true;
//
//SmithBTN
//
this.SmithBTN.AutoSize = true;
this.SmithBTN.Location = new System.Drawing.
    Point(129, 3);
this.SmithBTN.Name = "SmithBTN";
this.SmithBTN.Size = new System.Drawing.
    Size(97, 17);
this.SmithBTN.TabIndex = 3;
this.SmithBTN.TabStop = true;
this.SmithBTN.Text = "Smith-Winslett ";
this.SmithBTN.UseVisualStyleBackColor = true;
//
//JSBTN
//
this.JSBTN.AutoSize = true;
this.JSBTN.Location = new System.Drawing.
    Point(83, 3);
this.JSBTN.Name = "JSBTN";
this.JSBTN.Size = new System.Drawing.Size(40, 17);
this.JSBTN.TabIndex = 2;
this.JSBTN.TabStop = true;
this.JSBTN.Text = "J-S";
this.JSBTN.UseVisualStyleBackColor = true;
//
//SeaviewBTN
//
this.SeaviewBTN.AutoSize = true;
this.SeaviewBTN.Location = new System.Drawing.
    Point(12, 3);
this.SeaviewBTN.Name = "SeaviewBTN";
this.SeaviewBTN.Size = new System.Drawing.
    Size(65, 17);
this.SeaviewBTN.TabIndex = 1;
this.SeaviewBTN.TabStop = true;
this.SeaviewBTN.Text = "Seaview";
```

```
this.SeaviewBTN.UseVisualStyleBackColor =
    true;
//
//dataGridView1
//
this.dataGridView1.AllowUserToAddRows = false;
this.dataGridView1.AllowUserToDeleteRows = false;
this.dataGridView1.ColumnHeadersHeightSizeMode
    = System.Windows.Forms.
    DataGridViewColumnHeadersHeightSizeMode.
    AutoSize;
this.dataGridView1.Dock = System.Windows.
    Forms.DockStyle.Fill;
this.dataGridView1.Location = new System.
    Drawing.Point(0, 0);
this.dataGridView1.Name = "dataGridView1";
this.dataGridView1.ReadOnly = true;
this.dataGridView1.Size = new System.Drawing.
    Size(547, 254);
this.dataGridView1.TabIndex = 0;
//
//EncryptionBTN
//
this.EncryptionBTN.AutoSize = true;
this.EncryptionBTN.Location = new System.
    Drawing.Point(358, 3);
this.EncryptionBTN.Name = "EncryptionBTN";
this.EncryptionBTN.Size = new System.Drawing.
    Size(100, 17);
this.EncryptionBTN.TabIndex = 6;
this.EncryptionBTN.TabStop = true;
this.EncryptionBTN.Text = "MLR-Encryption";
this.EncryptionBTN.UseVisualStyleBackColor
    = true;
//
//QueryForm
//
this.AutoScaleDimensions = new System.Drawing.
    SizeF(6F, 13F);
this.AutoScaleMode =
    System.Windows.Forms.AutoScaleMode.Font;
this.ClientSize = new System.Drawing.
    Size(547, 450);
this.Controls.Add(this.splitContainer1);
```

```
            this.Controls.Add(this.toolStrip1);
            this.FormBorderStyle = System.Windows.Forms.
                FormBorderStyle.Fixed3D;
            this.Name = "QueryForm";
            this.Text = "Query";
            this.toolStrip1.ResumeLayout(false);
            this.toolStrip1.PerformLayout();
            this.splitContainer1.Panel1.
                ResumeLayout(false);
            this.splitContainer1.Panel1.PerformLayout();
            this.splitContainer1.Panel2.
                ResumeLayout(false);
            this.splitContainer1.ResumeLayout(false);
            ((System.ComponentModel.ISupportInitialize)
                (this.dataGridView1)).EndInit();
            this.ResumeLayout(false);
            this.PerformLayout();
        }

        #endregion
        private System.Windows.Forms.RichTextBox
            richTextBox1;
        private System.Windows.Forms.ToolStrip
            toolStrip1;
        private System.Windows.Forms.ToolStripButton
            toolStripButton1;
        private System.Windows.Forms.SplitContainer
            splitContainer1;
        private System.Windows.Forms.DataGridView
            dataGridView1;
        private System.Windows.Forms.RadioButton
            SeaviewBTN;
        private System.Windows.Forms.RadioButton
            JSBTN;
        private System.Windows.Forms.RadioButton
            SmithBTN;
        private System.Windows.Forms.RadioButton
            MLRBTN;
        private System.Windows.Forms.RadioButton
            BCMLSBTN;
        private System.Windows.Forms.RadioButton
            EncryptionBTN;
    }
}
using System;
```

```csharp
using System.Collections.Generic;
using System.ComponentModel;
using System.Data;
using System.Drawing;
using System.Linq;
using System.Text;
using System.Windows.Forms;
using GlobalClasses;
using System.Data.SqlClient;
using System.Collections;
namespace MLS
{
public partial class QueryForm : Form
{
        public QueryForm()
        {
        InitializeComponent();
}

        private void richTextBox1_TextChanged(object
           sender, EventArgs e)
        {
}

        private void toolStripButton1_Click(object
           sender, EventArgs e)
        {
        try
        {
                DateTime dt = DateTime.Now;
                string SqlStr = "";
                if (richTextBox1.Text.ToUpper().
                   Contains("SELECT"))
                {
                string oldSTR = MLSDB.
                   DMLSTR(richTextBox1.Text).Trim().
                   ToUpper();
                string newSTR = ""; ;
                if (SeaviewBTN.Checked)
                {
                        newSTR =
                           "UserVisibleSeaView" +
                           MLSDB.DMLSTR(richTextBox1.
                           Text).Trim().ToUpper();
                }
                else if (JSBTN.Checked)
```

```
        {
                newSTR = "UserVisibleJS" +
                    MLSDB.DMLSTR(richTextBox1.
                    Text).Trim().ToUpper();
        }
        else if (SmithBTN.Checked)
        {
                newSTR = "UserVisibleSmith"
                    + MLSDB.
                    DMLSTR(richTextBox1.Text).
                    Trim().ToUpper();
        }
        else if (MLRBTN.Checked)
        {
                newSTR = "VW" + MLSDB.
                    DMLSTR(richTextBox1.
                    Text).Trim().ToUpper();
        }
        else if (EncryptionBTN.Checked)
        {
                newSTR = "[Vw" + MLSDB.
                    DMLSTR(richTextBox1.
                    Text).Trim().ToUpper()
                    + "-Encryption]";
        }
        if (BCMLSBTN.Checked)
        {
                newSTR = "VBC" + MLSDB.
                    DMLSTR(richTextBox1.
                    Text).Trim().ToUpper();
        }
        BindingSource bindingSource1 = new
            BindingSource();
        SqlStr = richTextBox1.Text.ToUpper().
            Replace(oldSTR, newSTR);
        if (EncryptionBTN.Checked)
        {
                SqlStr = "exec dbo.usp_
                    EnableCellVisibility;"
                    + SqlStr;
        }
        bindingSource1.DataSource =
            GlobalClasses.DBOperations.
            GetData(SqlStr).Tables 0];
```

```
dataGridView1.DataSource =
   bindingSource1;
}

else if (richTextBox1.Text.
   ToUpper().Contains("INSERT"))
{
string name = GlobalClasses.MLSDB.
   GetInsertValue(MLSDB.
   AttributeSTR(richTextBox1.Text))
   [0].ToString();
string Dept = GlobalClasses.MLSDB.
   GetInsertValue(MLSDB.
   AttributeSTR(richTextBox1.Text))
   [1].ToString();
string Salary = GlobalClasses.MLSDB.
   GetInsertValue(MLSDB.
   AttributeSTR(richTextBox1.Text))
   [2].ToString();
string Class = GlobalClasses.
   globals.UserLabelID.ToString();
string Label =
   GlobalClasses.globals.UserLabel;
if (SeaviewBTN.Checked)
{
        string D2Str = "insert into
           dbo.[D2-" + GlobalClasses.
           globals.UserLabel + "]
           values(" + name + "," +
           Class + "," + Dept + ","
           + Class + ")";
        string D3Str = "insert into
           dbo.[D3-" + GlobalClasses.
           globals.UserLabel + "]
           values(" + name + "," +
           Class + "," + Salary +
           "," + Class + ")";
        GlobalClasses.DBOperations.
           SetData(D2Str);
        GlobalClasses.DBOperations.
           SetData(D3Str);
}
else if (JSBTN.Checked)
{
        string DStr = "insert into
           dbo.[D" + GlobalClasses.
```

```
                    globals.UserLabel + "]
                    values(" + name + "," +
                    Class + "," + Dept + ","
                    + Class +"," + Salary +
                    "," + Class+ ")";
             GlobalClasses.DBOperations.
             SetData(DStr);
    }
    else if (SmithBTN.Checked)
    {
    string DStr = "insert into dbo.
       [Smith-Employee] values(" + name
       + "," + Class + "," + Dept + ","
       + Salary + "," + Class + ")";
             GlobalClasses.DBOperations.
             SetData(DStr);
    }
    if (MLRBTN.Checked)
    {
    string DStr = "insert into dbo.
       [Employee] values(" + name + ","
       + Class + "," + Dept + "," +
       Class + "," + Salary + "," +
       Class + "," + Class + ")";
             GlobalClasses.DBOperations.
             SetData(DStr);
    }
    if (EncryptionBTN.Checked)
    {
             string DStr = "exec dbo.
                usp _ EnableCellVisibility;
                insert into dbo.[Employee]
                values(ENCRYPTBYKEY(KEY _
                GUID('" + Label +
                "SymmetricKey'),'" + name
                + "')," +
                "ENCRYPTBYKEY(KEY _ GUID('"
                + Label +
                "SymmetricKey'),'" + Dept
                + "')," +
                "ENCRYPTBYKEY(KEY _ GUID('"
                + Label +
                "SymmetricKey'),'" +
                Salary + "')," + Class+
                ")";
```

```
                GlobalClasses.DBOperations.
                    SetData(DStr);
        }
        if (BCMLSBTN.Checked)
        {
                string BCClass = MLSDB.
                    GetBCLabelNumeric
                    (globals.UserLabel.
                    ToUpper()).ToString();
                string DStr = "insert into
                    dbo.[BCEmployee]
                    values(" + name + "," +
                    BCClass + "," + Dept +
                    "," + BCClass + "," +
                    Salary + "," + BCClass +
                    "," + BCClass + ",0)";
                GlobalClasses.DBOperations.
                    SetData(DStr);
        }
}

        else if (richTextBox1.Text.
            ToUpper().Contains("UPDATE"))
        {
        string SelectSTR = "";
        ArrayList AttributeARR
            = GlobalClasses.MLSDB.
            GetAttribute(MLSDB.
            AttributeSTR(richTextBox1.Text));
        string PredicateSTR = MLSDB.
            PredicateSTR(richTextBox1.Text);
        if (SeaviewBTN.Checked)
        {
                string select = "";
                string updatePredicate = "";
                string UpdateStr = "";
                if (PredicateSTR.Split
                    (' = ')[0].Trim().ToUpper()
                    = = "DEPARTMENT" ||
                    PredicateSTR.Split("in".
                    ToCharArray(),2)[0].Trim().
                    ToUpper() = =
                    "DEPARTMENT")
                {
```

```
            select = "select name from
                dbo.[D2-" + GlobalClasses.
                globals.UserLabel + "]
                where " + PredicateSTR;
        }

            else if (PredicateSTR.
                Split(' = ')[0].Trim().
                ToUpper() = = "SALARY" ||
                PredicateSTR.Split("in".
                ToCharArray(),2)[0].Trim().
                ToUpper() = = "SALARY")
            {
            select = "select name from
                dbo.[D3-" + GlobalClasses.
                globals.UserLabel + "]
                where " + PredicateSTR;
        }

            foreach (DataRow DR in
                GlobalClasses.
                DBOperations.
                GetData(select).
                Tables 0].Rows)
            {
            updatePredicate =
                updatePredicate +"'" +
                DR["name"].ToString() +
                "','";
        }

            updatePredicate
                = updatePredicate.
                Remove(updatePredicate.
                Length - 1);
            updatePredicate = "("+
                updatePredicate +")";
            foreach (string s in
                AttributeARR)
            {
            if (s.Split(' = ')[0].
                Trim().ToUpper() = =
                "DEPARTMENT")
            {
                UpdateStr = "Update dbo.
                    [D2-" +
                    GlobalClasses.
                    globals.UserLabel +
```

```
              "] set " + s + "
              where name in " +
              updatePredicate;
          }
        else if (s.Split(' = ')[0].
           Trim().ToUpper() = =
           "SALARY")
          {
            UpdateStr = "Update dbo.
              [D3-" +
              GlobalClasses.
              globals.UserLabel +
              "] set " + s + "
              where name in " +
              updatePredicate;
          }
        GlobalClasses.DBOperations.
           SetData(UpdateStr);
    }
}
if (JSBTN.Checked)
{
          string UpdateStr = "";
          UpdateStr = "Update dbo.
             [D" + GlobalClasses.
             globals.UserLabel + "]
             set " + MLSDB.
             AttributeSTR
             (richTextBox1.Text) + "
             where " + PredicateSTR;
          GlobalClasses.DBOperations.
             SetData(UpdateStr);
}
if (SmithBTN.Checked)
{
          string UpdateStr = "";
          if (MLSDB.PredicateSTR
             (richTextBox1.Text) = =
             "")
          {
          UpdateStr = "Update dbo.
             [Smith-Employee] set " +
             MLSDB.AttributeSTR
             (richTextBox1.Text) + "
             where TC = " +
```

```
                              GlobalClasses.globals.
                              UserLabelID.ToString();
        }
                      else
                      {
                      UpdateStr = "Update dbo.
                          [Smith-Employee] set " +
                          MLSDB.AttributeSTR
                          (richTextBox1.Text) + "
                          where " + PredicateSTR +
                          " and TC = " +
                          GlobalClasses.globals.
                          UserLabelID.ToString();
                      }
                      GlobalClasses.DBOperations.
                          SetData(UpdateStr);
        }
        else if (MLRBTN.Checked)
        {
                      if (MLSDB.PredicateSTR
                          (richTextBox1.Text) = =
                          "")
                      {
                      SqlStr = richTextBox1.Text
                          + " where TC = " +
                          GlobalClasses.globals.
                          UserLabelID.ToString();
                      SelectSTR = "Select * " + "
                          From VW" + MLSDB.DMLSTR
                          (richTextBox1.Text).
                          Trim() + " where TC <>
                          '" + GlobalClasses.
                          globals.UserLabel+"'";
                      }
                      else
                      {
                      SqlStr = richTextBox1.Text
                          + " and TC = " +
                          GlobalClasses.globals.
                          UserLabelID.ToString();
        SelectSTR = "Select * " + " From vw" + MLSDB.
            DMLSTR(richTextBox1.Text).Trim() + " where
            " + MLSDB.PredicateSTR(richTextBox1.Text) +
            " and TC <> '" + GlobalClasses.globals.
            UserLabel+"'";
```

```
}
            GlobalClasses.DBOperations.
               SetData(SqlStr);
            foreach (DataRow DR in
               GlobalClasses.
               DBOperations.
               GetData(SelectSTR).
               Tables 0].Rows)
            {
            foreach (string s in
               GlobalClasses.MLSDB.
               GetAttribute(MLSDB.
               AttributeSTR
               (richTextBox1.Text)))
            {

               DR.SetField(s.Split
                  (' = ')[0].Trim(),
                  s.Split(' = ')[1].
                  Trim());
               DR.SetField("C" +
                  s.Split(' = ')[0].
                  Trim(),
                  GlobalClasses.
                  globals.UserLabelID);
            }
            DR.SetField("TC",
               GlobalClasses.globals.
               UserLabelID);
            string ColumnSTR = "";
            string ColumnValuesSTR = "";
            foreach (DataColumn DC in
               DR.Table.Columns)
            {
               ColumnSTR + =
                  DC.ColumnName + ",";
            }
            ColumnSTR = ColumnSTR.
               Remove(ColumnSTR.Length
               - 1);
            foreach (object value in
               DR.ItemArray)
            {
               if (value is string)
               {
```

```
        if (!value.ToString().
          Contains("'"))
        {
          ColumnValuesSTR + =
            "'" + value.
            ToString() + "',";
        }
        else
        {
          ColumnValuesSTR + =
            value.ToString() +
            ",";
        }
      }
        else
        {
        ColumnValuesSTR + =
          value.ToString() +
          ",";
      }
    }
ColumnValuesSTR =
    ColumnValuesSTR.
    Remove(ColumnValuesSTR.
    Length - 1);
string InsertSTR = "insert
    into " + MLSDB.
    DMLSTR(richTextBox1.
    Text).Trim() + "(" +
    ColumnSTR + ") values ("
    + ColumnValuesSTR + ")";
GlobalClasses.DBOperations.
    SetData(InsertSTR);
  }
  }

        else if (EncryptionBTN.
          Checked)
    {

        string Predicate = MLSDB.
          PredicateSTR
          (richTextBox1.Text);
        if (Predicate = = "")
        {
        SqlStr = richTextBox1.Text
          + " where TC = " +
```

```
            GlobalClasses.globals.
            UserLabelID.ToString();
        SelectSTR = "exec dbo.
            usp_EnableCellVisibility;
            Select * " + " From [VW"
            + MLSDB.
            DMLSTR(richTextBox1.
            Text).Trim() +
            "-Encryption] where TC
            <> " + GlobalClasses.
            globals.UserLabelID;
}

        else
        {
        string newPredicate = "
            CONVERT(nvarchar
            (MAX), DecryptByKey
            ("+Predicate.
            Split("in".
            ToCharArray(), 2)[0].
            Trim()+")) ";
        SqlStr = "exec dbo.usp_
            EnableCellVisibility;" +
            richTextBox1.Text.
            Replace(Predicate.
            Split("in".
            ToCharArray(), 2)[0].
            Trim(), newPredicate) +
            " and TC = " +
            GlobalClasses.globals.
            UserLabelID.ToString();
        SqlStr = SqlStr.
            Replace(MLSDB.
            DMLSTR(richTextBox1.
            Text).Trim(), "dbo.
            ["+MLSDB.
            DMLSTR(richTextBox1.
            Text).Trim() +
            "-Encryption]");
        //+ MLSDB.GetAttribute
            (MLSDB.AttributeSTR
            (richTextBox1.Text))[0].
            ToString()
        SelectSTR = "exec dbo.
            usp_
```

```
            EnableCellVisibility;
            Select * " + " From [VW"
            + MLSDB.
            DMLSTR(richTextBox1.
            Text).Trim() +
            "-Encryption] where " +
            MLSDB.PredicateSTR
            (richTextBox1.Text) + "
            and TC <> " +
            GlobalClasses.globals.
            UserLabelID;
    }

    GlobalClasses.DBOperations.
        SetData(SqlStr);
    foreach (DataRow DR in
        GlobalClasses.
        DBOperations.
        GetData(SelectSTR).
        Tables 0].Rows)
    {
    foreach (string s in
        GlobalClasses.MLSDB.
        GetAttribute(MLSDB.
        AttributeSTR
        (richTextBox1.Text)))
    {
        DR.SetField(s.Split(' =
            ')[0].Trim(),
            s.Split(' = ')[1].
            Trim());
    }
    DR.SetField("TC",
        GlobalClasses.globals.
        UserLabelID);
    string ColumnSTR = "";
    string ColumnValuesSTR =
        "";
    foreach (DataColumn DC in
        DR.Table.Columns)
    {
        ColumnSTR + =
            DC.ColumnName + ",";
    }
```

```
ColumnSTR = ColumnSTR.
   Remove(ColumnSTR.Length
   - 1);
foreach (object value in
   DR.ItemArray)
{
   if (value is string)
   {
   if (!value.ToString().
      Contains("'"))
   {
     ColumnValuesSTR + =
        "ENCRYPTBYKEY(KEY_
        GUID('" + globals.
        UserLabel +
        "SymmetricKey'),'"
        + value.ToString()
        + "'),";
   }
   else
   {
     ColumnValuesSTR + =
        "ENCRYPTBYKEY(KEY_
        GUID('" + globals.
        UserLabel +
        "SymmetricKey')," +
        value.ToString() +
        "),";
   }
}
   else
   {
   ColumnValuesSTR + =
      value.ToString() +
      ",";
}
}
ColumnValuesSTR =
   ColumnValuesSTR.Remove
   (ColumnValuesSTR.Length
   - 1);
string InsertSTR = "exec
   dbo.usp_
   EnableCellVisibility;
   insert into [" + MLSDB.
```

```
                        DMLSTR(richTextBox1.
                        Text).Trim() +
                        "-Encryption]("  +
                        ColumnSTR + ") values
                        (" + ColumnValuesSTR +
                        ")";
                    GlobalClasses.DBOperations.
                        SetData(InsertSTR);
        }
        }
        else if (BCMLSBTN.Checked)
        {
                    int TC = 0;
                    if (MLSDB.PredicateSTR
                        (richTextBox1.Text) = =
                        "")
                    {
                    SelectSTR = "Select * From
                        BC" + MLSDB.DMLSTR
                        (richTextBox1.Text).
                        Trim();
        }

                    else
                    {
                    SelectSTR = "Select * From
                        BC" + MLSDB.DMLSTR
                        (richTextBox1.Text).
                        Trim() + " where " +
                        MLSDB.PredicateSTR
                        (richTextBox1.Text);
        }

                    foreach (DataRow DR in
                        GlobalClasses.
                        DBOperations.
                        GetData(SelectSTR).
                        Tables 0].Rows)
                    {
                    TC = Convert.
                        ToInt32(DR[6]);
                    if (MLSDB.
                        GetBCprimarylevel(TC) =
                        = globals.UserLabel)
                    {
```

```
                GlobalClasses.
                    DBOperations.SetData
                    (richTextBox1.Text);
                }
        }
        }
}
        else if (richTextBox1.Text.
            ToUpper().Contains("UPLEVEL"))
        {
        string Query = richTextBox1.Text.
            Replace("\n", " ");
        string name = "";
        string Cname = "";
        string Dept = "";
        string CDept = "";
        string Salary = "";
        string CSalary = "";
        int TC = globals.UserLabelID;
        string SelectSTR = "";
        foreach (string s in GlobalClasses.
            MLSDB.GetAttribute(MLSDB.
            AttributeSTR(Query)))
        {
                string[] stringSeparators
                    = new string[]
                    {"FROM"};
                string Coulmn =
                    s.ToUpper().
                    Split(stringSeparators,
                    StringSplitOptions.
                    RemoveEmptyEntries)[0].
                    Trim().ToUpper();
                string CoulmnClass =
                    s.ToUpper().
                    Split(stringSeparators,
                    StringSplitOptions.
                    RemoveEmptyEntries)[1].
                    Trim().ToUpper();
                if (Coulmn = =
                    "DEPARTMENT")
                {
                SelectSTR = "Select
                    Name,CName,Department,
                    CDept from " + MLSDB.
```

```
                DMLSTR(Query).Trim() + "
                where " + MLSDB.
                PredicateSTR(Query) + "
                and TC = " + MLSDB.
                GetLabelID(CoulmnClass);
            DataRow DR = GlobalClasses.
                DBOperations.GetData
                (SelectSTR).Tables 0].
                Rows[0];
            name = DR.ItemArray[0].
                ToString();
            Cname = DR.ItemArray[1].
                ToString();
            Dept = DR.ItemArray[2].
                ToString();
            CDept = DR.ItemArray[3].
                ToString();
        }

            else if (Coulmn = =
                "SALARY")
            {
            SelectSTR = "Select
                Name,CName,SALARY,
                CSALARY from " + MLSDB.
                DMLSTR(Query).Trim() + "
                where " + MLSDB.
                PredicateSTR(Query) + "
                and TC = " + MLSDB.
                GetLabelID(CoulmnClass);
            DataRow DR = GlobalClasses.
                DBOperations.GetData
                (SelectSTR).Tables 0].
                Rows[0];
            name = DR.ItemArray[0].
                ToString();
            Cname = DR.ItemArray[1].
                ToString();
            Salary = DR.ItemArray[2].
                ToString();
            CSalary = DR.ItemArray[3].
                ToString();
        }
        }
        string DStr = "insert into " +
            MLSDB.DMLSTR(Query).Trim() + "
```

```
        values('" + name + "','" + Cname +
        ",'" + Dept + "','" + CDept + "," +
        + Salary + "," + CSalary + "," +
        TC.ToString() + ")";
    GlobalClasses.DBOperations.
        SetData(DStr);
}

    else if (richTextBox1.Text.
        ToUpper().Contains("VERIFY"))
    {
    string Query = richTextBox1.Text.
        Replace("\n", " ");
    string SelectSTR = "select * from BC"
        + MLSDB.DMLSTR(richTextBox1.Text).
        Trim().ToUpper() + " where " +
        MLSDB.PredicateSTR(richTextBox1.
        Text);
    DataRow DR = GlobalClasses.
        DBOperations.GetData(SelectSTR).
        Tables 0].Rows[0];
    string xkey = DR.ItemArray[0].
        ToString();
    int xlbOl = Convert.ToInt32(DR.
        ItemArray[1].ToString());
    int xtc = Convert.ToInt32(DR.
        ItemArray[6].ToString());
    int newLabel = MLSDB.
        VerifyBCUserbelief(xtc, Convert.
        ToBoolean(MLSDB.
        AttributeSTR(richTextBox1.Text)));
    string UpdateSTR = "Update BC" +
        MLSDB.DMLSTR(richTextBox1.Text).
        Trim() + " set CName = " +
        newLabel.ToString() + ", CDept =
        " + newLabel.ToString() + ",
        CSalary = " + newLabel.ToString()
        + ", TC = " + newLabel.ToString()
        + ", flag = " + newLabel.
        ToString() + " where " + MLSDB.
        PredicateSTR(richTextBox1.Text) +
        " and TC = " + xtc.ToString();
    GlobalClasses.DBOperations.
        SetData(UpdateSTR);
}
```

```
else if (richTextBox1.Text.
   ToUpper().Contains("DELETE"))
{
if (SeaviewBTN.Checked)
{
        string D2Str = "Delete From
           dbo.[D2-" +
           GlobalClasses.globals.
           UserLabel + "] where " +
           MLSDB.PredicateSTR
           (richTextBox1.Text);
        string D3Str = "Delete From
           dbo.[D3-" +
           GlobalClasses.globals.
           UserLabel + "] where " +
           MLSDB.PredicateSTR
           (richTextBox1.Text);
        GlobalClasses.DBOperations.
           SetData(D2Str);
        GlobalClasses.DBOperations.
           SetData(D3Str);
}
else if (JSBTN.Checked)
{
        string DStr = "Delete From
           dbo.[D" + GlobalClasses.
           globals.UserLabel + "]
           where " + MLSDB.
           PredicateSTR
           (richTextBox1.Text);
        GlobalClasses.DBOperations.
           SetData(DStr);
}
else if (SmithBTN.Checked)
{
        string DStr = "Delete From
           dbo.[Smith-Employee]
           where " + MLSDB.
           PredicateSTR
           (richTextBox1.Text) + "
           and TC = " +
           GlobalClasses.globals.
           UserLabelID;
        GlobalClasses.DBOperations.
           SetData(DStr);
```

```csharp
}
else if (MLRBTN.Checked)
{
        string DStr = "Delete From
            " + MLSDB.
            DMLSTR(richTextBox1.
            Text).Trim() + " where "
            + MLSDB.PredicateSTR
            (richTextBox1.Text) + "
            and TC = " +
            GlobalClasses.globals.
            UserLabelID;
        GlobalClasses.DBOperations.
            SetData(DStr);
}
else if (EncryptionBTN.Checked)
{
        string DStr = "Delete From
            [" + MLSDB.DMLSTR
            (richTextBox1.Text).
            Trim() + "-Encryption]
            where " + MLSDB.
            PredicateSTR
            (richTextBox1.Text) + "
            and TC = " +
            GlobalClasses.globals.
            UserLabelID;
        GlobalClasses.DBOperations.
            SetData(DStr);
}
else if (BCMLSBTN.Checked)
{
        string SelectSTR = "select
            * from BC" + MLSDB.
            DMLSTR(richTextBox1.
            Text).Trim().ToUpper() +
            " where " + MLSDB.
            PredicateSTR
            (richTextBox1.Text);
        DataRow DR = GlobalClasses.
            DBOperations.GetData
            (SelectSTR).Tables 0].
            Rows[0];
```

```
                    string xkey =
                       DR.ItemArray[0].
                       ToString();
                    int xlbOl = Convert.
                       ToInt32(DR.ItemArray[1].
                       ToString());
                    int xtc = Convert.
                       ToInt32(DR.ItemArray[6].
                       ToString());
                    if (MLSDB.
                       GetBCSecondarylevel(xtc)
                       = = "")
                    {
                    string DStr = "Delete From
                       BC" + MLSDB.DMLSTR
                       (richTextBox1.Text).
                       Trim() + " where " +
                       MLSDB.PredicateSTR
                       (richTextBox1.Text) + "
                       and TC = " + xtc.
                       ToString();
                    GlobalClasses.DBOperations.
                       SetData(DStr);
          }
                    else
                    {
                    int newLabel = MLSDB.
                       UnverifyBCUserbelief
                       (xtc);
                    string UpdateSTR = "Update
                       BC" + MLSDB.DMLSTR
                       (richTextBox1.Text).
                       Trim() + " set CName = "
                       + newLabel.ToString() +
                       ", CDept = " + newLabel.
                       ToString() + ", CSalary
                       = " + newLabel.
                       ToString() + ", TC = " +
                       newLabel.ToString() + ",
                       flag = " + newLabel.
                       ToString() + " where " +
                       MLSDB.PredicateSTR
                       (richTextBox1.Text) + "
                       and TC = " + xtc.
                       ToString();
```

```
                      GlobalClasses.DBOperations.
                          SetData(UpdateSTR);
                }
                }
        }
                MessageBox.Show(DateTime.Now.
                    Subtract(dt).ToString());
        }
        catch (Exception EX)
        {
                MessageBox.Show(EX.Message);
        }
}
private void toolStrip1_ItemClicked(object sender,
    ToolStripItemClickedEventArgs e)
        {
}
}
}
```

9.4.5 *Source Code of the Concurrency Control Form*

```
namespace MLS
{
partial class QueryForm
{
///<summary>
///Required designer variable.
///</summary>
        private System.ComponentModel.IContainer
            components = null;
///<summary>
///Clean up any resources being used.
///</summary>
///<param name = "disposing">true if managed resources
    should be disposed; otherwise, false.</param>
        protected override void Dispose(bool
            disposing)
        {
        if (disposing && (components ! = null))
        {
                components.Dispose();
        }
        base.Dispose(disposing);
}
```

```
        #region Windows Form Designer generated code
///<summary>
///Required method for Designer support - do not
   modify
///the contents of this method with the code editor.
///</summary>
        private void InitializeComponent()
        {
        System.ComponentModel.ComponentResourceManager
            resources = new System.ComponentModel.
            ComponentResourceManager
            (typeof(QueryForm));
        this.richTextBox1 = new System.Windows.Forms.
            RichTextBox();
        this.toolStrip1 = new System.Windows.Forms.
            ToolStrip();
        this.toolStripButton1 = new System.Windows.
            Forms.ToolStripButton();
        this.splitContainer1 = new System.Windows.
            Forms.SplitContainer();
        this.radioButton1 = new System.Windows.Forms.
            RadioButton();
        this.SeaviewBTN = new System.Windows.Forms.
            RadioButton();
        this.dataGridView1 = new System.Windows.Forms.
            DataGridView();
        this.toolStrip1.SuspendLayout();
        this.splitContainer1.Panel1.SuspendLayout();
        this.splitContainer1.Panel2.SuspendLayout();
        this.splitContainer1.SuspendLayout();
        ((System.ComponentModel.ISupportInitialize)
            (this.dataGridView1)).BeginInit();
        this.SuspendLayout();
        //
        //richTextBox1
        //
        this.richTextBox1.Dock = System.Windows.Forms.
            DockStyle.Bottom;
        this.richTextBox1.Location = new System.
            Drawing.Point(0, 26);
        this.richTextBox1.Name = "richTextBox1";
        this.richTextBox1.Size = new System.Drawing.
            Size(547, 141);
        this.richTextBox1.TabIndex = 0;
        this.richTextBox1.Text = "";
```

```
this.richTextBox1.TextChanged + = new System.
   EventHandler(this.richTextBox1_
   TextChanged);
//
//toolStrip1
//
this.toolStrip1.BackColor = System.Drawing.
   SystemColors.Control;
this.toolStrip1.Items.AddRange(new System.
   Windows.Forms.ToolStripItem[] {
this.toolStripButton1});
this.toolStrip1.Location = new System.Drawing.
   Point(0, 0);
this.toolStrip1.Name = "toolStrip1";
this.toolStrip1.Size = new System.Drawing.
   Size(547, 25);
this.toolStrip1.TabIndex = 1;
this.toolStrip1.Text = "toolStrip1";
this.toolStrip1.ItemClicked + = new System.
   Windows.Forms.ToolStripItemClickedEventHand
   ler(this.toolStrip1_ItemClicked);
//
//toolStripButton1
//
this.toolStripButton1.Image = ((System.
   Drawing.Image)(resources.
   GetObject("toolStripButton1.Image")));
this.toolStripButton1.ImageTransparentColor =
   System.Drawing.Color.Magenta;
this.toolStripButton1.Name =
   "toolStripButton1";
this.toolStripButton1.Size = new System.
   Drawing.Size(67, 22);
this.toolStripButton1.Text = "Execute";
this.toolStripButton1.Click + = new System.
   EventHandler(this.toolStripButton1_Click);
//
//splitContainer1
//
this.splitContainer1.Dock = System.Windows.
   Forms.DockStyle.Fill;
this.splitContainer1.Location = new System.
   Drawing.Point(0, 25);
this.splitContainer1.Name = "splitContainer1";
```

```
this.splitContainer1.Orientation = System.
   Windows.Forms.Orientation.Horizontal;
//
//splitContainer1.Panel1
//
this.splitContainer1.Panel1.Controls.Add(this.
   radioButton1);
this.splitContainer1.Panel1.Controls.Add(this.
   SeaviewBTN);
this.splitContainer1.Panel1.Controls.Add(this.
   richTextBox1);
//
//splitContainer1.Panel2
//
this.splitContainer1.Panel2.Controls.Add(this.
   dataGridView1);
this.splitContainer1.Size = new System.
   Drawing.Size(547, 425);
this.splitContainer1.SplitterDistance = 167;
this.splitContainer1.TabIndex = 2;
//
//radioButton1
//
this.radioButton1.AutoSize = true;
this.radioButton1.Location = new System.
   Drawing.Point(302, 3);
this.radioButton1.Name = "radioButton1";
this.radioButton1.Size = new System.Drawing.
   Size(70, 17);
this.radioButton1.TabIndex = 2;
this.radioButton1.TabStop = true;
this.radioButton1.Text = "Proposed";
this.radioButton1.UseVisualStyleBackColor =
   true;
//
//SeaviewBTN
//
this.SeaviewBTN.AutoSize = true;
this.SeaviewBTN.Location = new System.Drawing.
   Point(168, 3);
this.SeaviewBTN.Name = "SeaviewBTN";
this.SeaviewBTN.Size = new System.Drawing.
   Size(73, 17);
this.SeaviewBTN.TabIndex = 1;
this.SeaviewBTN.TabStop = true;
```

```
this.SeaviewBTN.Text = "Rajwinder";
this.SeaviewBTN.UseVisualStyleBackColor =
    true;
//
//dataGridView1
//
this.dataGridView1.AllowUserToAddRows = false;
this.dataGridView1.AllowUserToDeleteRows =
    false;
this.dataGridView1.ColumnHeadersHeightSizeMode
    = System.Windows.Forms.
    DataGridViewColumnHeadersHeightSizeMode.
    AutoSize;
this.dataGridView1.Dock = System.Windows.
    Forms.DockStyle.Fill;
this.dataGridView1.Location = new System.
    Drawing.Point(0, 0);
this.dataGridView1.Name = "dataGridView1";
this.dataGridView1.ReadOnly = true;
this.dataGridView1.Size = new System.Drawing.
    Size(547, 254);
this.dataGridView1.TabIndex = 0;
//
//QueryForm
//
this.AutoScaleDimensions = new System.Drawing.
    SizeF(6F, 13F);
this.AutoScaleMode = System.Windows.Forms.
    AutoScaleMode.Font;
this.ClientSize = new System.Drawing.Size(547,
    450);
this.Controls.Add(this.splitContainer1);
this.Controls.Add(this.toolStrip1);
this.FormBorderStyle = System.Windows.Forms.
    FormBorderStyle.Fixed3D;
this.Name = "QueryForm";
this.Text = "Query";
this.toolStrip1.ResumeLayout(false);
this.toolStrip1.PerformLayout();
this.splitContainer1.Panel1.
    ResumeLayout(false);
this.splitContainer1.Panel1.PerformLayout();
this.splitContainer1.Panel2.
    ResumeLayout(false);
this.splitContainer1.ResumeLayout(false);
```

```
        ((System.ComponentModel.ISupportInitialize)
            (this.dataGridView1)).EndInit();
        this.ResumeLayout(false);
        this.PerformLayout();
}

        #endregion
        private System.Windows.Forms.RichTextBox
            richTextBox1;
        private System.Windows.Forms.ToolStrip
            toolStrip1;
        private System.Windows.Forms.ToolStripButton
            toolStripButton1;
        private System.Windows.Forms.SplitContainer
            splitContainer1;
        private System.Windows.Forms.DataGridView
            dataGridView1;
        private System.Windows.Forms.RadioButton
            SeaviewBTN;
        private System.Windows.Forms.RadioButton
            radioButton1;
}
}
using System;
using System.Collections.Generic;
using System.ComponentModel;
using System.Data;
using System.Drawing;
using System.Linq;
using System.Text;
using System.Windows.Forms;
using GlobalClasses;
using System.Data.SqlClient;
using System.Collections;
namespace MLS
{
public partial class QueryForm : Form
{
        public QueryForm()
        {
        InitializeComponent();
}
        private void richTextBox1_TextChanged(object
            sender, EventArgs e)
        {
}
```

```csharp
private void toolStrip1_ItemClicked(object
    sender, ToolStripItemClickedEventArgs e)
{
}

private void toolStripButton1_Click(object
    sender, EventArgs e)
{
if (radioButton1.Checked)
{
        SqlConnection HighConnection = new
            SqlConnection("Data Source =.;
            Initial Catalog =
            ConcurrenCycontrol;Integrated
            Security = SSPI ");
        HighConnection.Open();
        SqlCommand HighCommand =
            HighConnection.CreateCommand();
        SqlTransaction LowTrans;
        SqlTransaction HighTrans;
//Start a local transaction
        DateTime datepefor = DateTime.Now;
        HighTrans = HighConnection.
            BeginTransaction();
        HighCommand.Connection =
            HighConnection;
        HighCommand.Transaction = HighTrans;
        HighCommand.CommandText = "select *
            from MLS where tc = 'Low'";
        HighCommand.ExecuteNonQuery();
        int counter = int.
            Parse(richTextBox1.Text);
        SqlConnection LowConnection = new
            SqlConnection("Data Source =.;
            Initial Catalog =
            ConcurrenCycontrol;Integrated
            Security = SSPI ");
        LowConnection.Open();
        SqlCommand LowCommand =
            LowConnection.CreateCommand();
        DateTime datepefor1 = DateTime.Now;
        LowTrans = LowConnection.
            BeginTransaction();
        LowCommand.Connection =
            LowConnection;
        LowCommand.Transaction = LowTrans;
```

```
                for (int i = 1; i < = counter; i++)
                {
                LowCommand.CommandText = "update MLS
                    set Salary = Salary where tc =
                    'Low'";
                LowCommand.ExecuteNonQuery();
        }

                LowTrans.Commit();
                string datelow = DateTime.Now.
                    Subtract(datepefor1).ToString();
                HighTrans.Commit();
                MessageBox.Show(DateTime.Now.
                    Subtract(datepefor).ToString() +
                    " low " + datelow);
        }
        else
        {

                SqlConnection HighConnection = new
                    SqlConnection("Data Source =.;
                    Initial Catalog =
                    ConcurrenCycontrol;Integrated
                    Security = SSPI ");
                HighConnection.Open();
                SqlCommand HighCommand =
                    HighConnection.CreateCommand();
                SqlTransaction LowTrans;
                SqlTransaction HighTrans;
//Start a local transaction
                DateTime datepefor = DateTime.Now;
                HighTrans = HighConnection.
                    BeginTransaction();
                HighCommand.Connection =
                    HighConnection;
                HighCommand.Transaction = HighTrans;
                HighCommand.CommandText = "select
                    top 300 * from MLS where tc =
                    'Low'";
                HighCommand.ExecuteNonQuery();
                int counter = int.
                    Parse(richTextBox1.Text);
                SqlConnection LowConnection = new
                    SqlConnection("Data Source =.;
                    Initial Catalog =
                    ConcurrenCycontrol;Integrated
                    Security = SSPI ");
```

```
LowConnection.Open();
SqlCommand LowCommand =
    LowConnection.CreateCommand();
LowTrans = LowConnection.
    BeginTransaction();
LowCommand.Connection =
    LowConnection;
LowCommand.Transaction = LowTrans;
LowCommand.CommandText = "update MLS
    set Salary = Salary where tc =
    'Low' and Name not in (select top
    300 Name from MLS)";
LowCommand.ExecuteNonQuery();
for (int i = 1; i < = counter; i++)
{
LowCommand.CommandText = "update MLS
    set Salary = Salary where tc =
    'Low' and Name in (select top 300
    Name from MLS)";
LowCommand.ExecuteNonQuery();
}

LowTrans.Commit();
HighTrans.Commit();
MessageBox.Show(DateTime.Now.
    Subtract(datepefor).ToString());
}
}
}}
```

References

1. Hao-Wei He. History of relational database. Available at http://www. studymode.com/essays/History-Of-Relational-Database-517921.html (last visit 2013).
2. Edgar Frank Codd. 1970. A relational model of data for large shared data banks. *Communications of the ACM* 13 (6): 377–387.
3. Gautam Bhargava and Shashi K. Gadia. 1993. Relational database systems with zero information loss. *IEEE Transactions on Knowledge and Data Engineering* 5 (1): 76–87.
4. Joseph M. Hellerstein, Michael Stonebraker, and James Hamilton. 2007. Architecture of a database system. *Foundations and Trends in Databases* 1 (2): 141–259.
5. Ramez Elmasri and Shamkant B. Navathe. 2010. *Fundamentals of database systems,* 6th ed. Boston: Addison–Wesley.
6. Elisa Bertino and Ravi Sandhu. 2005. Database security—Concepts, approaches, and challenges. *IEEE Transactions on Dependable and Secure Computing* 2 (1): 2–19.
7. Sohail Imran and Irfan Hyder. 2009. Security issues in databases. *Proceedings of Second International Conference on Future Information Technology and Management Engineering,* 541–545.
8. Pierangela Samarati and Sabrina De Capitani di Vimercati. 2001. Access control: Policies, models, and mechanisms. In *Foundations of security analysis and design.* Berlin: Springer, 137–196.
9. Ravi S. Sandhu. 1994. Relational database access controls. In *Handbook of information security management.* Boca Raton, FL: Auerbach Publishers, 145–160.

10. Ji-Won Byun and Ninghui Li. 2008. Purpose based access control for privacy protection in relational database systems. *Journal of VLDB* 17 (4): 603–619.

11. Cristi Garvey and Amy Wu. ASD—Views. 1988. *Proceedings of the IEEE Conference on Security and Privacy,* 85–95.

12. Zhu Hong and Feng Yu-Cai. 2001. Study on mandatory access control in a secure database management system. *Journal of Shanghai University* 5 (4): 299–307.

13. Mario Pranjic, KreSimir Fertalj, and Nenad Jukic. 2002. Importance of semantics in MLS database models. *Proceedings of 24th International Conference on Information Technology Interfaces,* 51–56.

14. Hasan M. Jamil and Gillian Dobbie. 2004. On logical foundations of multilevel secure databases. *Journal of Intelligent Information System*s 23 (3): 271–294.

15. Luigi Giuri and Pietro lglio. 1996. A role-based secure database design tool. *Proceedings of the 12th Annual Computer Security Applications Conference,* 203–212.

16. Li-xin Xu, Dong Sun, and Dan Liu. 2010. Study on methods for data confidentiality and data integrity in relational databases. *Proceedings of the 3rd IEEE International Conference on Computer Science and Information Technology* (ICCSIT), 292–295.

17. Walid Rjaibi and Paul Bird. 2004. A multi-purpose implementation of mandatory access control in relational database management systems. *Proceedings of the 30th VLDB Conference,* Toronto, Canada, 1010–1020.

18. Indrakshi Ray and Wei Huang. 2005. Event detection in multilevel secure active databases. *Proceedings of the International Conference* ICISS 2005, 177–190.

19. Ravi S. Sandhu and Sushil Jajodia. 1992. Polyinstantiation for cover stories. *Proceedings of Second European Symposium on Research in Computer Security,* Toulouse, France, 307–328.

20. Sushil Jajodia, Ravi S. Sandhu, and Barbara T. Blaustein. 1995. *Solutions to the polyinstantiation problem, in information security. An integrated collection of essays,* ed. M. Abrams, IEEE Computer Society Press, 493–529.

21. Doug Nelson and Chip Paradise. 1991. Using polyinstantiation to develop an MLS application. *Proceedings of the Seventh Annual Computer Security Applications Conference,* 12–22.

22. Mikko T. Siponen. 2002. Database security and the problem of polyinstantiation: A moral scrutiny. *Australasian Journal of Information Systems* 10 (1): 41–49.

23. Andro Galinovi and Vlatka Anton. 2007. Polyinstantiation in relational databases with multilevel security. *Proceedings of the ITI 2007 29th International Conference on Information Technology Interfaces,* 128–132.

24. Mark Heckman and William R. Shockley. 1990. The SeaView security model. *IEEE Transactions on Software Engineering* 16 (6): 593–607.

25. Sushil Jajodia and Ravi S. Sandhu. 1991. A novel decomposition of multilevel relations into single-level relations. *IEEE Symposium on Security and Privacy,* Oakland, California, 300–313.

26. Sushil Jajodia and Ravi Sandhu. 1991. Toward a multilevel secure relational data model. *Proceedings of ACM SIGMOD International Conference on Management Data,* Denver, Colorado, 50–59.

27. Joachim Biskup and Lena Wiese. 2009. Combining consistency and confidentiality requirements in first-order databases. *Proceedings of International Conference ISC* 2009, 121–134.

28. Ravi Sandhu and Fang Chen. 1998. The multilevel relational (MLR) data model. *ACM Transactions on Information and System Security* 1 (1): 93–132.

29. Nenad Jukic, Susan V. Vrbsky, Allen Parrish, Brandon Dixon, and Boris Jukic. A belief-consistent multilevel secure relational data model. *Information Systems* 24 (5): 377–402.

30. Teresa F. Lunt, Roger R. Schell, William R. Shockley, Mark Heckman, and Dan Warren. 1988. A near-term design for the SeaView multilevel database system. *Proceedings of the IEEE Symposium on Security and Privacy,* 234–244.

31. Frederic Cuppens and Kioumars Yazdanian. 1992. A natural decomposition of multi-level relations. *Proceedings of the IEEE Symposium on Security and Privacy,* 273–284.

32. Keith F. Brewster. 1996. Trusted database management system interpretation of the trusted computer system evaluation criteria. National Computer Security Center, NCSC technical report-005, 3 (5): 1–57.

33. Ravi Sandhu and Fang Chen. 1995. The semantics and expressive power of the MLR data model. *Proceedings of IEEE Conference on Security and Privacy,* Oakland, CA, 128–142.

34. Mario Pranjic, Nenad Jukic, and Krcsimir Fertalj. 2003. Implementing belief-consistent multilevel secure relational data model: Issues and solutions. *Proceedings of 25th International Conference Information Technology Interfaces* IT1, 149–154.

35. Nenad A. Jukic and Susan V. Vrbsky. 1997. Asserting beliefs in MLS relational models. *Proceedings of SIGMOD Record* 26 (3): 30–35.

36. B. Schneier. 1996. *Applied cryptography,* 2nd ed. New York: John Wiley & Sons.

37. L. Kocarev. 2001. Chaos-based cryptography: A brief overview. *IEEE Circulation Systems Magazine* 1 (3): 6–21.

38. D. Stinson. 2002. *Cryptography: Theory and practice,* 2nd ed. Boca Raton, FL: Chapman & Hall.

39. Y. Mao, G. Chen, and S. Lian. 2004. A novel fast image encryption scheme based on 3D chaotic Baker maps. *International Journal of Bifurcation and Chaos* 14 (10): 3613–3624.

40. S. Li. 2003. Analyses and new designs of digital chaotic ciphers. PhD thesis, School of Electronics & Information Engineering, Xi'an Jiaotong University, Xi'an, China.

41. National Bureau of Standards. 1980. Data encryption standard modes of operation, federal information processing standards publication 81. U.S. Government Printing Office, Washington, DC.

42. S. Li, G. Chen, and X. Zheng. 2004. Chaos-based encryption for digital images and videos. In *Multimedia security handbook,* chap. 4. Boca Raton, FL: CRC Press.

43. Y. Mao and M. Wu. 2006. A joint signal processing and cryptographic approach to multimedia encryption. *IEEE Transactions on Image Processing* 15 (7): 2061–2075.

44. Y. Mao. 2003. Research on chaos-based image encryption and watermarking technology. PhD thesis, Department of Automation, Nanjing University of Science & Technology, Nanjing, China.

45. J. Daemen and V. Rijmen. 1999. AES proposal: Rijndael. AES algorithm submission.

46. R. Kusters and M. Tuengerthal. 2009. Universally composable symmetric encryption, *2nd IEEE Computer Security Foundations Symposium* (CSF '09), 293–307.

47. H. Jin, Z. Liao, D. Zou, and C. Li. 2008. Asymmetrical encryption based automated trust negotiation model. *2nd IEEE International Conference on Digital Ecosystems and Technologies* (DEST 2008), 363–368.

48. S. G. Lian, J. Sun, and Z. Wang. 2004. A novel image encryption scheme based on JPEG encoding. *Proceedings of 8th International Conference on Information Visualization,* 217–220.

49. M. V. Droogenbroeck and R. Benedett. 2002. Techniques for a selective encryption of uncompressed and compressed images. *Proceedings of Advanced Concepts for Intelligent Vision Systems* (ACIVS), Ghent, Belgium, 90–97, September 9–11.

50. F. Dachselt, K. Kelber, and W. Schwarz. 1997. Chaotic coding and cryptoanalysis. *Proceedings of IEEE International Symposium on Circuits and Systems,* Hong Kong, 1061–1064, June 9–12.

51. S. Li and X. Zheng. 2002. Cryptanalysis of a chaotic image encryption method. *Proceedings of IEEE International Symposium on Circuits and Systems* (ISCAS) 2:708–711.

52. J. Wei, X. Liao, K. W. Wong, and T. Zhou. 2005. Cryptanalysis of cryptosystem using multiple one-dimensional chaotic maps. *Communications in Nonlinear Science and Numerical Simulation* 12: 814–822.

53. L. Kocarev and G. Jakimoski. 2001. Logistic map as a block encryption algorithm. *Physics Letters A* 289 (4–5): 199–206.

54. T. Xiang, X. Liao, G. Tang, Y. Chen, and K. W. Wong. 2006. A novel block cryptosystem based on iterating a chaotic map. *Physics Letters A* 349 (1–4): 109–115.

55. S. Contini, R. L. Rivest, M. J. B. Robshaw, and Y. L. Yin. 1998. The security of the RC6TM block cipher. RSA Laboratories, M. I. T. Laboratory for Computer Science, version 1.0.

56. M. Salleh, S. Ibrahim, and I. F. Isnin. 2003. Enhanced chaotic image encryption algorithm based on Baker's map. *Proceedings of 2003 International Symposium on Circuits and Systems* (ISCAS '03), 2: 508–511.

57. D. Chen. 2009. A feasible chaotic encryption scheme for image. *International Workshop on Chaos-Fractals Theories and Applications* (IWCFTA'09), 172–176.

58. A. Palacios and H. Juarez. 2002. Cryptography with cycling chaos. *Physics Letters A* 303 (5–6): 345–351.

59. H. E. H. Ahmed, H. M. Kalash, and O. S. Faragallah. 2007. Encryption efficiency analysis and security evaluation of RC6 block cipher for digital images. *International Conference on Electrical Engineering* (ICEE '07), 1–7, April 11–12.

60. Min-A Jeong, Jung-Ja Kim, and Yonggwan Won. 2003. A flexible database security system using multiple access control policies. *Proceedings of the 4th International Conference on Parallel and Distributed Computing, Applications and Technologies*, 236–240.

61. Bruce Benfield and Richard Swagerman. 2001. Encrypting data values in DB2 universal database. Available at http://www.ibm.com/developerworks/data/library/techarticle/benfield/0108benfield.html (accessed March 2011).

62. Transparent data encryption. Available at http://docs.oracle.com/cd/B19306_01/network.102/b14268/asotrans.htm (accessed July 2011).

63. Worawit Meanrach and Suphamit Chittayasothorn. 2007. A bitemporal multilevel secure database system. *Proceedings of IEEE African 2007 Conference*, 1–7.

64. Art Rask, Don Rubin, and Bill Neumann. 2005. Implementing row- and cell-level security in classified databases using SQL server. 2005. Available at http://technet.microsoft.com/en-us/library/cc966395.aspx (accessed April 2011).

65. Yuval Elovici, Ronen Waisenberg, Eras Shmueli, and Ehud Gudes. 2004. A structure preserving database encryption scheme. *Proceedings of International Conference SDM*, 28–40.

66. Xiao-Dong Zuo, Feng-Mai Liu, and Chao-Bin Ma. 2007. A new approach to multilevel security based on trusted computing platform. *Proceedings of the Sixth International Conference on Machine Learning and Cybernetics*, Hong Kong, 2158–2163.

67. Navdeep Kaur, Rajwinder Singh, and H. S. Saini. 2009. Design and analysis of secure scheduler for MLS distributed database systems. *Proceedings of IEEE International Advance Computing Conference* (IACC 2009) Patiala, India, 1400–1404.

68. Ramzi Haraty and Natalie Bekaii. 2006. Towards a temporal multilevel secure database (TMSDB). *Journal of Computer Science* 2 (1): 19–28.

69. Pinal Dave. 2008. Introduction to SQL server encryption and symmetric key encryption tutorial. Available at http://dotnetslackers.com/articles/sql/IntroductionToSQLServerEncryptionAndSymmetricKeyEncryption Tutorial.aspx (accessed May 2011).

70. Moses Garuba. 2003. Performance study of a cots distributed DBMS adapted for multilevel security. PhD thesis, Department of Mathematics, Royal Holloway, University of London, Egham, Surrey. Available at http://digirep.rhul.ac.uk/items/f076f347-2036-6bd0-98c8-e1d2dc-9cf4ab/1/ (accessed April 2011).

71. Moses Garuba, Edward Appiah, and Legand Burge. 2004. Performance study of a MLS/DBMS implemented as a kernelized architecture. *Proceedings of the International Conference on Information Technology: Coding and Computing* (ITCC'04), 566–570.

72. Zahid Rashid, Abdul Basit, and Zahid Anwar. 2010. TRDBAC: Temporal reflective database access control. *Proceedings of 6th International Conference on Emerging Technologies* (ICET), 337–342.

73. Vinti M. Doshi, William R. Hemdon, Sushil Jajodia, and Catherine D. McCollum. 1996. Benchmarking multilevel secure database systems using the MITRE benchmark. *Proceedings of IEEE Transactions on Knowledge and Data Engineering* 8 (1): 46–55.

74. Leon Pan. 2008. Using criterion-based access control for multilevel database security. *Proceedings of International Symposium on Electronic Commerce and Security,* 518–522.

75. Ravi S. Sandhu and Sushil Jajodia. 1993. Referential integrity in multi-level secure databases. *Proceedings of 16th NIST-NCSC National Computer Security Conference,* Baltimore, MD, 39–52.

76. Marco Vieira and Henrique Madeira. 2005. Towards a security benchmark for database management systems. *Proceedings of the 2005 International Conference on Dependable Systems and Networks,* 1–10.

77. Gunther Pernul, A. Min Tjoa, and Werner Winiwarter. 1998. Modeling data secrecy and integrity. *Data & Knowledge Engineering Journal* 26 (3): 291–308.

78. Zhu Hong, Zhu Yi, Li Chenyang, Shi Jie, Fu Ge, and Wang Yuanzhen. 2008. Formal specification and verification of an extended security policy model for database systems. *Proceedings of Third Asia–Pacific Trusted Infrastructure Technologies Conference,* 132–141.

79. Xiaolei Qian and Teresa F. Lunt. 1997. A semantic framework of the multilevel secure relational model. *IEEE Transactions on Knowledge and Data Engineering* 9 (2): 292–301.

80. Leon Pan. 2009. A unified network security and fine-grained database access control model. *Proceedings of the Second International Symposium on Electronic Commerce and Security,* 265–269.

81. Kamel Barkaoui, Rahma Ben Ayed, Hanifa Boucheneb, and Awatef Hicheur. 2008. Verification of workflow processes under multilevel security considerations. *Proceedings of Third International Conference on Risks and Security of Internet and Systems,* 77–84.

82. Baohua Wang, M. A. Xinqiang, and L. I. Danning. 2008. A formal multilevel database security model. *Proceedings of International Conference on Computational Intelligence and Security,* 252–256.

83. Yongzhong He, Zhen Han, Huirong Fu, and Guangzhi Qu. 2010. The formal model of DBMS enforcing multiple security policies. *Journal of Software* 5 (5): 514–521.

84. Veluchandhar Vadivelu, R. V. Jayakumar, M. Muthuvel, K. Balasubramanian, A. Karthi, Karthikesan, G. Ramaiyan, Alagarsamy Deepa, and S. Albert Rabara. 2008. A backup mechanism with concurrency control for multilevel secure distributed database systems. *Proceedings of Third IEEE International Conference on Digital Information Management* (ICDIM), 57–62.

85. Aidong Zhang and Ahmed Elmagarmid. 1993. A theory of global concurrency control in multidatabase systems. *Journal of VLDB* 2 (3): 331–359.

86. Bharat Bhargava. 1999. Concurrency control in database systems. *IEEE Transactions on Knowledge and Data Engineering* 11 (1): 3–16.

87. Sharon Lewis and Simon Wiseman. 1993. Database design and MLS DBMSs: An unhappy alliance. *Proceedings of the Ninth Annual Computer Security Application Conference,* 232–243.

88. Khaled Maabreh and Alaa AI-Hamami. 2008. Increasing database concurrency control based on attribute level locking. *Proceedings of the International Conference on Electronic Design,* 1–4.

89. Qilong Han, Haiwei Pan, and Guisheng Yin. 2008. A concurrency control algorithm access to temporal data in real-time database systems. *Proceedings of the International Multisymposiums on Computer and Computational Sciences Conference,* 168–171.

90. Fritz Laux and Martti Laiho. 2009. SQL access patterns for optimistic concurrency control. *Proceedings of the Future Computing, Service Computation, Cognitive, Adaptive, Content, Patterns Conference,* 254–258.

91. Xiaoyu Qi. 2010. A fast concurrency control algorithm in embedded real-time database system. *Proceedings of the International Conference on Computer Engineering and Technology* (ICCET), 608–610.

92. Qiansheng Zheng and Xiaoming Bi. 2010. An improved concurrency control algorithm for distributed real-time database. *Proceedings of the International Conference on Advanced Management Science* (ICAMS), 364–367.

93. Qiuyu Zhang, Sanjun Sui, and Jingrong Li. 2007. Research and realization of transaction concurrency control in grid database. *Proceedings of the Sixth International Conference on Grid and Cooperative Computing,* 168–172.

94. Navdeep Kaur, Rajwinder Singh, Manoj Misra, and A. K. Sarje. 2006. A secure concurrency control for MLS/DDBSs. *Proceedings of the International Conference on Digital Information Management,* 41–46.

95. Navdeep Kaur, Rajwinder Singh, A. K. Sarje, and Manoj Misra, 2005. Performance evaluation of secure concurrency control algorithm for multilevel secure distributed database systems. *Proceedings of the International Conference on Information Technology,* 249–254.

96. Navdeep Kaur, Rajwinder Singh, Manoj Misra, and A. K. Sarje. 2007. A feedback based secure concurrency control for MLS distributed database. *Proceedings of the International Conference on Computational Intelligence and Multimedia Applications,* 8–12.

97. Navdeep Kaur, Rajwinder Singh, Manoj Misra, and A. K. Sarje. 2009. Concurrency control for multilevel secure databases. *International Journal of Network Security* 9 (1): 70–81.

98. Markus Morgenstern. 1987. Security and inference in multilevel database and knowledge-base systems. *Proceedings of the ACM SIGMOD International Conference on Management of Data,* San Francisco, CA, 357–373.

99. Sang-Won Lee, Yong-Han Kim, and Hyoung-Joo Kim. 2004. The semantics of an extended referential integrity for a multilevel secure relational data model. *International Journal of Data & Knowledge Engineering* 48 (1): 129–152.

100. Nenad Jukic, Svetlozar Nestorov, Susan V. Vrbsky, and Allen Parrish. 2005. Enhancing database access control by facilitating non-key related cover stories. *Journal of Database Management* 16 (10): 1–22.

101. Vijayalakshmi Atluri, Sushil Jajodia, and Elisa Bertino. 1997. Transaction processing in multilevel secure databases with kernelized architecture: Challenges and solutions. *IEEE Transactions on Knowledge and Data Engineering* 9 (5): 697–708.

102. Jonathan Millen and Teresa Lunt. 1992. Security for object-oriented database systems. *Proceedings of the IEEE Symposium on Research in Security and Privacy,* Oakland, CA, 260–272.

103. Thomas Keefe and Wei-Tek Tsai. 1996. A multiversion transaction scheduler for centralized multilevel secure database systems. *Proceedings of the 1st High-Assurance Systems Engineering Workshop* (HASE '96), Niagara, Canada, 206–213.

104. Eduardo Fernandez, Ehud Gudes, and H. Song. 1989. A security model for object-oriented databases. *Proceedings of the IEEE Symposium on Security and Privacy,* 110–115.

105. Eduardo Fernandez, Ehud Gudes, and H. Song. 1994. A model for evaluation and administration of security in object-oriented databases. *International Journal of IEEE Transactions on Knowledge and Data Engineering* 6 (2): 275–292.

106. Jeffrey Parsons and Jianmin Su. 2006. Analysis of data structures to support the instance-based database model. *Proceedings of Design Science Research in Information Systems and Technology* (DESRIST), Claremont, CA, 107–130.

107. Jeffrey Parsons and Jianmin Su. 2010. The instance-based multilevel security model. *Proceedings of International Conference DESRIST,* 365–380.

Index

A

Access controls (authorization), 6
Advanced encryption standard
    (AES), 81–83
  resulting ciphertext, 81
  Rijndael algorithm, 81
  rounds, 81
  S-box, 81
  subkeys, 82
AES, *see* Advanced encryption
    standard
Associate relation, 2
Asymmetric cipher, 68
Asymmetric encryption, 69
Attack
  brute-force, 70
  ciphertext-only, 70
  known-plaintext, 70
  "meet-in-the-middle," 73
  Trojan horse, 10
Attribute polyinstantiation, 22
Auditing, 6
Authentication, 6
Availability, 6, 65

B

Base tuple, 28, 29
BCMLS model, *see* Belief-consistent
    multilevel secure data
    model
Belief-based semantics model, 28
Belief-consistent model, 109, 173
Belief-consistent multilevel secure
    (BCMLS) data model,
    29–30
  base tuple, 28, 29
  false tuple, 29
  primary security level, 29
  secondary levels, 29
  verify mechanism, 30
Belief-consistent multilevel secure
    relational data model,
    53–63
  basic procedures for operations,
    53–57
  delete operation procedure,
    62–63
  flow chart, 55, 61, 63
  Ib (label) procedure, 57

Printed and bound by CPI Group (UK) Ltd, Croydon, CR0 4YY

21/10/2024

01777085-0009